D1713453

Praise for *Running into the Wind*

"For Bronco Mendenhall, this book shares his values and virtues as a husband, a father, and a man of strong faith who can touch and shape all with whom he associates. He provides the leadership, motivation, and energy for student-athletes to balance their lives and develop athletically, academically, and socially. His daily life reflects his unselfish attitude and also emphasizes that always doing what is right is a path that can lead to lifetime success for student-athletes and their families."

—Urban Meyer, Ohio State head football coach

"An engaging book that will take readers deep into the heart and mind of Bronco Mendenhall where they'll see firsthand Bronco's extremely unique approach to running a college football program. Not only will this book give readers insight into Bronco, it will also lay out Paul's renowned organizational principles—Five Smooth Stones—that Bronco learned and applied, and that also can guide any leader to organize and move teams to successful outcomes."

—Stephen M. R. Covey, *New York Times* and *Wall Street Journal* #1 best-selling author of *The Speed of Trust* and coauthor of *Smart Trust*

"BYU's record is a reflection of Bronco's relentless quest to create the optimal environment for his players and staff to achieve their shared vision. This quest took him far from the field of football and into the science of sustainable high performance—researching the mindset and systems behind the leading global organizations and thought leaders to create BYU Football's winning culture. There is a lot to be learned from this rare, winning combination of aligned leadership and a team optimizing its performance on and off the field."

—Mark Verstegen, president and founder, Athletes' Performance/Core Performance

"What a fun and insightful book! Like chocolate and peanut butter, this book brings together two great subjects—football and management. It weaves together marvelous stories about how Bronco applied leadership principles to create a band of brothers and a winning tradition."

—Dave Ulrich, University of Michigan professor, Ross School of Business; partner, the RBL Group

"Bronco Mendenhall is a great football coach who obviously knows how to win a lot of games. More important, Bronco is a true leader and a unique coach who has a broader focus than just winning games. He is about life skills, teamwork, excellence."

—Chris Peterson, Boise State head football coach

"A masterful demonstration of how to win in sports by placing character first. Insightful, provocative, timely. A must-read for leaders."

—Jim Loehr, performance psychologist and best-selling author

RUNNING INTO THE WIND

RUNNING INTO THE WIND

BRONCO
MENDENHALL

5 STRATEGIES FOR BUILDING A SUCCESSFUL TEAM

Paul Gustavson and
Alyson Von Feldt

SHADOW
MOUNTAIN

The Five Smooth Stones concept was previously published in *Five Smooth Stones: Strategy and Organization Design Guidebook* by Paul Gustavson and Alyson Von Feldt (San Jose, CA: Organization Planning and Design, Inc., 2009). © 2009 by Organization Planning and Design, Inc.

Photo credits: Pages 74, 110, 134 by Mark A. Philbrick/BYU Photo; pages 51, 97, 229 by Jaren Wilkey/BYU Photo.

"Building and Sustaining High Performance Teams" DVD by Bronco Mendenhall and Paul Gustavson © by Intellectual Reserve, Inc. Used by permission.

Text © 2012 Organization Planning and Design, Inc., Crimson Corporation, and Tri Bear Holdings LLC.

All rights reserved. No part of this book may be reproduced in any form or by any means without permission in writing from the publisher, Shadow Mountain®. The views expressed herein are the responsibility of the authors and do not necessarily represent the position of Shadow Mountain.

Visit us at ShadowMountain.com

Library of Congress Cataloging-in-Publication Data
Gustavson, Paul, author.
   Running into the wind : Bronco Mendenhall : 5 strategies for building a successful team / Paul Gustavson and Alyson Von Feldt.
      pages cm
   Includes bibliographical references and index.
   ISBN 978-1-60907-162-2 (alk. paper)
1. Teams in the workplace. 2. Organizational behavior. 3. Mendenhall, Bronco, 1966–
I. Von Feldt, Alyson, author. II. Title.
   HD66.G875 2012
   658.4'022—dc23   2012029548

Printed in the United States of America
Worzalla Publishing Co., Stevens Point, WI

10   9   8   7   6   5   4   3   2   1

For my late parents,
Arle and Doris Gustavson,
who taught me about principles and
inspired my career's work

—PG

For Jacob.
This book has been for you
since its inception

—AVF

Contents

SECTION 1
ON THE FIELD

Contents

SECTION 2

IN THE FOOTBALL OFFICES

Foreword

WHEN BRONCO MENDENHALL took over one of the country's best-known and yet precariously declining football programs, he faced a challenge of enormous magnitude. First of all, he was a coach. That can't be a fun job. Imagine having a career in an industry where your success depends on the daily choices of people who are now, or recently were, teenagers. And you have to practically fight to get them to come work for you. And these new employees then do their jobs in front of millions of crazed customers who scrutinize their every move, along with the actions of their bosses. These customers are so opinionated about what they like and don't like, that when things don't meet their approval, they routinely call for the bosses to be fired. Many, in a highly transparent effort to gain power, donate tens of thousands of dollars to the company, and then demand a say in how it's run.

Welcome to the world of college coaching.

Then you have the problem of an organization in decline. A screeching crowd of rabid customers has called for and received the head of the previous boss. You, the new leader and hope of the future, are going to enjoy a "honeymoon period" of a few weeks while people express their love for you because, well, you aren't the previous boss who led the company through several years of disappointment—and anything's better than that.

Then, as the rhetoric of how great you're going to be is unceremoniously washed away by the harsh reality of "these are mostly the same folks who failed to perform well the last year," you realize that your resources are severely limited, despite all the promises you were given. For one, most of those with whom you will be working directly, you didn't hire. It's the former guy's employees you'll be reshaping into a new entity, and we've all seen what they can do.

Maybe, just maybe, if you had four to six years to recruit and train your own employees, you'd turn the company around. But your crazed, ever vigilant, hyper-opinionated, and heavily invested customers aren't going to wait for six years. They're in your face with a list of demands after about, say, six weeks. And don't forget the press. These members of the "fourth estate" write whatever comes into their head, whenever they like, as often as they like—and much of it is about your leadership style. After all, for the first few months you aren't going to be demonstrating your product, so all they have to talk about is the cut of your jib, your strut, the clothes you wear, and other equally inane topics. And, oh yes, they too will be calling for your job if they don't see big changes soon.

Such were the circumstances Bronco Mendenhall faced when he took over the helm at BYU. It had been a great team, had declined into something far less, and now Bronco was supposed to make it all better. And fast.

Which Bronco did.

And he didn't do it through magic, rhetoric, or luck. He did it (and who's going to believe this?) by applying sound leadership principles and techniques. Bronco is one of those rare leaders who not only reads about his industry, he also eats management theory for breakfast. While it's true that he looks and sounds like the poster guy for football (his name is Bronco, for crying out loud), he's equally comfortable talking about empowerment, change theory, high performance teams, and the like. Who would have thought?

In short, Bronco Mendenhall is a guy every leader who wants to lead a team to victory ought to study.

—KERRY PATTERSON
MANAGEMENT THEORIST AND
New York Times BEST-SELLING AUTHOR OF
Change Anything, Crucial Conversations,
Crucial Confrontations, AND *Influencer*

Preface

THIS STORY is not just about football.

I first heard Bronco and Paul tell about their adventures with the Brigham Young University football team at a conference for students and professionals in the fields of human resources and organizational behavior in the spring of 2008. The conference, sponsored by BYU's Marriott School of Management, was held at Aspen Grove in the Wasatch Mountains just above Sundance. I remember standing outside in the crispness of early April and calling my thirteen-year-old son at his school in Mexico, Missouri, to brag about the scenery. He was indeed impressed.

Bronco and Paul electrified the audience. They electrified me. Paul is a good friend of mine, my mentor and matchmaker. When I was a graduate student, he acted as an agent for the company known then as Hill's Pet Products, now Hill's Pet Nutrition, a division of Colgate-Palmolive, in hiring me as an intern to write the story of the unprecedented $80 million start-up of a new plant in Richmond, Indiana. I botched my interview badly by admitting that our family cat was not much of a fan of Science Diet, the company's flagship product. (All our pets since have eaten Science Diet and found it delicious as well as highly nutritious.) Regardless, Paul persevered with the inquiry. Before he concluded our discussion, however, he diplomatically explained that Richmond was a small town and that the size of its congregation of members of The Church of Jesus Christ of Latter-day Saints (the Church) was unknown to him. He suggested that the dating opportunities might be limited. This turn in the conversation was unexpected, but understandable and easily dispatched. I was coming to the end of my seventh year at BYU—six as an undergraduate and one as an organizational behavior graduate student—and yet I was still glaringly single. Readers who are not members of the Church may not fathom the significance of my failure to hitch by that point, but the culture at BYU at that time was such that folks would take notice of this state of affairs and find friendly ways to try to understand it or remedy it. Given this culture, Paul knew that dating might be on my mind, and as you will read in the upcoming pages, he believes that it is crucial to be clear about expectations up front. He wanted my expectations to be realistic. I could honestly assure him that the criteria for my selection of a summer internship did not encompass the likelihood of a wedding.

Nevertheless, the story of my tenured relationship with Paul cannot be disconnected from the story of my family, for indeed I met my future husband at the Hill's plant in Richmond, Indiana, dated him, introduced him to the Church members who baptized him, and was married to him by the next Christmas.

Two enduring matches had been made: a mentorship pairing and a matrimonial pairing. Paul and I continued on professionally, and my husband, Doug, and I shared a friendship with him and his lively wife, Kris Anne, as well. As I began to have children, Paul happily accommodated my wish to do less work and more of it at home, until finally, sometime after our third child, I pulled out of the workforce for what I thought would be forever.

It was after my retreat from employment that Paul first volunteered his time with Bronco. I kept up through e-mails from Paul and the occasional article he would send. But I was immersed in my role as a stay-at-home mom and followed only casually.

This story now takes a very personal and painful turn. Soon after my oldest son turned twelve, we found that we had trouble seeing eye-to-eye, and that's a big understatement. He thought we were ridiculously strict and out of touch; we thought he was angry and antagonistic. Jacob did not fail school, do drugs, or hang out with the wrong crowd, thankfully. But our home life became most chaotic. Doug and I redoubled our efforts to be loving and listening, firm and consistent. We devoted much time to prayer, reflection, and scripture study. We read books about adolescent discipline and adolescent neurochemistry. As our home life became more and more turbulent, we sought help. Jacob stayed with his grandparents for some time. We also received earnest support from counselors, hospitals, doctors, bishops (the Church's analog to a pastor), social workers, policemen, medicines, and vice-principals.

My pain was excruciating. I felt as if my son were lost to me. Daily life in our family was exhausting as we struggled to maintain family rituals and family rules, to cultivate love and kindness in what felt like a war zone. Jacob felt disrespected and desolate. It was extraordinarily debilitating for all of us. I am sure that many parents and young people reading this will have first-hand experience with exactly what I am describing.

After over a year and a half of this pattern, my husband and I could see that nothing we had tried so far had been effective in bringing our family into a sustainable equilibrium. In fact, we were in decline. We had certainly given an honest go to everything we and the professionals could think of. I remember talking with the psychiatrist about increasing the dosage of Jacob's medication when I found myself turning away from the mental health path that we had been following, diagnosing our family malady with words I had used often as an organizational design consultant: "We do not need any more incremental change. We need radical change." I knew that organizations—including families—are perfectly designed to get the results that they get. This is a saying of Paul's that comes up early in this book. If our results for eighteen months had been overwhelmingly inadequate in the face of our distress, then what the situation demanded was a quantum change in the design elements in place in our family.

We set up appointments at boarding schools.

In my circle of family and acquaintances here in the Midwest, boarding school is perceived as an option for children with learning disorders or serious and chronic disciplinary issues. Jacob did not fit these categories. At first we wondered if sending Jacob to boarding school was giving up on him. The idea made us feel disloyal and cruel. But as we talked, we came to believe that it would be more as if we were inviting a whole big institution to help us in our plight—that we would simply be putting the forces of the educational establishment into our service rather than those of the mental health establishment. And when we looked at it in this way, especially in retrospect, it seemed to us as if our bright, powerful son had all along been commandeering these forces to him, marshaling the toughest and most demanding circumstances on his behalf. It had just taken us some time to see that that was the direction he was headed all along. Prayer and fasting confirmed the viability of this change in plans.

Jacob eagerly entered boarding school within two weeks, and, since this adventure carried a price tag not covered by insurance, two months later I was in the audience when Bronco and Paul, standing against window-walls framing freshly leaved quaking aspens, excited and united their audience with tales of sustaining the recent successes of the BYU football team. It was an energizing entrée back into the work force after nearly ten years.

A few weeks earlier, as I had sat across the desk from the highly decorated Major General Robert Flanagan, the president of Missouri Military Academy, discussing the prospect of my son attending his school, I had noticed two books stacked on the edge of his tidy desk: Jim Collins's *Good to Great*, and *Boys Adrift* by Leonard Sax, author of *Saving Cain*. I ordered them when I got home. I started with *Boys Adrift*. Sax, a family physician and research psychologist, describes the forces in our world contributing to the decline in the motivation and achievement of boys and young men. The book resonated with me. My boy certainly seemed adrift, and the mental health model that suggested he was ill did not offer solutions that had proved adequate to rescue our family as we sunk. By the time I heard Bronco and Paul talk, I knew that my son's all-boy military school had us securely in hand and we at last were on solid ground. It was an enormous relief and one of the greatest blessings of my entire life. No wonder the peaks and foliage of Provo Canyon seemed so especially spectacular that April.

Here is the crux: both the program and the players of the BYU football team are most certainly NOT adrift. Their mission is so clear and compelling, the players' commitment to it so tenacious, and the message of their head coach so undaunted, that I wanted parents and adolescents everywhere to hear their story. I wanted my boy to hear their story. After Paul and Bronco's talk, I urged the two of them to be sure to get the story told.

What a pleasure it is for me to join them in telling it.

Jacob, by the way, had a successful semester at Missouri Military Academy and continued on to a coed nonmilitary boarding school for a full year. He returned home to complete his last three years of high school, and by that time we were able to establish an equilibrium that we could all live with. He flourished at school as a gifted student, debater (not surprising), and wrestler. By the time he graduated in 2012, he was confident of his path moving forward. He now attends the University of Kansas, where he was admitted to the business leadership program and plans to study finance. He astonishes us all with his wit, enthusiasm for learning, and self-sufficiency. Occasionally, he even takes out the trash.

Alyson Von Feldt
May 2012

Introduction

I T IS NOT UNCOMMON to find metaphors about sports in the business world. Speakers use them to motivate, posters use them to invigorate, and writers use them to articulate important ideas. Commonplace business vocabulary such as "teamwork" and "coaching" and "competitor" is borrowed from the world of sports and effectively captures the spirit of certain business realities, even when you are after a sale or a contract rather than a trophy.

So it was not a bad idea when Bronco Mendenhall pulled a reverse maneuver and turned to the world of business for knowledge about how to coach a football team.

It was coauthor Paul Gustavson's great privilege to be the one Bronco turned to for this new knowledge. Bronco and Paul first made contact just prior to a visit Bronco was paying a potential quarterbacks coach. Bronco had ten minutes when he first phoned Paul. He said, "This is my first time as a head football coach. I want to be a great head football coach. You're somebody I was told I can learn from."

Paul, who for more than thirty-five years has helped leaders design organizations to carry out their chosen strategies, was impressed with Bronco's obvious enthusiasm for learning. They briefly talked over a set of principles that Bronco could use as he approached his decision. He put insights from their discussion to use right away, that very evening, when he conducted the interview. The candidate was Brandon Doman.

Thus a vital relationship burgeoned between Bronco and Paul. The hours Paul volunteered with Bronco came to be the most rewarding and joyful of his career, his friendship with Bronco a highlight of his life.

Coauthor Alyson Von Feldt got involved with this story some years later. She heard Bronco electrify a professional audience with his forthright conviction that an elite football program can be run with upstanding athletes committed to academic excellence and a strict code of honor. At the time, her oldest son was a young teen and a mighty football fan. What mom wouldn't want the kind of athlete Bronco was describing to stand as a model for her impressionable offspring?

So Alyson—a long-time colleague of Paul's—took up her voice recorder to find out what was behind the magic happening on the green grass gridiron in Provo, Utah. Bronco invited her into the football offices over several years to discover what kind of organization design had brought Bronco's unusual strategy to fruition.

Her findings come together in this book with Paul's and Bronco's perspectives about what challenges arose behind the scenes and what approaches Bronco and his staff took to meet them.

We share here the principles and tools the Cougars relied on. Because Paul's background is in organization design, the perspective on leadership that he brings to the table leans with a heavy tilt toward the importance of a carefully crafted organization architecture, not just the personal savvy of leaders, for top-notch organization performance. This book will show how Bronco put these ideas to work. It will describe the thoughtful strategic positioning that was behind a robust set of aligned design choices that he, his assistant coaches, and even his player-leaders developed and institutionalized as part of BYU Football.

Did the principles result in success?

Taking over a program coming off three consecutive losing campaigns, Bronco led BYU to a 6–6 record in his first season at the helm. The next four years brought three eleven-win seasons and a ten-win season (out of a total of thirteen games played each year). Never before in the history of the program—despite the 1984 national championship and the legacy of top coaching and player awards—had BYU teams achieved four consecutive seasons of at least ten wins each. They won double-digit games again in 2011, earning a 10–3 record and a place in the final *USA Today* Coaches' Poll for the fifth time in six seasons, something only eight other programs out of 120 had accomplished. Under Bronco the Cougars ranked in the final top twenty-five in the *USA Today* Coaches' Poll for five of Bronco's first seven years and were nationally ranked in-season during six of his first seven campaigns. Of all 120 NCAA Division 1 teams, only fourteen won more games than BYU over those seven years.

Since Bronco took the lead, the team has played in a bowl game every year, going 5–2 in the postseason. The Cougars claimed the top spot in the Mountain West Conference twice—the first consecutive titles in the league's history earned by way of back-to-back undefeated conference records. BYU then declared independence for its football program and signed a contract with ESPN that would bring Cougar Football into hundreds of millions of homes over the course of a season.

Consistent athletic performance is not the only area in which the team has excelled. Seven Academic All-American citations were received among six BYU Football athletes between 2005 and 2011—the third highest in NCAA Division 1 programs. In the years 2007–2011, twenty-five players were admitted by the National Football

Foundation and College Hall of Fame (NFF) to the Hampshire Honor Society. This honor is given to collegiate players who maintain a cumulative 3.2 GPA or better throughout their college career. BYU had the most honorees among Division 1 schools in 2010 and tied for the most in 2011. In 2012 it was tied for the second-most honorees.

In Bronco's first seven years, he coached or recruited 258 players who had either served or were currently serving a two-year mission for The Church of Jesus Christ of Latter-day Saints. One hundred thirty-three players were married and a good number started their families during their tenure on the team. This is drastically different from other college football programs where only a handful of players are married, if any at all.

For Bronco, success cannot be measured without statistics that evidence the full range of his players' achievements. He has said that he is not interested in this high-profile coaching job if he is working with "just anybody." He would rather be with young people who are stellar representatives of their institution, faith, and community. When the team is winning, some view his players' personal qualities as a strength. When the team is losing, some view those qualities as the cause of their weakness.

This book is about how Bronco Mendenhall made strongly held personal values and balanced achievement the very foundation of the sustained success of the BYU Cougars and how he carried this out by applying principles and practices from the world of business. It was difficult. Sometimes it felt like running head-on into a very strong wind.

The story unfolds in two sections. Section 1, On the Field, is similar to going backstage at a special event. It begins with Bronco's personal history, which comprises the first two chapters. Chapters 3–10 describe at length how Bronco and his staff put organization design concepts to work for the football program. Chapter 11 sums everything up with a recounting of the results of Bronco's first seven years and his vision for the future.

Section 2, In the Football Offices, goes into greater detail about the principles that Bronco relied on. This is where you can turn for your own personal coaching. If you are interested in knowing more about the background, research, or references behind the principles and tools from section 1, turn to section 2 for more. Here we offer examples, suggestions, and questions to help you face your challenges using the same tools that Bronco used to face his.

As you read, you will find Quick Response (QR) Codes scattered throughout the text. You may scan these two-dimensional barcodes with a reader on a smartphone or other mobile device to view segments in a presentation that Bronco and Paul gave to a group of professionals. Alternatively, you may go directly to the URL to see the clips. These segments complement the story at the point where the QR code is printed. (QR readers are available as downloadable apps.)

Bronco is passionate about what has happened with the team over the last seven years and enthusiastic about telling the story. From his first day as head coach, he utterly submitted himself to the all-too-public persona of his position, believing it to be one of the duties of the job.

At the same time, he has sought to keep his personal life private and shield his family from undue exposure. So we thank Bronco for letting us tell his story, including the personal background that we give at the beginning of section 1. He has been generous in sharing with us but reluctant to take center stage. At one point he bowed out as a coauthor because he thought we were being too generous with our praise. We have had to convince him that by letting readers know more about his past and some of the most cherished experiences of his life, they could more easily put themselves in his shoes and dare to design their own organizations as he did his.

I WAS INVITED to be interviewed by Mike Wallace, a tough senior reporter for the CBS *60 Minutes* program, which is broadcast across America to more than 20 million listeners each week.

I recognized that if I were to appear, critics and detractors of the Church would also be invited to participate. I knew we could not expect that the program would be entirely positive for us.

On the other hand, I felt that it offered the opportunity to present some affirmative aspects of our culture and message to many millions of people. I concluded that it was better to lean into the stiff wind of opportunity than to simply hunker down and do nothing.

—GORDON B. HINCKLEY
PRESIDENT OF THE CHURCH OF JESUS CHRIST
OF LATTER-DAY SAINTS, 1995–2008

SECTION 1

ON THE FIELD

CHAPTER 1

Warrior Coach

Coach Mendenhall was in charge of the Lobos' kickoff team. He had a standard that everybody finishes at the end zone. No matter who it is, you had to finish at the end zone—full speed. Coach Mendenhall stood by that every day. He taught us to finish the job.

He passed out green [Maori] *tiki* warrior totems to us on the defensive side. We wore them around our necks. He told a story about the tiki warrior and the New Zealand All Blacks rugby team. That was intense and emotional. That touched me personally. This is a game that's fun, but at the same time, I wanted to give him my all. I wanted to give him my all because of the stories, and how important they were to him, and how he shared them with us. I was always trying to give it my all in everything that I did when I was out there playing for Coach Mendenhall.

I don't have my tiki warrior with me right now in Albuquerque. It's in my bedroom in Dallas, on my dresser. Some of my things from football I left behind in Dallas, like my jersey. But what I do carry with me right now are the principles that Coach Mendenhall instilled in me. Those principles have helped to get me through the PhD program that I'm in right now. I'm working on a PhD in Special Education at the University of New Mexico. The skills that I gathered in football, and the leadership experiences, and those principles I learned, I really, really do rely on. I thank Coach Mendenhall for those. I've never had an opportunity to earnestly tell him, but I go back to the discipline that assisted me in preparing myself to play football, and the discipline to go into a practice with Coach Mendenhall. I rely heavily on those things.

Some nights when I feel laid out, I think, "This is just me practicing. This is just the training piece right here. It's me toning myself to get in shape." I don't physically use my body. I'm using my brain right now to get me through these different exercises that I'm going through as I pursue this degree. Attention to detail. Get the job done. As I work with people, review articles, and put together papers, it takes discipline. It takes staying up longer, or getting up earlier in the morning to get back to what I'm doing. There's no time for me to say, "I gotta rest." It's time for me to get the job done.

—Charles Moss
UNM linebacker 1999–2002

WHAT WOULD you do first if you found yourself to be the head coach of a college football team? What would your strategy be?

Would you design amazing new schemes? Fire all the coaches and hire a new set of the best in the nation? Throw yourself into recruiting with such a degree of enthusiasm and panache that no five-star recruit would turn you down? Redesign fall camp? Deliver a series of locker-room talks to motivate your players to unprecedented performance?

Is there a college football program that you would choose to emulate? Are you a fan, for example, of Nick Saban's program at Alabama? Do you admire the efforts of Chris Petersen at Boise State? Or maybe Mark Richt at Georgia?

Bronco Mendenhall was named head coach of the Brigham Young University football team in December of 2004. He and everyone else knew he was not the first choice. It was widely reported that Kyle Whittingham was at least one who had been offered the position before Bronco, and Kyle had nearly taken the job before choosing instead to fill the vacancy left at the University of Utah when Urban Meyer departed for Florida.

Bronco was young, without head coaching experience. He was only thirty-eight when appointed, which made him the second-youngest head coach in Division I college football. He had a grand total of one bowl game under his belt as either a player or a coach.

As head coach he became perhaps the most public face of BYU (sometimes called the "Y"), the largest religiously affiliated university in the United States and the third-largest private university, owned and operated by The Church of Jesus Christ of Latter-day Saints (the Church). But Bronco is a pensive and reserved kind of person who had only very recently first imagined himself at the head of a team. He channels his extraordinary focus and tenacity in private directions except when coaching. To rather suddenly find himself in such a visible role was sobering. And he was already a sober man by nature.

The Church emphasizes values of high character such as honesty, charity, modesty, chastity, temperance, and other classic virtues. These values take their shape in an honor code at BYU in terms of dress and grooming standards; prohibition on the use of alcohol, drugs, and tobacco; and abstinence from extramarital sexual relations, among other requirements. Bronco is a model of these virtues. He would need to ensure his football players were as well, especially since troubling scandals involving BYU team members had recently played out in the media, resulting in the suspension or dismissal of fourteen young men from the roster and from the university.

Bronco was replacing Gary Crowton, a good friend. They went way back. Bronco had played cornerback at Snow College in Ephraim, Utah, when Crowton was the offensive coordinator; some years later, when Crowton was head coach at Louisiana Tech, he had hired Bronco as the secondary coach. Crowton had put in four seasons at BYU. His first was bright and promising; the Cougars opened with a twelve-game winning streak before losing their last two games, including a bowl game. In each of the next three years the team lost more games than they won and never became bowl eligible. Bronco at first balked at the notion of taking his friend's job. But a persuasive assistant athletic director and some persistent players who advocated for Bronco finally changed his mind.

The three losing seasons had stung the BYU fan base, which is spread across the nation. Predating this downturn, BYU Football had a venerable history of winning and innovating. The beloved LaVell Edwards, legendary for his twenty-nine-year BYU dynasty that delivered a 257–101–3 record, had retired only four years earlier as the sixth-winningest football coach in NCAA history. Early in his tenure, LaVell had championed the development of a passing attack to challenge big schools that could recruit top-tier players. It was a brilliant move. Before LaVell became head coach, the team had won *only one* league championship in its entire school history. In contrast, LaVell's teams went on to claim conference titles in nineteen of his twenty-nine seasons, playing in twenty-two bowl games, and winning the national championship in 1984. He coached one Heisman trophy winner, two Outland Trophy recipients, three

Davey O'Brien award winners, seven Sammy Baugh Trophy honorees, and thirty-two All-Americans. BYU became known as a quarterback factory—"Quarterback U"—for its steady production of top-performing NCAA offense leaders including Heisman Trophy winner Ty Detmer. Celebrated NFL quarterbacks Steve Young, Jim McMahon, Marc Wilson, and Gifford Nielson were all products of the LaVell Edwards era.

Thus Bronco found himself at the turn of the year. The fan base was reeling from scandal and losses, and Bronco's inexperience weighed heavily on him. Yet BYU Football's rich history stood to prod a new generation to reclaim national prominence. Bronco faced the formidable challenge of finding top athletes eager for that challenge, who at the same time could enthusiastically embrace the strict BYU Honor Code.

What would you have done if you had found yourself in his shoes?

Here's what Bronco did: he went in search of ideas. He began a study of concepts and practices from the domain of business strategy and organization design that had applicability in the world of sports. He used these practices to build a football organization that could succeed because of its unique moral values, not in spite of them.

But we are getting ahead of ourselves. First let's trace the journey that led Bronco to this unanticipated moment in his life.

• • •

In a corner of Bronco Mendenhall's light-filled office on the campus of Brigham Young University in Provo, Utah, leans a Maori totem called a *tokotoko*. Bronco first studied the culture of the Maori tribe, indigenous to New Zealand, when his father was overseeing missionary activities in the South Pacific for the Church. For years the BYU football program has heavily recruited young men of Polynesian descent, but the association between Latter-day Saints and Polynesians goes back much further. Joseph Smith, founder of the LDS Church, sent missionaries to French Polynesia in 1843, a year before his death and three years before the Mormons embarked on their famous trek to Utah under the guidance of Brigham Young. While Brigham Young was building a society in the desert West and establishing an academy that would later become Brigham Young University, the Church was spreading in the South Pacific. Bronco's appropriation of Maori cultural artifacts as teaching devices for his young football warriors flows in an elegant continuum from the earliest days of Church history.

Bronco's *tokotoko* was a gift from a Maori fan living nearby who also volunteered, with Bronco's encouragement, to create a *tokotoko* for each 2008–09 senior, decorated with tokens of the player's football legacy and the team's core values.

Another totem stands in the opposite corner of Bronco's office—a custom surfboard emotionally presented to Bronco after the 2007 win over Utah. It was airbrushed for him by a fan, who attributed the roots of a life turnaround to a talk Bronco had given at one of the ritual pregame "firesides" presented by the team.

In Bronco's drawer: a keychain with the emblematic orange-and-black Harley-Davidson logo. Bronco rides a Harley Road King to work. It's a family tradition. Two of his three older brothers have long been hog enthusiasts and chopper owners. He dons leather from head to toe, and as the roar of the 110-inch-cubic engine surrounds and isolates him, he commutes thirty-five miles along the winding streets of his rural neighborhood in the foothills of the Wasatch Mountains to the linear strips of the meticulous pioneer grid of Provo, Utah. He arrives at the Student Athlete Building on the campus of BYU every morning early enough to study his scriptures before the daily staff meeting. In Bronco's first years as coach, he also fit in an early workout at the office, but he moved that to his home gym as his sons grew older and he found the morning hours with them too precious to be away.

Bronco's short-cropped hair is bleached anew each summer in the waters of the Pacific. He loves to surf and vacations at the beach each July with his wife, Holly, and their three towheaded boys, Cutter, Breaker, and Raeder. His smooth face is weathered, skin sunburned, and lips often chapped from afternoons outside on the practice field. He is blue-eyed. A dimple in his right cheek appears at the end of statements, retracting sharply and deeply as if to punctuate his sentences.

Perhaps Bronco's identity is most revealed not by the artifacts in his office or the weathering of his face but by the way he learned to care for horses as a child. When he was ten years old, after the youngest of his three older brothers graduated from high school, his family moved from Salt Lake City to a ranch in Alpine, Utah. His father, Paul Mendenhall, soon had him mucking out the stalls, hauling hay, and feeding the animals. Bronco was so painstaking and perfectionist by nature that he would at times get down on his hands and knees to clean up horse manure piece by piece.[1] "I've always had a really obedient and conscientious spirit," says Bronco. "I desire to please. I want to do things right. I want to do a job exactly as it needs to be done." His dad came to thoroughly trust him and gave him chores usually suited to an adult or a responsible teenager, such as training a dozen horses, administering their shots, and driving the pickup truck on the farm to help manage a hundred head of cattle.[2]

Following in the footsteps of his older brothers, Bronco also got involved in sports. "In my family, my brothers were all such strong and vibrant people. They all were either racing motorcycles, skiing competitively, or playing great baseball or football. I wanted badly to be like them." Bronco adds, "I tried hard to gain acceptance. I wanted people to say of me, 'That's one of the Mendenhalls. You can just tell.' As a little kid, I put all this pressure on myself because I wanted to be like my brothers, and I wasn't sure I could." So along with his conscientious spirit and his family pride came some self-doubt. "I was always very self-critical, thinking, 'What if I don't play well?'"

Bronco ultimately became captivated most of all by football. His dad had been a defensive end for BYU in the 1950s. Two of his older brothers were successful players who provided inspiration as well. Mat, a starting defensive lineman for BYU, was picked in the second round of the NFL draft by the Washington Redskins, where he played for two years and started in Super Bowl XVII. Marty, closest in age to Bronco, played first at Snow College, then at Weber State and the University of Utah.

Bronco grew up attending BYU football games. "My mom and dad used to take me out of school on Fridays to travel to Fort Collins [Colorado] and Laramie [Wyoming] to watch my brother Mat play," he says. "It was a big deal. When I'd get up to leave class, it was a huge thing to the other kids because my brother played at BYU, and I got to leave school because of that. It made me feel special. I idolized my brother. My identity was tied to sports performance."

And Bronco did play well. He became the captain of the American Fork High School football team where he was a tight end and defensive back. He showed unrelenting dedication at practice and put in extra conditioning hours on the weekends. He was hailed by his coach as a fierce competitor, reliably conscientious and tough, but also "a genuinely thoughtful person" and an earnest friend to the underdog.[3]

Though he was only 6 feet tall and 170 pounds, Bronco made plans to become a career player. He believed that if he worked hard enough, he could set his sights on the NFL.

Bronco's dreams of playing for BYU were dashed, though, when the Cougars did not offer him a scholarship. The only scholarship that came, in fact, was from two-year Snow College in Ephraim, Utah. So Bronco followed in Marty's footsteps. Starting both years as cornerback, he contributed to the 1985 team's perfect 11–0 season and National Junior College Athletic Association (NJCAA) national championship. He earned top laurels including a first-team all-conference spot, second-team NJCAA All-America accolades, and Junior College Gridwire Academic All-America honors. Still, when several scholarships offers were extended to him as his career with the Badgers concluded, BYU again failed to pony up. Bronco was irritated. He chose Oregon State mostly because BYU was on its schedule. Now he longed for a win *against* the Cougars.

For the Beavers, Bronco again started both years—this time as free safety, strong safety, and linebacker—and captained the team his senior year. Bronco's longed-for win over BYU came in his junior year. He was so thrilled that, after the game in Provo, he threw himself spread-eagle on the stadium grass to savor the victory, looking skyward.[4]

He continued pursuing the dedicated work ethic he had cultivated with the horses as a youth, but what foreshadowed his future path was not his success as a player, but as a leader. At Oregon State, he won the Leo Gribkoff Memorial Award, an honor given to the team's most inspirational player. Having received solid recognition during his college career, he eagerly anticipated the spring NFL draft, hoping to be selected by a team recognizing his work ethic, his leadership potential, and his whole-hearted playing style. When draft day arrived, though, Bronco's name was never called. He was devastated.

But he held out hopes of getting on as a free agent. He graduated with a bachelor's degree in physical education and then continued at Oregon State, pursuing a master's in education with an emphasis in exercise physiology. He took a job as a graduate assistant in the football program. He was biding his time as he waited for the NFL offer to come, training intensely every day. "Realistically, looking back," says Bronco, "it was a waste of time. I wasn't a good enough college player, nor were my chances strong enough. I was just chasing a dream that wasn't realistic."

As graduation approached and the NFL dream withered, Bronco did not know where he would get a job. That last semester, to save money, he lived in his office. "I had a little piece of foam for a bed," he remembers. "Literally everything I needed was there. My work was there, the gym, the weight room, the showers." Oregon State was a struggling football program at the time, so work was intense. Living at school and working feverishly, Bronco was so engrossed in football that he actually lost his car. He recalls:

> On weekends, during that semester, we were playing games, and then I was staying afterward to break down the film late at night. The weekend would come and go. I mean it's Monday, and all I'd done on Sunday was go to church and come back and work. Because Sunday was a workday, I really didn't have weekends. So I found that one week went by, then two, then three, then four, and I hadn't ever driven my car. It went from weeks to months, and that's how all-encompassing what I was doing was. And eventually when it came time to leave to go home, I didn't know where I had put my car! It wasn't where I thought it was.

Bronco reported it stolen to the police. They found it in the school parking lot, covered with leaves.[5] "I'm pretty obsessive, and I have a one-track mind. Even for people who know me, they still think it's weird that I lost my car. But I'm kind of all or nothing when it comes to doing things." So for Bronco, failing to drive his car for an entire semester was all in the course of a season's work.

After that season, the entire coaching staff at Oregon State was fired when Jerry Pettibone was brought on as the new head coach. All of the professionals that any other year would have been Bronco's advocates as he sought a job were themselves on the hunt. So he went home to Alpine to train horses again with his dad. "I loved being with my dad and I loved the horses, so I was just kind of doing it as a filler. He was paying me a salary because I was working the colts for him."

Then a call came from Paul Tidwell, the head coach at Snow College, who had been Bronco's defensive coordinator when Bronco played for the Badgers. Paul offered him the secondary coach and defensive coordinator spot. It was a ninety-minute commute worth only $4,500 a season, so the rest of the year Bronco continued to work with the horses. After a couple seasons of this, "I just was kind of at the end of my rope, thinking, you know, I don't even know if I want to coach." But then Steve Kragthorpe, who had been a graduate assistant along with Bronco at Oregon State and was now offensive coordinator at Northern Arizona, helped him secure an interview in Flagstaff. Bronco got the secondary coaching job, and that started his full-time coaching career. Bronco loaded up his dad's horse trailer and moved himself south. He was named codefensive coordinator the following year.

Soon contacts at Oregon State brought him back to his alma mater. He became the defensive line coach under coordinator Rocky Long, with Jerry Pettibone still in the head coach slot. The Rocky-Bronco pairing would prove to be a long and fruitful collaboration. When Rocky landed the head coaching spot at UCLA, Bronco was promoted at Oregon State and became the youngest defensive coordinator in PAC-10 history, at only twenty-nine years old. Pettibone was fired a year later, though, so once again Bronco was in search mode. Louisiana Tech head coach Gary Crowton had been an assistant coach at Snow College when Bronco was a cornerback there, and Gary offered Bronco a job coaching the secondary in Ruston, Louisiana.

It was during this time that Bronco reconnected with Holly Johnston. Holly had introduced herself to Bronco ten years earlier when he was playing for the Beavers in Oregon. Mutual family friends, members of the cutting horse circle in which the Mendenhalls and Johnstons moved, had sized up the young Holly—an outdoorsy freshman from Montana who loved horses, skiing, and travel—and declared their intent to find her a "Mormon cowboy" to marry. They urged her to contact Bronco, whom she had never met. That is, they urged her *repeatedly.* So finally she put pen to paper. "I am not kidding you," she says. "I wrote him a letter that said, 'Dear Bronco, my name is Holly.'"

They soon met and dated for a time but then parted ways for a decade. They reunited again by chance at an airport. While waiting for her flight, says Holly:

> I saw this guy who had an Oregon State jacket on. I was just sitting there waiting, so I said, "Hey, do you happen to know Bronco Mendenhall?"
>
> He said, "He's right there." I walked over, and Bronco was reading a book. I was just so impressed, because it kind of broke the football mold. He'd been a player when I dated him before, and my parents thought he was a knucklehead, a football jockhead. We had both really changed.

Bronco proposed just after being fired from Oregon State. The couple's honeymoon was the romantic drive from the Northwest down south to Louisiana Tech. "It was a terrible drive down there," says Holly. "It was just long, and we had really bad roads, and there were blizzards all through Montana and Wyoming. Then when we got to Kansas, we stayed in a tiny motel, because that's all there was. They had just washed the carpets. So our feet were squishing in water. It was the only room they had, and we were in the middle of nowhere."

The drive to the South may have been cold and wet, but the couple was happy. Still, they both had second thoughts about

Bronco's career choice. He and Holly were far from home and family. They did not have as much time together as they wanted. Of that early period in their marriage, Holly says:

> I grew up in a family where my dad was totally on his own schedule. If he wanted to go on a family trip, he blocked out the time. Bronco's schedule was rigid, strict. He was never home. He'd leave at 6:00 in the morning and come home at 10:00 at night. I'd left my family, left everyone; I didn't know anyone in Louisiana. It was an extremely different culture than what I was remotely used to. Bronco was gone all the time. I had no friends. I thought there was a competition between the men to see who could get to the office first and who could stay the latest. There was one coach's wife who took me under her wing and taught me the ropes. I will forever be grateful to her for being a good friend and teaching me what a coach's wife does and what the season is about. I mean, we went 9–2. I had no idea how great that was!

Besides all the time away from Holly, Bronco was also dismayed by other facets of his work life. The cockroaches scurried when he flipped on the lights in his office; the projector screen in his meeting room doubled as a barrier to the visitor's restroom, which was noisome and often strewn with dirty laundry.

There, in muggy north-central Louisiana, Bronco Mendenhall's commitment to coaching was profoundly shaken. Was this really what he wanted? Were the sacrifices worth it? How had he ended up here? Bronco plumbed his depths, striving to grasp hold of a purpose that could help him find peace, to call forth the inspiration to invigorate the pursuit of his current course.

Though passionate about football, a deep-rooted aspect of Bronco's personality is spiritual. Grandfathers on both sides served in careers for the Church, one as the Presiding Bishop (the leader of the administrative arm of the Church), and one as an administrator of the Church's labor missionary program. His father had recently completed a three-year term as a mission president, where he had directed the labors of dozens of missionaries serving within the boundaries of the Church's New Zealand Auckland Mission. Then he had become a stake patriarch, which is a formal appointment to be the mouthpiece for inspired blessings and counsel to Church members, particularly young people. As Bronco and Holly contemplated having children, Bronco now realized that his work was no longer and could never be ultimately meaningful to him for his personal advancement alone, but only as it furthered something of intrinsic worth.

Did he find that higher purpose, something that could attach him to football coaching in a way that satisfied his desire to reach beyond himself, to serve others, and to contribute to a transcendent cause? He did indeed. After much contemplation and prayer, Bronco came to believe that the greatest value of his work was the opportunity to develop and shape young men, to teach them to consistently put forth their best effort. Perhaps this was a fulfillment of his inclination since a youth to reach out to the underdog. When Bronco envisioned this as his paramount goal rather than the winning of football games, when he realized that he could define his life's work as dedicated service to others, then the intense devotion he was giving to the game seemed worthwhile.

"At some point, I had to decide why I was doing this," he says. "I concluded that I like to see kids try hard. I like to see them develop. I don't coach for Saturdays. I coach for the day-to-day thrill of watching them show up and do the very best they can. That's how I gain the greatest satisfaction. Since I came to that conclusion, I've been at peace with what I'm doing."[6]

In a few years, Bronco's understanding of the meaning of his career would be augmented in important ways. But this initial burst of inspiration refreshed him and provided a backdrop for the unusual leadership approach that he would go on to develop at UNM and BYU. Some of the principles that would later prove startling and fascinating to the national media grew out of his inner struggles in Ruston, Louisiana.

After a year at Louisiana Tech, Bronco heard again from Rocky Long, who was now the head coach at the University of New Mexico in Albuquerque. "Hallelujah!" thought Holly. "We're headed back north! I'll be two days from Montana!" Bronco took the job eagerly, if nothing else, to get Holly closer to home.

By the time Bronco left Albuquerque, where he was the defensive coordinator, he had become known for his gifted ability to help even disadvantaged players reach unexpected heights of performance. His recruits at UNM came from Los Angeles and Texas—rough, street-smart survivors who cared mostly about football and little about academics. "They were a very diverse group of young men trying to survive life experiences that you and I can't even imagine," says Bronco. "I'd coached all these other young men in my career, but I hadn't really *looked* yet." At UNM, Bronco saw deep into the hearts of his players. He felt he might be able to connect with youngsters who but for the game of football would be difficult to reach.

The defensive players may have come to the meetings for the game, but what they began to get from Bronco was something else: a message about who they fundamentally were deep inside. "We were from different faiths," Bronco says, "and it wasn't appropriate in that setting for me to be talking about religion." Instead, he turned to the world's great warrior cultures to capture the attention of his players. He began an informal study of the Zulu, Apache, Samurai, and Pacific Islanders. He found that presenting stories from these cultures and examining their bonding and rites of passage were engaging and intriguing to his young men. On Fridays, Bronco would share a quote with his players about a warrior group. He would expound on the story, the culture, and the principles or practices lived by these heroes.

For example, he told a story his father had repeated throughout his childhood of Maori Battalion 28 that in 1943 faced the German troops of Field Marshall Erwin Rommel in Egypt. Surrounded one day by Rommel's tanks and greatly outnumbered, the Maori forces coalesced at dawn before the invading army and performed the *haka*, a ceremonial war dance, fiercely chanting *Ka Mate! Ka Mate!* and brandishing their tattooed bodies before the stunned Germans. Though casualties were high that day, the Maori troops broke through the German lines, opening a passage for their battalion's trucks and guns.[7]

"The point I made with the players is that in moments of absolute uncertainty and indecision, warriors revert back to who they really are. I trained the kids so hard and gave them such great challenges to bring them right back to the question, 'Who am I?'" In the same way that Bronco challenged himself relentlessly as a youngster in order to prove himself, he now worked his players mercilessly so that they, too, could discover who they were deep inside.

Bronco arranged for a visit from Maori officials. "The leader stood up in front of our team and told a great story about his father, and how he fought off a thousand men," says Nick Speegle (UNM outside linebacker 2001–04; team captain). Nick recalls:

> It was just so inspiring. At the end of that speech, the other tribesmen did the *haka* in front of us. I mean, they were spitting on the people in the first row. It was awesome. Then we flew up to Colorado and played a great game. They went on the flight with us and watched the game. That's just one more example of going that extra distance for us—just us.

Bronco cared so much about us that he would go that extra mile.

"We called the style of defense we were playing at UNM an effort-based system," says Bronco, "meaning you worked as hard as you could. We went to great lengths to make sure there wasn't anybody, anywhere, who was practicing harder or trying harder than we were. It was the rite of passage. There was something special waiting for them that was not for everybody. Those who really wanted it had to demonstrate their desire."

Bronco gave each defensive player a Maori *tiki*—a small, carved pendant—to betoken the World War II Maori Battalion story. They wore them around their necks to remind themselves of their true identities. "These kids were from all different cultures and walks of life, and they valued these emblems," says Bronco. "They knew how to be warriors. They knew how to act tough. But did they know how to be resilient? To persevere? To continue on when *really* challenged? The common message I had for them was simply that they each have greatness inside of them. They are blessed with unique and different gifts, but inside each of them at those critical moments is where they need to look. These moments are when their greatest growth will happen."

Bronco adds:

I allowed them to watch themselves go from wondering about their abilities, to carrying themselves with confidence and viewing themselves as someone of value, as someone who could make a difference, rather than just another kid from this area or street. They actually had great potential. I saw the change manifested most in camaraderie, in cooperative behavior, in caring for one another. Did I change their off-the-field behavior? Did they still drink? Almost every player there did. Were there tattoos from head to toe? On almost every kid. Did they attend strip clubs? Probably. But when they walked through the doors of the building, they found this unique other place that they liked. Not only a physical place, but a mental place.

For all this talk of changing lives and helping youth, Bronco is not a particularly gregarious person. He could never be described as easygoing (though Holly sometimes teases him by calling him "Mr. Happy-Go-Lucky"). By his own admission he does not naturally reach out to others. He is slow to chuckle when amused; his father brags that he is one of the few who can get Bronco to laugh outright. Still, he can be outgoing and friendly in the right circumstances. "You could see this expression on Coach Mendenhall's face when things would go well and everything was clicking on the football field," says Charles Moss (UNM linebacker 1999–2002). "He would smile. You'd see that smile come out. Then he'd run around and have fun on the football field. It was fun to see him. He was just a very stern guy, but he approached life with the belief that there's a time and a place for everything."

Bronco is über-intense. He is captivated by the game, engrossed and absorbed. He cannot easily put it out of his head.

Also, in the words of his wife, Holly, he is "extremely private." He is not one for small talk. Even players who greatly admire him have described him as "standoffish." BYU players would later notice that he avoided extraneous social contact by exiting out the back door of the athletic building. On the whole they would find him unapproachable, especially during his earlier years of coaching. Yet in a few years, the same BYU defensive team he intimidated would feel such admiration and loyalty that they would eventually step up to formally advocate his promotion to head coach.

The apparent paradox is resolved by an understanding that Bronco's successful connection with young men comes not so much through his informal relationships with them, nor through any random moments of jocular exchange or social banter. Rather, his deep concern for their well-being is revealed by his unlimited hope for their potential and his willingness to help them learn about their true selves. He never asks more of them than he asks of himself, never expects them to be or give any less than everything of which they are capable. His hope for their everyday greatness emits like a fiery furnace, warming them even without beckoning them to come too close. When he does invite them in, his concern is perceptive and sincere.

"He expected perfection," says Nick. "There are a lot of coaches who coach by fear. He didn't coach that way." Nick continues:

He just demanded perfection because in his mind, that's what it takes to win. It was a whole new level that he brought his players to. Everybody wanted to win. I mean, you say you play for yourself, but a lot of us were playing for him. We wanted to win for Coach Mendenhall, because of how hard he worked and the type of person he was. He led by example. He would never do the lazy thing. He would always be the first one out at practice. He would never take the elevator; he'd only take the stairs. He'd always do things the hard way because it would make you that much better. As a player, I would think, if there's a lazy option and a hard option, Coach Mendenhall would always take that difficult, hard path. So I was inspired to do the same.

As Bronco's experience as a coach broadened and he honed his ability to coax a farm work ethic, technical precision, and a new sense of personal worth from players of all backgrounds, his brand of character development never wavered from an unyielding expectation of excellence in football performance. Bronco's players worked hard *and* did well. He himself continued to innovate defensive strategies. At New Mexico, he and head coach Rocky Long developed a new defensive scheme for the Lobos. The defense there amassed impressive stats including a three-year run in the Mountain West Conference as the top rushing defense, while leading the league in total defense in 2002 and in sacks in both 2001 and 2002. Bronco coached "Lobo-back" Brian Urlacher, who was picked in the first round of the NFL draft by the Chicago Bears, claimed the 2000 NFL Defensive Rookie of the Year Award, and was voted into eight pro bowls (as of the 2011–12 season). At UNM, Bronco coached in his first-ever bowl game: the 2002 Las Vegas Bowl.

Finally, Bronco's achievements earned him an offer at BYU in 2003—not as a player, as he had dreamed as a youth—but as a coach.

"It was difficult to leave New Mexico," he says. "In fact, Holly and I didn't want to leave. I'd just been promoted to be the assistant head coach and things were going great. The players were making tremendous progress." But after some deliberation, he and Holly made the decision to return to Bronco's native Utah. He was rejoining head coach Gary Crowton, this time as defensive coordinator.

Bronco was glad to be back home after more than ten years of living far from his roots. He and Holly were now the parents of two little sons, and it was good for the boys to be so near at least one set of grandparents. A third son was born to Bronco and Holly a few months after their return to Utah. Bronco was also pleased to be reconnected with Crowton.

But that first season at BYU, when he found himself in Albuquerque playing against the Lobos, he felt like a traitor. The Lobo defenders were wearing their *tikis*. Bronco remembers, "I had coached the kickoff team there, and the whole kickoff team turned to face me and saluted me with upraised fists, which is what we used to do."

Nick Speegle comments:

That was our thing. In the huddle we would raise our fists in the air. That was *his* thing. When he was gone, the team didn't want to do that anymore. When we played BYU, I just remember myself standing and looking at him with my fist raised. I was just showing him: "Coach Mendenhall, we still love you. You did what you had to do for your family, and we're still going to run down on kickoff."

"That will be a moment I will never forget," says Bronco. "They were remembering. That was all I needed to see to continue that same approach, applied now in a completely different setting, to a greater extent, including faith at the very core, but with the same motive of inspiring people to reach their true potential."

All was well.

But at the end of Bronco's second season at BYU, the world turned upside down once more. Crowton resigned in the wake of three losing seasons. Bronco shed tears at the press conference when his friend stepped down. He had hoped that Crowton would be given more time to prove himself at BYU, and he regretted not being able to do something that would have prevented this turn of events.

Driving in his car shortly thereafter, an unnerving impression came to Bronco. He immediately called Holly, who was in the kitchen making dinner. He said, "This is going to sound really crazy, Holly, but I think I'm supposed to be the next head coach here."

She said, "You're kidding! What do you mean? What are you talking about?"

Bronco replied, "Nothing. I'm just saying, I just had a really strong feeling as I was driving around that I'm in line." He had never mentioned a desire to be the head coach before.

"For a long time he had wanted to be a coordinator in the

NFL," Holly says. "He was a great coordinator." But he had never spoken of being a head coach.

Nevertheless, when the media reported that Kyle Whittingham, a former BYU star linebacker and then defensive coordinator at the University of Utah, had been chosen as Crowton's successor, Bronco and Holly prepared the family to move on. Holly says:

> We brought the kids together—it was around Christmas—and we sat them down and said, "We're probably going to move. We'll have a new adventure. We'll meet new friends." You know, in coaching, you just go wherever. You're grateful to have a job. Then we got in the truck and we went to look for a Christmas tree.
>
> Bronco had the radio on, which was really unlike him, because he never listens to the sports shows. The broadcaster said, "We expect to hear any moment the announcement that Kyle Whittingham will be named the head coach of BYU."
>
> Bronco shut it off. I said, "Amen! We don't need to listen to that!"

But then Urban Meyer decided to leave Utah, and Whittingham abruptly took the head coaching spot for the Utes instead of for the Cougars.

Now Bronco's defensive players at BYU made a play for their co-ordinator. They had come to love and respect him, grueling practice regimen and all. "Twenty-five guys knocked on my door one day, all defense," says then-assistant athletic director Tom Holmoe. He had seen these guys "getting their butts whipped" each day on the practice field by their uncompromising coach, yet it was Bronco's "victims" who now pled that he be considered for the job. Tom says, "He was very hard on his defense, but as a unit they wanted him. And that left a very strong impression on me." Tom met with

Bronco, but he was a reluctant candidate. He was deeply loyal to Crowton and peeved by his dismissal. He could not fathom himself as a head coach. He was pointed and frank in initial interviews, even downright abrasive. He rejected the suggestion that changes needed to be made with the team.

So Tom pressed Bronco for a second interview. "He was so loyal to Coach Crowton that he didn't want to say anything bad," says Tom. "I said, 'Bronco, by you suggesting that there are different ways to lead a team, that's not disrespectful to Coach Crowton. I *fired* him, okay? I don't *hate* him. I'm concerned about this program. If you're going to lead it, I've got to know what you're going to do. What are your thoughts? What are your passions? Show me something.'" Bronco reoriented himself and opened up, sharing more of his personal philosophy, of his passion for serving young men, and sketching a possible vision for the team.

Tom offered him the job. "I think we got the perfect guy," says Tom, whose first choice had unequivocally been Whittingham. "In hindsight, Bronco is our guy. This is the perfect fit. I wouldn't have hired him if I didn't think he was going to be successful. But I must say that it happened faster, way faster, than I thought it would."

CHAPTER 2

Head Coach

Being around Coach Mendenhall just made you want to be a better person. He made you want to be a better athlete, a better man overall. It was not really what he said, it was just the way he carried himself as a person. You saw it within his family—he had his first boy when he was at New Mexico— and the way he talked about himself and his wife. Here's a great story: I was a redshirt freshman, and my very first game as a Lobo, actually playing, we lost to Texas Tech. We were on a bus back from the airport in Albuquerque, and I was sitting next to him. We had just lost, and everybody was quiet. He started asking me if I had a girlfriend. He started talking to me about family. I didn't have a girlfriend at the time, and he said, "Never settle for anything but the best. That's the best advice I can give to you." He was talking about my future wife, and we'd just lost a game. He's our D-coordinator, and I'm a freshman. That was a touching moment for me, because it was more than just about football. It was about real life.

—Nick Speegle
UNM linebacker 2001–04

Head Coach

BRONCO'S FIRST DAYS at the helm were marred by what he sensed was a sagging of aspirations all around him. He was not the school's first choice for head coach. No one seemed to have much confidence that he could produce a team that would win a conference championship and regain national prominence. Though it was never communicated to him explicitly, he had a feeling that he would be judged successful by school administrators if he merely inspired the players to behave, taught them to try hard, made sure they went to class, and offered up a group of young men who could respectably represent the university and the Church.

The hopes and dreams that the school and Church leaders had for their new coach amounted to anticipation of a clean and honorable program, or so Bronco felt. Winning football ranked lower on the list of expectations.

Nothing could have motivated Bronco more powerfully than this lackluster outlook, real or imagined. He could envision much more for the team. He could feel it. He could see it. His *raison d'être* may have been day-to-day coaching triumphs rather than Saturday thrills, but that did not mean that he aspired to anything less than victory on those Saturdays. Though he was fully aware of his own inadequacies, at the same time he was filled with ardor about the potential, really the imperative, of a return to glory.

This ardor, which would propel Bronco through his first years at BYU, had been augmented during his final interview in the hiring process with Church leader Henry B. Eyring. President Eyring was, at the time, a member of the Quorum of the Twelve Apostles, which is the one of the highest ecclesiastical governing bodies of the Church, second only to the Church president and his two counselors. (President Eyring is currently in the LDS Church presidency.) Bronco had carefully prepared for this important interview, rehearsing his response to possible questions about how he would turn the football team around, what approach he would take to managing Honor Code violations, and what his recruiting tactics would be.

He was spirited off to meet with President Eyring at a small personal residence near Saratoga Springs, Utah. President Eyring and his wife greeted Bronco, and then the Church leader guided him to a modest office. There were only two chairs, facing each other and nearly touching. As they sat, Bronco tried to slide back to make knee room, but President Eyring reached out to his leg to hold him in place. A thin, smiling, gentle man with round scholarly glasses who had once been a college president, he surprised Bronco by not asking about football at all. He was kindly, but serious and stern. He began the interview with a simple question: Did Bronco believe The Church of Jesus Christ of Latter-day Saints to be true? Bronco could answer that with conviction in the affirmative.

Bronco had never questioned his family's faith nor been tempted by practices such as drinking and smoking, abstinence from which are the most visible evidences of devotion to the Church. But it was not until he was a senior at Oregon State, sharing a house with five football players who were not members of the Church, that he had the overwhelming urge to solidify his religious beliefs. The house was a typical college environment where parties were occasionally held. "I'd get up the next morning to go to church," he says, "and I'd be kicking through bodies and beer cans literally to get out the door." At one point in this incongruous situation he said to himself, "I gotta know."

I closed the door to my room and I stayed in there for two days. I got the Book of Mormon out, and I went from the first page to the last page. Didn't go to class. Didn't do anything else. Because I had to know. Eating was a burden. Sleep was a burden. It was like that. Then, I knew! I remember it was the first time in my life I really *wanted* to know. And I did.

So when President Eyring asked him about his testimony, Bronco had this and all his experience since to draw upon to answer a solid "Yes!" to the question. Bronco took this inquiry itself as guidance about how the BYU football program should be run. It was the closest thing to direction he would ever receive from the Church, the university, or the athletic department.

At the end of the powerful interview, President Eyring exclaimed, "Well, then, you're our man!"

And as the reality of unfolding events loomed large before Bronco, he thought, "I don't know if I want to be anyone's man right now." Could he rise to the task? Could he adequately provide the head coaching the team required? Could he shoulder the pressure of being the most public face of BYU? Could he signify to his players, through his own words and behavior, the importance of choosing right and representing the team well?

Bronco asked for a blessing, and President Eyring obliged. Walking around Bronco's chair to stand behind him and placing his hands on Bronco's head, he offered a prayer, giving comfort and encouragement from the Divine. Bronco was calm for the first time in weeks.

The interview stoked the Bronco Mendenhall furnace, and he embarked on the biggest challenge of his first year as BYU Football's head coach: convincing the players, the coaching staff, university administrators, fans and foes in Utah and throughout the land that the football team and individual players could not only reflect the precious values of the educational and ecclesiastical institutions of the

Scan this QR code to see "Becoming BYU's Head Coach" or go to http://bit.ly/LslYBS

Church, but that these values could be openly championed and were fully compatible with the winning of football games.

It is not as though the community did not already know that such a thing was possible. Bronco had inherited a team that had only recently careened away from its rich history of victory and triumph over the odds. LaVell Edwards's legendary achievements had been obtained at the same time he had reversed the program's historical practice of encouraging players to postpone their two-year missions until after their four years of football eligibility were up. LaVell allowed players to interrupt their football careers for their missions and to retain their scholarships, redshirt after their return, and play again when they were ready. He felt that football and religion could not only coexist but also thrive together. So there was no sense of any incongruity between football excellence and Church values under LaVell's leadership, and the team had indeed played successfully at a national level for years at a time.[1]

• • •

After the first press conference announcing his promotion to head coach, Bronco went to his office. The experience of landing the job had been sudden and amazing, and he was overwhelmed. Leading a program would be worlds different from coordinating only a part of it. His walls were as bare as his plans for how to proceed. The burden of what he had just assumed pressed down on him. He lacked know-how, and he knew it. He felt exhausted. He again wondered if he really did want this job after all. Already, 170 phone messages from Church leaders, administrators, and alumni were waiting. He went home that afternoon without answering even a single one.

Bronco arrived at 5:45 the next morning. He knelt in prayer and spent two hours pleading ardently for guidance and assistance. He needed inspiration about how to begin.

Near eight o'clock, he heard a soft knock on his door. LaVell

Edwards himself had come by to provide support and counsel. Who better? The sagacious old coach was aptly the first angel sent to bear up the sagging Bronco Mendenhall!

They sat knee-to-knee, just as in the interview with President Eyring. LaVell looked him in the eye and said, "You have a tough job." It was not what Bronco was hoping to hear, but he knew the truth in those words, because the weightiness of his work had already descended so heavily. LaVell paused for what seemed to be a long time, his eyes penetratingly searching Bronco, and then added, "But you have a great job." In the years to come, Bronco would indeed feel both the depths and the heights of his responsibilities.

LaVell reveals what went through his mind during the conversation: "I thought, 'This guy is young. He's never been a head coach. It's going to be almost like a learn-as-you-go experience.' You just hope to make more good decisions than you do bad decisions. That's the way I felt, anyway, because I made both, you know, along the way."

Advice immediately flooded in. Bronco's inbox overflowed with e-mails from fans. Well-meaning administrators visited his office bringing new themes for him to adopt for the program. His phone rang incessantly with callers eager to have his attention for a few minutes to chip in their opinions. Visitors bent his ear in the grocery store and even stopped by his home to make suggestions.

Bronco was not opposed to the input—who could be dismayed at such passionate interest from the fans?—but much of it was packaged with stinging criticism. In their e-mails and letters, fans impressed upon Bronco how unqualified he was and what a big mistake BYU had made. He still craved qualified guidance that would resonate with his own unequivocal aspirations for the team.

It was during these earliest days of Bronco's new assignment that he followed a tip offered by Tom Holmoe. Following Tom's suggestion, Bronco phoned coauthor Paul Gustavson. Paul was a former BYU player who had been primarily a deep snapper and special teams player. He had been a Cougar during LaVell's first years as head coach. In the decades since, he had pursued a career in management consulting, helping businesses create marketplace advantage through their organization design.

Bronco and Paul had initially spoken when Bronco was in San Francisco, where he had arrived to interview Brandon Doman, then a 49ers quarterback. Bronco was hoping to persuade Brandon, who had led the Cougars to a bowl game only three years earlier as "The Domanator," to consider becoming the Cougars' quarterbacks coach.

Paul felt honored to hear from Bronco. He had been the first walk-on returned missionary during the LaVell Edwards years. He was a lifelong Cougar fan who had ached along with the rest of the BYU community when the team had recently ailed. He wanted to see the program return to the achievements of its heyday as much as Bronco and all the other fans did. He volunteered to help in whatever way he could.

So they set up some time to talk back in Provo.

During their first meeting early one January morning, Paul told Bronco about five key practices pertinent to any organization, any time, any place. Paul compared them to the weapons used by the unlikely hero David when he conquered Goliath. Before David faced the giant, he threw away the heavy accoutrements of battle that others pressed on him and instead selected five smooth stones from a nearby stream for his sling. We know what happened next.

Paul suggested that Bronco would need five smooth stones for his bag as well. Each stone would be a nitty-gritty tool-at-hand for him in his new leadership capacity. Bronco and Paul discussed each

Scan this QR code to see "Paul and Bronco" or go to http://bit.ly/MI6DaA

at length over the next few months and years, mostly during sunrise sessions in Bronco's office, and then Bronco steadily found the best ways to use each stone in the world of college football.

"I'm not a trusting person," says Bronco. "I'm not an openly social person in terms of reaching out. Why I called and decided to set up a time with Paul, I can't tell you, other than it changed my life, and it changed the direction of the program. What we've been able to achieve would not have been possible without that influence. We've spent hundreds of hours together, most of the time early in the morning, before our workday starts. I've learned organizational principles and behavior and leadership through Paul. But I'm the one responsible for the application."

The story of what Bronco did to apply the things he learned unfolds in the remaining pages of this section.

CHAPTER 3

Different

When Coach Mendenhall came in from New Mexico, he would not play me because I didn't work hard enough for him. So I ended up red-shirting, but I was happy because then I could get ready for him and his standards. Then my senior year came, and he literally changed the way I looked at football. It wasn't just a game for talented kids. He was looking for people who were willing to work their hardest. He changed my perspective on football and also on life.

I always had a good work ethic, but he took it to a whole different level. There are no shortcuts. I tried to get away from Coach Mendenhall and the standards that he set. He has a pursuit drill that he does, and I hated that thing. When we first did it, I hid under the filming lift because I hated it so much. The next day he called me into his office. I forgot that there was another camera on the other side that caught me hiding!

After my redshirt year, every kid who was on the team said I was one of the best defensive linemen. But after spring ball, I went in to have an interview with Coach Mendenhall, and he told me that I wouldn't play on his defense. I said,

"Coach, I don't know if you know this, but this is my senior year."

He told me, "I don't really care. I think you're very athletic, but you find your way out of drills. You're kind of lazy at times. I'd rather play other kids that go all out."

I'll never forget sitting in his office; I was crying. I was telling him, "This is my senior year; you can't put me on fourth team."

He said, "You have the whole summer and three weeks of camp to prove to me that you really want to start."

So that summer I worked my butt off. I watched what I ate; I worked hard. When I came back for fall camp, he still put me on the fourth team. I had three weeks of fall camp to prove myself. I didn't hide from the drills; I finished every one. He made me repeat them over and over again. He tested me so hard at fall camp, I ended up starting. He saw that I worked my way up. I actually gained his respect.

I got Second Team All-Conference that year, and I got drafted. Those things made me happy, but my biggest pride was to finally start on his defense. That was my accomplishment that I was most proud of.

After I played for him, I had a short career with the Pittsburgh Steelers. He played a big role in me making it there. We went to the Super Bowl. After the NFL, I came back and literally begged him for almost four months to hire me as a graduate assistant. He eventually did. Working for him was the exact same thing, and the standards for the staff are the same as the standards he sets for his players. If I turned in a report to him and he saw a misspelled word, he'd make me go through it all over again. There are no shortcuts. If you're going to do a job, do it right. If you're going to get into something, do it with all your heart. Be your best at it.

What I learned from him opened up a lot of doors for me. I hope I can inspire and help kids who are in the same situation I was.

—Shaun Nua
BYU defensive line 2002–04;
current Naval Academy
assistant defensive line coach*

I MAGINE YOURSELF in Bronco's position. You were the underdog candidate. You have never been a head coach before. There is tremendous pressure from fans to return the team to its former status and from administrators to keep the players out of trouble. You know it can be done. What would you do first?

Much of the early advice Bronco received had to do with programs BYU should emulate. E-mails talked up the merits of Mack Brown's work at the University of Texas. Folks at the grocery store suggested he benchmark the fine program at Florida or the Sooners' way of doing things at the University of Oklahoma.

STRATEGIC DIFFERENTIATION

Nearly ten years before Bronco found himself in this situation, Michael Porter, an international expert on business strategy, wrote an article for the *Harvard Business Review* entitled, "What is Strategy?" Porter emphasized there is only one way to obtain enduring advantage over your competitors, and it is not by copying them. Modern corporations, he said, have all become very good at what they do. They also have become adroit at recognizing and copying the best practices of their rivals.[1]

So, if at first blush, it seems as if finding and emulating the best practices from the NCAA football world would be a laudable way to begin a head-coaching career, after a little consideration you might

* See his story at "BYU Athletics—Shaun Nua" on YouTube.

conclude what Porter described in his *HBR* piece—that if you can copy superior programs and amass the techniques of other teams, then you also can be copied. That if you do the *same things* as your competitors do, but *better*—you'll be good, but you won't be good forever. It won't be long before another team will outperform you at your own game, so to speak.

Porter explained that superior performance can only be sustained by doing *different things* than your rivals, or by doing the same things *differently.* To be sure, everything you do must be done well, but certain chosen activities must be completely different from what anyone else does, or if they are similar to what others do, they must be done differently.

Smooth Stone #1

Organizations can craft a sustainable competitive advantage through differentiation.

The first smooth stone for Bronco's shepherd's bag was a lesson about how to achieve *sustainable competitive advantage.* Paul sent him Porter's classic article ahead of their first meeting. When the morning of the appointment arrived, as Paul busied himself setting up his PowerPoint presentation, Bronco set the article on the table in front of him. He had gone through the entire document, highlighting relevant sentences on every page and throwing down ideas for BYU in the margins. Never in Paul's experience had an executive prepared so thoroughly and with such utter enthusiasm. In that first two-hour meeting, Paul never got past his prepared overview of the five smooth stones. Bronco was bursting with thoughts about activities that could be done differently in recruiting, spring camp, fall camp, and more. This would become a pattern. In all the years and hundreds of hours with Paul, Bronco was every time ebullient with ideas about how to create a competitive advantage in some facet of the program. (You can read more about Smooth Stone #1 in section 2.)

As Bronco continued developing what is or could be distinct about BYU Football, Paul encouraged him to nurture that distinctiveness and find a way to compete that would be impossible for any other football program to replicate. Rather than pointing Bronco to other programs to imitate, he urged him to differentiate. Do something entirely different, he said, echoing Porter, or else do something similar but in an entirely different way.

To say Bronco embraced the concept of strategic differentiation would be an understatement. It was like a spark igniting his mind and setting off an enormous explosion of insight and ideas for the Cougars. Bronco suddenly saw that in his two years as an assistant coach at BYU, the program had been intent on imitating others. The coaches had brought the practices that had been successful for them elsewhere—at Oregon State, at Louisiana Tech, at Texas Tech, at New Mexico—and tried to use them again in a completely different environment. They had recruited the same young men as everyone else, had held them to the same academic standards to which they would be held anywhere else, and asked them to do the same things that anyone else would. Yet BYU is an educational institution unlike any other, so these copycat practices meant only that the staff had been working against the potential strengths of the team.

It is probably unnecessary to point out that BYU is a unique university, but it's worth reviewing some of the points of radical divergence.

BYU is attended by 33,000 students, so it's a large school, but nothing unusual there. Thirty-three percent of the students come from

Scan this QR code to see "Differentiation" or go to http://bit.ly/NyO7h2

Utah, the rest from elsewhere in the United States and 115 countries around the world. A nice global reach, but nothing that's not obtained by many large state or private schools. Most obviously unusual about BYU is the religious composition of its student population. Ninety-eight percent are members of The Church of Jesus Christ of Latter-day Saints, though students of any religion—as well as gender, race, or nationality—are welcome as long as they meet admission requirements and agree to abide by the school's standards of behavior.

BYU ranks the highest of any major college or university on the *Princeton Review*'s list of most religious students.[2]

Admission is very competitive. Many more of the 14-million-member Church's young people wish to come to Provo than can be accommodated. The average entrant ACT and SAT scores are 28 and 1250, respectively; the average GPA is 3.8. Applicants also must obtain a recommendation from their ecclesiastical leader, whether or not they are Latter-day Saints, and show a well-rounded record of accomplishments.

BYU annually ranks first or second (behind Harvard) as the most popular university in the nation, which means that the yield of accepted students who go on to enroll is exceptionally high—about 75 percent.[3]

The BYU Honor Code is big news in the national media, but it does not require behavior that is unfamiliar to young people who have either grown up in or even recently joined the Church. Church programs for youth and religion classes for high school students emphasize the same values encoded in the Honor Code. Young Latter-day Saints are taught to be honest, dress modestly, abstain from the use of alcohol and drugs, and eschew premarital sex.

BYU has held for more than a decade the number-one spot on the *Princeton Review*'s list of "Stone-Cold Sober" schools.[4]

Of the BYU student population, 78 percent of males are returned missionaries, and 10 percent of females have served a mission. These young people have volunteered to spend eighteen months (for women) or two years (for men) in an effort to share the message of the gospel and to provide community service to the citizens of the globe, mostly at their own expense. A great many serve in countries other than that of their own origin, often learning a second language and being thoroughly immersed in a foreign culture.

These missionaries leave family, friends, school, work, and perhaps a romantic interest behind and journey to a faraway place, where they quite possibly are just learning the language, are unfamiliar with the food, and aren't able to communicate with loved ones at home more than once a week—and then only in writing. On arrival, they don't know a soul. They spend long days knocking on doors and sitting in the living rooms of the world, testifying of their hearts' dearest sentiments, or ladling in soup kitchens, or cleaning up after natural disasters, or providing other service in the community. This is an extraordinary formative experience for a young man or woman. If you had been a star high school football player, though, you might find that a body toned by many years of dedicated conditioning is quickly transformed by great Mexican cooking into more than a few extra pounds, or that an athletic frame is diminished into sinewy leanness while you pad and pedal around the countryside of Guatemala or the streets of Singapore.

But to Coach Mendenhall and many others, the most important and defining aspect of BYU is its mission, which is "to assist individuals in their quest for perfection and eternal life."[5] (This, by the way, is where BYU Football's 2008 "Quest for Perfection" theme had its origins.)

Among the specific aims of the university—in addition to intellectual goals—is to spiritually strengthen and build character in its students.[6] Pioneer leader and Church president Brigham Young himself urged the first president of the school "to remember that you ought not to teach even the alphabet or the multiplication tables without the Spirit of God," for, as he said on another occasion, "a firm, unchangeable course of righteousness through life is what secures to a person true intelligence."[7] The school's charge is "to educate students who are renowned for what they are as well as for what they know. . . ."[8] BYU "fulfills its promise only when 'the morality of the graduates of this University provide[s] the music of hope for the inhabitants of this planet.'"[9] Indeed, a service ethic is another aim of a BYU education. "BYU should nurture in its students the desire . . . not only to enrich their own lives but also to bless their families, their communities, the Church, and the larger society. Students should learn, then demonstrate, that their ultimate allegiance is to higher values, principles, and human commitments rather than to mere self-interest. By doing this, BYU graduates can counter the destructive and often materialistic self-centeredness and worldliness that afflict modern society."[10]

After learning about the first smooth stone from Paul, Bronco suddenly saw that the principles of BYU's rich mission could and should be extended to guide the football program no less than any other department or college at the university. He believed that he must lead his staff and his players into alignment with the school's highest purposes, and that such a move would kindle a brilliant flame that would fuel the highest level of individual and team achievement possible, as it had kindled in himself a desire to see the team reach its ultimate potential.

FLAG BEARERS

He wasted little time in gathering his assistant coaches together to study the BYU mission statement and aims and to articulate the football program's own singular purpose. "We talked about this: What is it exactly, with the end in mind, that we hope to do?" says Bronco. "What is our mission? What is our path?" An hours-long session resulted in a mission statement and the identification of the core values that would be cherished, nurtured, and even proclaimed above all others.

The mission adopted by the BYU football program, then, is "to be the flag bearer of Brigham Young University through football excellence, embracing truth, tradition, virtue, and honor as a beacon to the world." Bronco's studies of military history provided the image of the flag bearer. The warriors who carry the flag to battle are on the front lines leading the charge. They represent the cause, the entire army, an entire people. As the most visible group from BYU and arguably the most visible LDS group aside from the Mormon Tabernacle Choir, the BYU football team, whether in fact they choose the role for themselves or not, are indeed flag bearers. From that moment, the coaching staff embraced the charge. "We carry the colors in everything we do," says Bronco. "We'll carry the flag high, and we'll carry it with the right intent."

Bronco and his coaches identified three core values for the program as well: Tradition, Spirit, and Honor.

Tradition, because of the program's rich history of football excellence: twenty-three bowl games since 1974, a national championship, twenty conference championships, forty-five All-American citations awarded to thirty-eight players, four members of the College Football Hall of Fame, including a Hall of Fame coach, a Heisman trophy winner, a Doak Walker Award winner, four Davey O'Brien Award winners, two Outland Trophy winners, seven Sammy Baugh Trophy honorees, a two-time National Coach of the Year, thirteen NCAA Post-Graduate Scholars, and twenty-four Academic All-Americans who had earned a total of thirty-one Academic

Scan this QR code to see "Mission Statement" or go to http://bit.ly/SHMWKU

Tradition–Spirit–Honor wall

All-American citations. Bronco wanted the program under his direction to show no less success achieving awards such as these.

Spirit, meaning the Spirit of God, not the enthusiastic loyalty usually meant by school spirit. The football program would affirm its commitment to seeking the Spirit, living by the Spirit, turning to the Spirit, and keeping football affairs "bathed in the light and color of the restored gospel."[11]

Honor, as inspired by the university's Honor Code. The football program would be committed to cultivating an "atmosphere consistent with the ideals and principles of the gospel of Jesus Christ," which would mean players and coaches would be selected who would voluntarily "maintain the highest standards of honor, integrity, morality, and consideration of others in personal behavior."[12] That would mean, among other things, observing the dress and grooming standards (short hair, clean-shaven faces), shunning foul language, abstaining from alcohol and tobacco use, participating regularly in church services, and encouraging others in their commitment to comply with the Honor Code.

It was a personal triumph for Bronco and his staff to have worked together to clarify and develop their own mission for the team. "Why should the program be like any other place in the country?" he said passionately at the time. He explained,

> Why should it be the same? It should be different and distinct. The expectations of our players should be different in every area. That's the way we're going. Has it been done before? It's been dabbled with, and I think there's been strong leadership for a number of years. But it was a defining moment in BYU's future, the way I see it, when we aligned our mission and values with that of our parent institution.

Not long after settling on these principles, some senior athletic department administrators, who had been recommending possible strategies to Bronco, gathered in his office. He enthusiastically shared the new mission and three core values. To Bronco's utter astonishment, these administrators met his news with reluctance. It wasn't the flag-bearing stance that they objected to, nor the idea of deriving inspiration from BYU Football's history, nor committing to its Honor Code. But they squirmed at the overt emphasis Bronco was planning to place on the Spirit.

"I'll never forget it," says an astounded Bronco. "I said, 'What are you talking about? From my understanding, you might argue that the football program is the most visible part of the institution, which is owned by the Church, so how does that not connect? Isn't that why the institution was formed?'"

What they feared, as they warned Bronco that day, was that he would become "a target"—a target of criticism, a target of ridicule, a target of media gawking and sniggering.

Bronco's pioneer past loomed as a response formed in his mind. When have Church members *not* been a target? When had severe persecution, from the embattled days of mob violence in the Missouri frontier to the wrecked dreams and temples in Ohio and Illinois, ever deterred Church members from doing what they believed to be right? The administrators feared that championing the influence of the Spirit of God so openly was perhaps inappropriate in the current college football milieu.

Bronco simply ended the conversation. He obtained the warm support of Tom Holmoe, who was now the athletic director, and never looked back. This is not to say that the criticism, which did, in fact, ensue as the administrators had predicted, was not irksome to Bronco. Since then, both foes and fans have indeed accused him of being self-righteous or pompous.

It is understandable, in a largely secular society, that some observers would be arrested by Bronco's brand of religious talk. Sentiments of faith are perhaps even less expected or tolerated in the bold and boisterous world of sports broadcasting. The team's theologically tinged 2008 theme, "Quest for Perfection," was resoundingly ridiculed by some as ostentatious, especially when the team's exciting initial performance yielded a 10–3 season in the end, somewhat short of flawlessness. Bronco explained to national sports talk show host Jim Rome that this expression, lifted verbatim from BYU's mission statement, had less to do with the team's designs for their record and more to do with Bronco's persistent encouragement for team members to strive to meet their potential in every area of their lives.

To conclude that Bronco or his team or individual players are imperiously pious is to misunderstand their focus. To carry the flag for them is an act of determination and courage. Their intent is to open their mouths about the beliefs that guide them and to go ahead of others in doing so—not just members of The Church of Jesus Christ of Latter-day Saints, but all people of faiths who believe themselves—allow themselves—to be guided daily by a loving influence that transcends this often bawdy arena in which we live. Whether or not your beliefs resound with this worldview, perhaps you can appreciate Bronco's forthright conviction that in order to be true to his commission as the head coach of BYU Football, there was really no other option than to take a stand openly about the divine influence that he and his players believe they need and feel every day.

"I had no idea of the exposure," Bronco says of the limelight in which he now finds himself. "I might as well just carry a flag around all day and all night. And what a great opportunity it is. When we play, that's the most visible way to demonstrate who we are. Winning gives credibility to our message. Some might say that there is no connection between football and religion. I promise you, that is not the case."

And what is that connection? "Maybe faith can move mountains," read a 2005 *ESPN: The Magazine* article on Bronco. "But can it blanket a 4.4 receiver on a fly pattern? Because that's what Mendenhall really needs." The article, written in the fall of Bronco's first season at the helm, expressed deep skepticism that stricter adherence to university standards would be anything other than an insurmountable handicap to Bronco in restoring the team's performance as he so very much hoped he could. It cynically suggested that a team couldn't hold players accountable to high moral standards and play conference-topping seasons at the same time.[13]

But Greg Wrubell, KSL Newsradio's "Voice of the BYU Cougars," has an explanation that works whether or not your philosophy is religious. After Bronco's second season at the helm, Wrubell explained:

Bronco doesn't expect perfection from every individual on his team, but he does expect a commitment. If you're committed, you're trying, you're working hard—he expects to see results, and indeed the results have been demonstrated. It's not illogical to say that this team is being rewarded for that commitment. People often ask, "Does God care about the outcome of sporting events?" That point may be debated for a long time! But I think God does care about each individual trying to make himself a better individual. If you have 105 of those individuals working together, you're going to have a pretty good football team, and one that can say to itself, "Yeah, we are seeing the rewards. We're seeing the results of that commitment."[14]

Bronco asks: "Was it difficult to face the criticism when we carried the flag out and then explained what that act represented? Was it difficult to share two accounts, scriptural accounts, as we unveiled the new uniform in front of the cameras? No question. Did it take courage? No question." But he adds:

From my understanding, people of faith are to be representatives at all times, in all things, in all places. That to me means as football players and football coaches as well. I'm not so sure it's different if you're a student or an employee in any other business. If the spiritual nature that we carry with us in our countenance isn't first and foremost in our lives, then I don't think our priorities are correct. We have a very clear idea of the mission of this institution and the mission of our football program, which is to be the flag bearers of Brigham Young University through football excellence, embracing truth, tradition, virtue, and honor as a beacon to the world. That's our mission. And that leads to a sense of calm and a sense of purpose and a sense of determination. It's not about the other team. It's about us. And we're just simply trying to do the best we can to represent this institution at its highest level, and with the special message we have that's behind that.[15]

According to Bronco, football means little but as a vehicle to help others receive a message of real value and substance.[16]

And *that's* Bronco's strategy for sustainable competitive advantage in college football—a strategy and approach that fully embraces Michael Porter's admonition to do *different things* than your rivals, or to do the same things *differently.*

CHAPTER 4

On the Bus

Bronco had a huge impact on me personally. I had respect for him immediately. He demanded that respect. A little story for you: I'm a guy who likes to use slang a lot when I talk to people. It's just my way of letting them know that I want to be friendly. When I would see coaches in the hallway, I'd say, "Hey, bro," or, "What's up, man?" Bronco still looks young today, and he looked about my same age then. When he first showed up, I looked at him as the kind of guy who would probably like to be called bro, dude, man, or whatever. One day, I was walking down the hallway, and I saw him, and I said, "Hey, what's up, man?"

He stopped abruptly and s-l-o-w-l-y turned around with a very focused look. He stared right through me, and he said in a very Clint Eastwood, stoic, monotone voice, "It's 'Coach' to you, son." He turned around and walked away, and I stood there pretty much frozen.

I thought, "Okay. I will never call that guy dude, man, or bro again! It will be 'Coach' from here on out!"

—BRADY POPPINGA
BYU LINEBACKER 2001–04

I N THE BUSINESS WORLD, an organization doesn't aim to have a good year and then plan for a couple of down cycles before coming back. An organization strives to be on the top of the market year in and year out because that's what investors require. That was Bronco's goal as well. That's what BYU Football was once able to achieve. When the team won the national championship in 1984, this ultimate achievement was preceded by nine conference championships in a row and a total of ten in the eleven years before the national title.

To again achieve this kind of sustained success, Bronco began to develop a unique model to take advantage of the unique strengths of his unique players. Not only would the recruiting process be different but so would every other facet of the program—off-season conditioning, spring practice, team meetings, and more. Bronco's intent was to ensure the program was separate and distinct. That's what it had been in its heyday under LaVell Edwards, but as time had marched on an even greater intensification of the Y's distinctiveness was called for. Bronco's aim was to remake the program, relaunch its strengths, and recapture the prominence of the past.

So, having tuned in to the flag-bearer identity, how did Bronco apply the principle of being different into gaining competitive advantage?

Paul and Bronco discussed how it takes an *array* of activities linked together to achieve long-term success. But the first thing to do even before weaving a signature fabric of organizational practices is to choose the artisans who will weave and wear that cloth.

RECRUITING THE RIGHT PEOPLE

The first step Bronco took was to get the right people on the bus, allow the wrong people off the bus, and get the right people in the right seats. This is a metaphor from *Good to Great*, the book by Jim Collins that describes how companies achieve enduring high performance. The Cougar staff studied the book together. Collins discusses how great companies begin with "who," not "what." He says, "*First* get the right people on the bus (and the wrong people off the bus) *before* you figure out where to drive it."[1]

In actual fact, the process of allowing the wrong people off the bus began in the early hours of Bronco's first morning on the job. Emerging from his office after his heart-to-heart with LaVell Edwards, Bronco faced the most touted, highly recruited player on the team, waiting for him dressed in a suit and tie.

Bronco invited the player into his office and listened. "This isn't going to be for me," the young man began. Bronco had not yet had a team meeting, not spoken a word to his players about how things might be different as they moved forward, but the player knew well enough. "I've watched you as the defensive coach. We're going to have to try harder. We'll be expected to excel in the classroom. The Honor Code is going to be important. You're going to ask a lot, right?"

Bronco confirmed, "All those things are true."

The player responded, "This is not for me. I would like to be released from your program." Bronco said simply, "You're right then. This isn't for you. I'll be glad to help you find a place that meets your expectations."

That same day at 3:30 in the afternoon, after the first team meeting, two other players quit. Bronco by now had had a chance to share clearly what the expectations would be—harder work, stricter adherence to commitments, more rigorous academic monitoring. It wasn't for everyone. Bronco didn't push them out; he simply explained what to anticipate in the weeks and months ahead, and then the players "self-selected" for outplacement. Bronco helped them move on to a school that was a better fit.

First day, three players off the bus.

"I'm not going to make any apologies for it," said Bronco at the time, after yet another player had exited the program. He explained to a group of fans in the community:

> So many of you sent me e-mails [asking], "What's the problem? Why are these guys leaving?" I don't think it's a problem. I think it's a strength. The expectation was set very clearly to them, and they chose not to meet it, either [because of] the academic standard, the Honor Code standard, or . . . the work demand. Self-selection. They chose to leave the program. I was more than willing to help them find a place that met their expectations.[2]

As Bronco turned his attention to getting the right players on the bus, he crafted a new set of stringent qualifications for recruits.

In terms of athletic ability, recruits would be required to have Division 1 talent. The coaching staff would pay little attention to a high school athlete's star rating. He need only be fit for Division 1 football.

In terms of academics, BYU would set the bar high in order to give players the best chance of academic success and to assess their commitment to goals broader than athletics. Roughly a 3.0 high school GPA would be the criterion. Bronco believes this was the most stringent GPA recruiting target in the country, and it's only gotten stricter since Bronco's first year.

In terms of behavioral standards, recruits would not be brought to campus until they had obtained an endorsement from their ecclesiastical leader, regardless of faith. This endorsement would now be required near the beginning of the recruiting process. It would no longer be a minor part of the package of paperwork put together at the end. It would be one of the first hurdles and would send an early signal.

Many observers might conclude that these strict requirements would limit the pool of qualified talent. But Bronco had decided to be different, and he also knew what his trade-offs would be as well. He knew exactly what kind of young man he was after for the team. He says this move was not limiting. It was efficient. There was no good in cajoling reluctant youths to sign an Honor Code that they had no intention of upholding, only to lose them a year or two later to Honor Code violations. Better to let them internalize it from the start. Better to identify the pool of qualified players as early in the process as possible.

Sounds noble, doesn't it? Consider this: in Bronco's first recruiting season, the program had twenty-four scholarships to give. How many qualified recruits did they find? The year before, when Bronco was still an assistant coach, the database of potential recruits was a thousand strong. A year later, with the new requirements in place, that pool shrunk to thirty-four. Just thirty-four athletes in the entire United States and Tonga and Samoa who could potentially play for BYU on scholarship! The difference is breathtaking. But Bronco describes it as efficient. Different criteria. Different screening. Different mission.

The next step in Bronco-style recruiting would be to choose those athletes who would welcome flag bearing as an opportunity, not a burden. The tactic would be to let the mission choose the team. Young men would come because they *wanted* to carry the colors of Brigham Young University, embracing truth, tradition, virtue, and honor as a beacon to the world.

The coaches' recruiting duties, after screening all the candidates who passed the recruiting criteria, would be to educate potential players about the expectations they would face at BYU. They would describe how players would need to be conscientious and hardworking and embrace the rigor demanded by the program. Then they would let the young men decide if this was a challenge that beckoned them. Did they connect with the team's mission as flag bearers? Did they concur that football is only a vehicle by which to do a fundamentally more important work? Bronco wanted to be convinced that the recruit had a burning desire to come play for BYU. He did not wish to engage in the dubious work of wooing a foot-dragging star athlete.

Bronco tests recruits for this desire in moments unique to the BYU recruiting *modus operandi*. When they sit in Bronco's office flanked by their parents, he asks them to read statements made by Church presidents regarding the mission of BYU. They read the words of Gordon B. Hinckley, Church president from 1995 until his death in 2008:

Here we are doing what is not done in any other major university of which I am aware. We are demonstrating that faith in the Almighty can accompany and enrich scholarship in the secular.[3]

They also read the words of President Thomas S. Monson, President Hinckley's successor:

You have the blessing of receiving your education at an institution . . . where one of the goals of the university is to build testimonies of the restored gospel of Jesus Christ and encourage living its principles.[4]

"Every young man is asked to read that out loud," says Bronco. "Just by watching them, we have a great idea whether this is for them or not." He talks to them about the principles of the program, stressing the Cougar Football order of priorities: Faith first, then family, then finding knowledge, then friends, and finally football. "Often there is just disbelief that that's how the program is really run," says Bronco.

"As kids come in here," he adds, "many times their parents are in tears. The recruit is not. The parents have yearned for years and years for this opportunity for their son." Bronco tells of one father who, after his son accepted the scholarship, asked if they could all kneel in prayer so that he could immediately thank the Lord that his prayers for his son had been answered. "So I'm the head coach, talking in a recruiting setting, and the dad stops us. He kneels, and the younger brother, who has come in as well, kneels, and his son that was just offered the scholarship kneels, and I kneel." The father then offered a prayer.

"That is the ideal for these kids," says Bronco. He wants kids and families whose absolute dream is being fulfilled by the football scholarship, but who also believe this opportunity is an essential accomplishment to form the foundation for the rest of the player's life. "When I go into homes on recruiting trips, the families that have this dream, it's almost like I'm welcomed as a Church authority," says Bronco. "They have brought their entire families there and they expect a spiritual message! They say, 'Now we'd like to turn the time over to Coach Mendenhall!' They're not wanting to talk BYU Football—they're wanting a sermon. And it's an amazing thing. But those are the right kids."

Is Bronco ready with a sermon? Always.

With these and other recruiting tactics emphasizing the broader mission of the university, Bronco is able to identify players who would come to BYU because of the values, not in spite of them. Therefore, they would be already united in a common cause before the first team meeting, before the first practice, before the first win. Bronco says that when you get the right people on the bus and they are passionate about the mission, you can ask them for anything. It is critical to have the right people committed to the right cause.

TRANSITION TO THE RIGHT CULTURE

These new tactics would eventually refine the composition of the team and streamline recruiting efforts. But Bronco already had a solid base of team members who were potentially the right people for the bus and would likely resonate with Bronco's renewed emphasis on faith and values. Each year, of 105 or so players, roughly 65–75 have served full-time missions for the Church. This was true when Bronco became head coach as well. When Paul played for BYU in 1972, there were only a couple of returned missionaries on the team, and he was one of them! These are young men who have chosen on their own to set out across the world for two years, knocking on doors, sharing their faith, and offering community service. A dozen or so languages are spoken in the locker room as a result of these adventures. A set of experiences is held in common between these men unlike at any other football program at any other university.

Owing to these two-year absences from football, the average age of the BYU player is a bit advanced. Debate erupts periodically about whether this is an advantage or disadvantage. Bronco has perspective on the matter. When he was the defensive coordinator at New Mexico in 2000, the coaches gathered to prepare to play against LaVell Edwards in his last home game at the BYU stadium. As they all sat around the staff room table in Albuquerque, one of the coaches said, "How are we going to beat these guys? They have all these returned missionaries!" From UNM's perspective, the returned missionaries had a competitive advantage because they were bigger and more mature.

Three years later, Bronco was an assistant coach at BYU, getting ready with his colleagues to play USC at the Los Angeles Memorial Coliseum. Sitting around the staff table, one of the coaches asked,

Scan this QR code to see "Unique Recruiting Requirements" or go to http://bit.ly/NA3UsW

"How are we going to beat USC? We have all these returned missionaries!"

Is a team of returned missionaries wiser and bigger and more seasoned than the usual profile of players? Or, on the other hand, do they lose their edge when they step out of play for a couple seasons and then face the daunting challenge of up to a year of reconditioning just to return to their former strength and agility? Bronco chose to stop comparing them to the alternative and instead identified the strengths of this demographic. And the primary strength he saw in them was a *service* mindset. It's who they *are* as men. And though their muscles may have atrophied and their football momentum may have stalled while they'd been gone, during that time many had gained significant leadership experience. They had adhered to strict daily schedules, reached deep to keep themselves going when proselytizing success was scarce, trained new ("green") companions in the mission field, and served in mission offices where they managed and motivated their peers. They may have come home slack of muscle but strong of mind.

Cameron Jensen (linebacker 2004–06; team captain) was one such player. Out of high school in Bountiful, Utah, Cameron was a linebacker for Ricks College (now BYU–Idaho), and then served a two-year mission in Russia. Returning from his mission, he was recruited by the likes of Oklahoma, UCLA, Arizona—and BYU. He chose BYU because he felt a connection to its mission.

He had grown taller and skinnier on his mission. Cameron says he had watched his body "withering away" while in Russia, but he knew it would come back. He tried to do as much as he could at the time, getting up earlier than required for push-ups and other conditioning exercises. "But I knew I'd be blessed if I gave it all to my mission," he says. He was in pads on the practice field only a week after his return. "It was a very humbling experience."

Bronco remembers watching Cameron at fall camp in 2003.

He had an eager heart and demonstrated strong motivation, but his body was sadly unprepared. When the rest of the team filed back to the locker room after practice, Cameron appeared with two big sandbags. Hoisting one on each shoulder, he commenced lunges, hauling himself and his sandbags around the whole practice field. "My legs weren't coming back as quick as I wanted them to," explains Cameron.

Observing this, Bronco predicted then that Cameron would make the first defensive team and would be a starting player. Bronco also knew that day that Cameron would strongly influence the team and because of his commitment would emerge as a powerful leader. And he did. Anchoring the defense for three years and leading the team in tackles each season, he became a three-time All-MWC honoree and captained the team for two years. Bronco says he was the best leader he ever coached.

Though Cameron excelled on the team, his first years, when Bronco was still the defensive coordinator, were not everything he had expected. Cameron remembers, "When I came to BYU Football I was surprised by the lack of activities with a spiritual component. I really felt as though something was missing. I wanted that to be part of the program; it's one of the reasons I came to BYU."

Lasting success comes by getting the right people on the bus and crafting organizational practices that capitalize on their strengths. So the question became, how could Bronco connect those strengths to the guys on the bus—guys such as Cameron Jensen and others? When Bronco took the helm, the team was dispirited by defeats and scandal, and now they had lost some key players. Plus, as a former defensive coach, Bronco had much to do to build relationships with the offensive side of the team.

The change would not be easy or instantaneous. Bronco would be altering the culture of the organization. Culture change is ponderous. It cannot be accomplished without extraordinary tenacity on the part of an organization's leaders. But Coach Mendenhall was up to the assiduous husbandry required.

He began right away by commencing team meetings with a prayer. This was welcome to many players. But it was met with resistance by others, even returned missionaries. When prayer was held in the locker room, a few of these young men would slip away from the area. They did not wish to integrate their football experience with their faith. It was a different way of doing things that they did not immediately embrace.

Bronco and Paul discussed culture change in one of their early morning meetings. They talked about how big changes in life occur in stages: an unfreezing of the old ways is followed by a period of transition and learning, and then new routines eventually refreeze into established practices and traditions.[5] As a leader, Paul said, Bronco could help change take hold by creating memorable events to emphasize each stage of the transition process. And the three best facilitators of long-term memory are *significant emotional experiences* (you remember where you were on 9/11), *music* (you learned your alphabet with the help of a familiar song), and *metaphor* (you remember the mission of Cougar Football more clearly because it incorporates the metaphor "flag bearer").[6]

They talked through ways to bring a divided team together into a unified whole and considered team-building activities as one way to help the players experience how working together and trusting each other might feel.

They also reviewed research on individual and team performance. Athletes, entertainers, and other individuals who attain greatness, Paul explained, can see it in their minds before it happens. The diver can see the dive before jumping; the mountain climber can envision the ascent to the top of the mountain before embarking; the dancer can imagine a perfect performance before stepping on stage.[7]

So to apply these ideas, Bronco set out to create a series of memorable events, at times using music and metaphor, that would help the team leave the ignominy of the recent past behind and envision for themselves an exciting future.

The first event was staged during off-season conditioning in early 2005. The team loaded into buses and set off for a mystery destination, which turned out to be Provo Canyon, just a short drive up the road. On a chilly evening in mountain terrain still subdued by the quiet desolation of winter, players huddled close to a bonfire with poster paper and markers and, under Bronco's instruction, wrote out lists of things that had recently gone wrong with BYU Football. Bronco had team leaders read the lists aloud—painful stuff for both players and coaches to review. Then he had them throw the lists in the fire.

Quarterback John Beck (2003–06; team captain) remembers that "next, Coach Mendenhall tossed his own defensive coach ball cap in, then the BYU helmet—the old blue one—as well. Coach said, 'That's all gone. What's done is done. We're starting anew, and we're going to build this place right, and we're going to do everything the right way from now on out.'"[8]

Bronco had the team draw up new lists of the commitments they were willing to make. Then he asked them as they departed in the dark not to look back, but to move forward toward the new program and their own new promises.

Journalist Peter B. Gardner captured John Beck's reaction. "As quarterback, he had experienced the brunt of the team's darkest years," says Gardner, who then quotes Beck: "'When we came to BYU, we had dreams of great things. We wanted to accomplish so much—and it wasn't happening. . . . To burn it all up and say, "That's it. It's done with"—that was a great thing.'"[9]

Prior to the start of spring ball, the team headed for the hills again—this time to the base of the famous white-washed "Y" that is imprinted in concrete on the mountain just east of the university. Bronco's instructions: "Get to the top as fast as you can."

Running uphill a thousand feet or so over the course of a mile has a way of creating a significant emotional experience. As players arrived, dripping sweat, they sat side by side on the Y's white concrete to rest, looking out over a panoramic view of Utah Valley and Utah Lake. Bronco then unveiled a new white helmet, emblazoned over the ears with a Y much like the enormous symbol on which they sat. He said, "This is the view from the top. Take it in. We haven't had this view in a while. Our view has been from the bottom. *The view from the top is different than the view from the bottom.*" Bronco presented their climb to the Y as a metaphor of their uphill battle toward a successful season. He said, "This is going to be what it looks like for us now."

Not long afterward, a new uniform was unveiled in full—another fitting symbol of a fresh start. With season play less than a year away, Bronco had had to move heaven and earth at Nike to secure their agreement to redesign the uniforms, eventually turning to LaVell Edwards to pull strings. (The press labeled the duds "miracle unis.")[10] The new design hearkened back to uniforms of previous decades, reminiscent of those worn by the 1984 national championship team.

At a high-profile press conference to which Bronco had invited 1,700 former Cougar football players, the playbook he brought was a Book of Mormon. He said of the new uniforms, "This is about honoring tradition. This is about respect for and accountability to the coaches and players who have made BYU one of the national pillars of college football. They represent a tradition of over thirty years

 Scan this QR code to see "Transition and Change" or go to http://bit.ly/OaQq5W

of excellence, both on and off the field. . . . This is the look people associate with the great BYU teams of the past. I refuse to entertain anything that does not represent the greatness of BYU Football."[11]

Then he compared the team's mandate to two scripture stories from the Book of Mormon, first about the great prophet-general Moroni and his courage to fight for what was right, and second about the 2000 impressive young men who fought in Moroni's army and garnered divine protection because of their faith and obedience. Some local sports writers hooted at this in the days that followed, but Bronco doggedly muscled through their criticism.

Of course, Bronco was also, predictably, instituting an arduous practice regimen for the full team. One day he tried a "beep test" that the new quarterbacks coach, Brandon Doman, brought with him from the 49ers. Bronco wanted to compare the performance of the Cougars to the standards the 49ers had established for each position. In the test, players race between two cones when a beep sounds, returning at the sound of the next beep. The beeps speed up, requiring players to move faster and faster. But Bronco was frustrated to see players giving up easily.

After practice, there was a discussion among staff members. Some said, "How can we use the standards the 49ers use? They're paid millions of dollars. They are the best athletes in the world. How can our kids compete against that standard?"

"My argument was just the opposite," says Bronco. "Money is [a pro player's] motivation. That's their job. These kids are playing at BYU to represent this place and represent the Spirit. I said, 'We'll blow those standards away.'" Bronco was vindicated when, two weeks later, every BYU position but one could beat the 49ers' standards.

Bronco expected phenomenal effort from every player. He planted himself firmly in this stance and steeled himself for resistance. He explained indignantly at the time:

I've had so many chances to tell the players, "You know what? I'm not going to get tired." When there's a new coach who takes over, [players] want to start poking and prodding and trying to find where the holes are. Where can they make it easier? Where can they get away from the discipline? Where can they get away from the expectation? Where can they go? Well, the answer is, "Nowhere."

He expected them to reach daily for perfection. He raised the level of intensity on the practice field as well as the requirements for academic performance. He enforced new standards of accountability. A brazen Bronco told an audience just prior to the start of spring ball:

If [players] don't go to class—and I'm talking about *everyone*—if they don't report to their 7:30 meeting in the morning, if they don't [visit] with their academic advisor, if they don't get their study hall hours, you're not going to see them at practice. Is that going to hurt our program? [I will] not . . . compromise a principle of right and wrong. I'm not going to be held hostage by [athletic] ability. So I don't know how many are going to be out there when we start spring practice. That's the players' choices. . . .

I know the expectation right now is, "You've got to win next year." Yeah, I do. But the kids that we're going to put out there, they're going to go to class, they're going to live the Honor Code, and they're gonna try like crazy. . . .

I don't intend to ask these kids to do anything different than I would do or am willing to do. I'll beat them to the top of the mountain. I'll live the lifestyle that I'm asking them to live. I'll portray excellence day in and day out, and I'll be driven to return the program to where it's supposed to be. . . . If I don't do that, how do I expect to have any credibility?

Run to the top of the mountain he did—as well as bike and swim. He invited the full team to participate that June in a defensive team tradition: the Eco Challenge. This was something Bronco had devised at UNM, a suggestion of his brother Marty, who is a fitness expert. "The idea of the event is an intimate rite of passage to connect a group to a common cause," says Bronco. In Provo, the triathlon, which was open to the public, involved a mile swim, a thirty-eight-mile bike ride up Provo Canyon, and a six-mile run to the top of Sundance Resort.

It was a voluntary test of will for both players and coaches, which of course Bronco also hoped would contribute to team unity. The aerobic race was a particular challenge for athletes such as football players, whose training emphasizes anaerobic fitness. Part of the tradition was for early finishers to wait the several hours it takes for all players to complete the race in a show of support. "There's never been anyone who started that hasn't finished," says Bronco.

Because NCAA rules prohibit coaches from mingling with players on such events, the coaching staff began the event an hour earlier than the players. Bronco's brother Marty finished first, but Bronco was not far behind, finishing in five hours. Other team members persisted despite challenges and mishaps such as broken hands, flat tires, and missed turns; the last participant crossed the line in ten hours.

Newspaperman Dick Harmon reported team members' reflections on the event:

> "To see those guys finish, with what they went through, well, it was inspiring," quarterback John Beck said. "To go through it, to see teammates sweating alongside you with the effort, it does something to you as a team," Beck continued. "I asked myself several times, 'Why am I doing this, it's just crazy, what did I get myself into?' Then you know the guy alongside you is thinking the same thing. I was so

sore I could hardly get back on my bike and ride. But you go through something like that and you get close to your friends. I don't think you can duplicate it any other way."[12]

Bronco was in the mountains again not long before fall camp, this time to work on staff cohesiveness. All the coaches and their wives joined Paul and his wife, Kris Anne, for a two-day retreat near Park City. Outside, during beautiful August days, they previewed a number of team-building exercises they might use, as well as spent some time getting to know each other better.

Afterward, Bronco was still not done crafting significant emotional experiences. Because the team's three-year losing record precluded adequate experience with victory, he created one activity in particular to help them envision success. As fall camp geared up, he had them lying spread eagle on the grass at the LaVell Edwards Stadium. The prior season in that same venue, after losing a crucial game to New Mexico, Bronco had observed BYU players walking up the ramp, laughing and joking. Disgusted, he had made a vow then to catalyze in players a devotion to that place and its history so intense that they would never again have the heart to find something funny in the wake of a defeat on their own turf. So now he asked his team to lie down on their backs and close their eyes. Over a backdrop of inspiring music, the loudspeaker broadcast important moments of the significant victories won in that stadium. Even LaVell appeared and walked down the ramp to join the team on the grass and speak to them about the traditions of the place.

Quarterbacks coach and future offensive coordinator Brandon Doman remembers that day: "Our players have the responsibility . . . [to] carry on their shoulders the great plays, the great moments, the memories that our fans have [had] in this stadium of ours." They have to remember their roots. Getting back to those roots starts with "reminding . . . players that . . . they have a responsibility to uphold that tradition."[13]

"In my opinion," says Nate Meikle (wide receiver 2004–06), "this experience was directly correlated with the success the 2006 team experienced at home. This was the night that we decided we were going to win at home. Period."

Bronco even devoted some fall two-a-day practices to the work of moving the team mindset to a new outlook. It was a precious sacrifice, since the NCAA limits fall training to twenty hours a week. That limitation is meant to include all meetings, practices, and weight training. Compliance was important to Bronco, and he was committed to strict adherence to the twenty-hour limit. So when he commenced team-building activities, it was in place of tackling. It was in place of lifting weights. It was in place of throwing the ball. All this after three losing seasons, and Bronco a rookie head coach. So it was risky.

He and his staff counseled together to decide which activities to use first. They determined that developing trust was a priority. The exercise that they selected from their retreat was called the "Trust Fall." The team was divided into groups, each standing in front of a ladder. They were told to climb to any rung of their choice, close their eyes, and fall backward into the receiving arms of their teammates.

Bronco was discouraged with the team as players repeatedly refused to fall from any higher than the lowest rungs. After the third or fourth guy could not bring himself to risk anything more than the second rung, Bronco crawled to the top of a ladder himself and threw himself backward. "I wasn't sure that I was going to be caught," says Bronco, "but why not *now* put my trust in my team?" To his astonishment, even after his own example, the players went back to their low-risk behavior, clinging to the second and third rungs.

He tried another activity another day. He gave teams a set of Tinker Toys, twenty minutes for planning, and forty seconds to build the tallest self-sustaining tower in the room. Again, he was

Trust fall

disappointed when the results were short, one- and two-foot towers built to the accompaniment of a good deal of bickering and blaming.

Despite his efforts to date, he had a team whose members did not trust each other and did not know how to work together. Meanwhile, he had his assistant coaches wondering if he was crazy after all to waste precious practice time with Tinker Toys. "But was it time well spent?" asks Bronco. "It allowed us time to address our culture. . . . It's easy to pretend everything's okay. It's harder to take time out of practice when you are only given twenty hours."

Scan this QR code to see "Stadium" or go to http://bit.ly/NGbJj0

The Cougars did not have a great year their first season under Coach Mendenhall. It was a tough year. Bronco saw compliance with his new policies, but many of his players were only "maliciously obedient." Others, though willing and cooperative, were not yet fervently committed.[14] But only a small slice of an organization—just 5 to 15 percent—needs to be passionate about change for it to take hold.[15] Bronco had that many. The work ethic, the leadership, and the commitment were showing from these few. "If you think that it takes a majority, that's not the case," says Bronco. "I had maybe five players who were passionate about the change. And they were the right people. If you have the right people and they are passionate about the change, it will work."

Enough of the right people were on the bus. A new recruiting process was in place to bring in even more. As season play began, team members had together experienced powerful emotional scenes that communicated new expectations and united them around a new vision. Bronco had additional changes up his sleeve, and the purpose of many of these reached far beyond initial team-building exercises and transitional events. BYU Football began to implement practices that would eventually become ingrained as the new and *different* way of doing things.

Scan this QR code to see "Team Unity" or go to http://bit.ly/NA4Z3V

CHAPTER 5

What You Design For

We make a family trip to the BYU bowl game each year if BYU plays close by. In 2007, the Cougars played in the Pioneer Las Vegas Bowl, and we were there. It got very cold, but three of my grandsons (and their fathers) hung in there when other family members went home at halftime. James was eleven, Pete was nine, and Alex was ten.

[With BYU leading 17–16, UCLA drove eighty-seven yards in the final two minutes and set up for a field goal.] Had they made the kick, they would have won. We were really discouraged and down in the dumps, because teams don't miss too many of those kicks. But lineman Eathyn Manumaleuna blocked that kick. The crowd went crazy, and all of the BYU fans just swarmed the field. Our boys wanted to go down there, too. We said, "Fine." So we all hopped down there.

We were meeting and congratulating several of the players, and then we recognized Eathyn. He was standing there, and a lot of people were slapping him on the back, congratulating him, and we cornered him. There we were with these three boys. Completely spontaneously, I said to

Eathyn, "Wow! This will probably be the greatest moment in your life."

He responded in front of these three grandsons, "No, I just got my mission call, and the most important thing I'm going to do in my life lies ahead of me on my mission." These three boys heard that, and it made quite an impression on them. It was just a real thrill.

—Paul Gilbert
BYU 1968; former BYU student body president;
former BYU Alumni Association president

Symbolic activities, for all their power and purpose, are not sufficient alone to transform a losing team or organization into a winning team or organization. Drama can communicate a lot about what is important to a leader. It can touch people and awaken emotions that have been stifled or dormant. It can inspire them. It can ignite their noblest passions. It can provide the impetus to change, but the change itself is played out in daily decisions and routines. If a leader doesn't find a way to change the daily way of doing things, the energy from even the most enthralling and unifying of team outings can fade like the twinkling trails of fireworks against a black summer sky.

In other words, culture change happens through adjustments to everyday tasks and relationship structures. Culture cannot be changed *directly*. A leader cannot send a memo or give a speech outlining the new attitudes and behaviors he or she would like to order up and expect them to be delivered. But without a doubt, culture can be changed. Though it is impacted by forces outside of the organization over which the organization does not have direct control, including community traditions, economic trends, and regulatory boundaries, culture is also shaped by forces inside the organization. Culture can be nudged by directing attention to these elements—the organization's guiding mechanisms and its systems of work, information, and reward.

In short, if a group or organization wants different results, its processes, structures, and systems will need to change. Leaders have the power to change them.

Which brings us to Smooth Stone #2: Organizations are perfectly designed to get the results that they get.

Smooth Stone #2

Organizations are perfectly designed to get the results that they get.

This means that if an organization's results are disappointing, the explanation lies in an understanding of its choices: the strategies and systems that drive its culture. And the good news is, that's where the remedy lies as well because the way an organization works can be changed. People can overhaul the rules that they have put in place about how to do things. They can change procedures, remodel, rework, restore, revamp, reconnect. By making thoughtful choices about organization design—by adjusting design elements such as the goals and principles that provide guidance, work activities and facilities, decision-making processes, approaches to recruiting and training and rewarding and learning—a team can remake itself systematically.

Even while Bronco was orchestrating poignant experiences to mold a new culture, he also set about designing a new organization. The football program had gotten the results that it was designed for. Better results would require a distinctly different design.

Scan this QR code to see "Organizations Are Perfectly Designed to Get the Results That They Get" or go to http://bit.ly/OmrqKF

He knew that design choices must be *aligned* with each other. They must work in unison to bring about the aspirations of the organization. He believed that the football program's mission and values must align with the mission of BYU; likewise, routines carried out daily in the football department must also align with the team's values and goals. It would be no good to advocate BYU's Honor Code but allow football players leeway in adhering to these standards because of their special athletic talents. It would be contradictory to work on Sunday when Church members throughout the world strive to keep the Sabbath day holy. It would be foolish to recruit players with leadership talent and fail to get them involved in coaching peers and running councils and developing service programs.

If organization design choices are at odds with each other, their intended effects can be cancelled out. Meanwhile, a lot of confusion and frustration can result.

Bronco and his staff pictured a step-by-step path to improved results (below). He knew that if the team were to obtain different outcomes, he would need to influence the culture of the football program. But since no leader can control all of the forces outside a team and within its individual members that impact the culture, he set out to do what he could to influence that culture by redesigning elements of the organization that he could directly change, such as goals, routines, and policies. Thus, he made *design choices* to affect *culture*, which in turn drove new *outcomes*.

Bronco and his staff used this path to chart the Cougars' way back into winning territory. You can find an expanded version of this path in section 2 and a more detailed discussion about how to use it to improve an organization.

In the remainder of this chapter, we describe some of the dozens of design choices that have come to characterize the BYU football program.

CULTURE AND OUTCOMES

To start, Bronco identified the cultural characteristics that he believed were most important for achieving the outcomes he envisioned for the team. And he didn't keep them a secret. He distributed rubber bracelets to players engraved with the letters "ADE" for accountability, discipline, and effort. Reporter Jeff Call recorded Bronco's comments at the time, just prior to the opening of Bronco's first spring practice as head coach:

> "The performance level of this team needs to be raised to where they are accountable to each other, they're playing with discipline and they're playing with effort," said [Bronco]. "Those three [cultural attributes] will lead to an execution that is much different than what it is now . . . on both sides of the ball. And that should lead to a consistency of a sustainable competitive advantage over time. The program right now has ups and downs. There are games where the ball is turned over, there are games where we've had personal fouls, and there are games where, just in general, we're not achieving to the level necessary to win a close football game. So as I look at those things going into spring—the ultimate goal is to be able to execute and play in a consistent manner to win football games. That is where we need to go."[1]

But of course rubber bracelets alone do not foster accountability, discipline, and effort, so as Bronco moved through his first year, he and the Cougar coaching staff were busy crafting practical design choices that they hoped would institutionalize these qualities.

MISSION

We have already introduced one of the first design choices laid down by Bronco and his staff: their mission statement. A mission will energize an organization when it awakens and entices them toward something extraordinary.[2]

Set firmly in place in the first months of Bronco's tenure, the Cougars' mission "to be the flag bearer of Brigham Young University through football excellence, embracing truth, tradition, virtue, and honor as a beacon to the world" was already beginning to influence player performance.

Cameron Jensen recounts when Bronco introduced the mission early in 2005 during a team meeting:

> I remember the first time Coach Mendenhall showed the mission statement on the board. He said, "This is what we're going to be about." I remember reading it and thinking, "I'm really excited about the way the program's going." Every day he showed that on the board. I remember he had us stand up and say it a couple of times.

Scott Johnson (defensive back 2006–9; team captain) describes how the new mission impacted him:

> I had played a semester before my mission, before Bronco was head coach, and it was so hard for me. I was eighteen years old. There were other players who had three kids. I just didn't relate to them. I was on the bubble, meaning that come fall I might not be on the team anymore, and I didn't have a scholarship. I knew that academics were important. I was going to make a career in something besides football. I knew that from day one, but I wanted to play, and I loved it. Initially, getting just beat up on the field and being a small

guy out there—that was hard for me. That was super hard. Right when I got back from my mission, I came in to tell Coach Mendenhall that I wasn't going to play anymore. He explained to me how the program had changed and what his vision was. That was something that was in embryo, but it began to mature inside of me, and I figured it out. That's when everything changed. It was awesome.

Scott went on to eventually earn a scholarship and was a starter his junior and senior years. He received the Robbie Bosco Award for Determination as a junior and as a senior team captain finished third on the team with seventy-one tackles, including forty-seven solo stops. Among other honors, he was also named an ESPN Academic All-American.

Even Brian Logan (defensive back 2009–10), not a member of the Church, would in future years find himself inspired by the team's mission. Brian says, "I take it upon myself, just like any other guy on this football team who's a member of the Church, to stand for more. We're more than just football players. Like Coach Mendenhall said, because of football, and because of the success we have, people will tend to listen and tend to look."

For example, teammate Brandon Bradley (defensive back 2006–10) heard that a friend's teenage son was struggling, so he invited the youth to shadow him for a day, bringing him to classes, the Cougars' team meeting, and practice. Brian remembers the day, laughing at how the youngster surprised defensive coordinator Jaime Hill with his football knowledge and reflecting on the messages that Brandon shared with him about the importance of education. He says, "When that kid came to us and spent the day with us, if we didn't have the success we had throughout football, there's no way he would have wanted to hang out with us."

Before 2005 season play began, Bronco asked every player on

the team if they were willing to put their names on a symbol that represented the team mission and then to play from that place. The players agreed, and they all signed a Cougar "Y" flag. "I believe in the mission: flag bearer," says Bronco. "I believe in it literally."

Beginning with the 2005 season and to this day, the team captains choose a player to run the flag out of the tunnel and into the stadium before each game. It is an honor to carry the flag. "I think the significant thing was that the team signed the flag and committed to the goals of the program, the mission of the program, and guiding principles of the program" says Cameron Jensen. "That was the significance of the flag and running it out."

VALUES AND GUIDING PRINCIPLES

In signing the Y flag, the team was committing to be flag bearers and to the core values of tradition, spirit, and honor. Values are another design choice. They now tower above the stadium neighborhood, printed on the back of the end zone scoreboards. They welcome game-day fans as they approach the stadium, emblazoned on mega-sized banners. They embellish the sideline railings of the playing field.

Most of all, Bronco constantly emphasizes that football is not the first priority of the BYU football program. He writes:

> The most important thing in our lives as members of the BYU football team and of this church is our *faith*. Faith is the first principle of the restored gospel. Without the internal foundation of testimony, belief, and action, it doesn't matter what the outside façade portrays. Faith is the very essence of who a person is. . . .
>
> Second is our *family*. After you leave this earth you have a chance to be as a family together. Another name for this blessing in the scriptures is "eternal life."

Third is *finding knowledge* and learning. I am proud that our football team has one of the highest grade point averages in the country as a team and how they work so hard to achieve that. I believe it's so important because when we leave this earth, our knowledge and our spirit are what we take with us, not the championships or anything else.

Fourth is *friends.* It is so important to surround yourself with greatness—not perfection, but those who are trying very hard to help you return to our Father in Heaven. The friends you select and the friends you associate with are huge factors in what type of behavior you choose to be involved in. In the young adult years, friends can often have the biggest influence on the behavior of an individual. Choosing good friends may be the most important decision you make as a young adult.

And so, fifth is *football.* Fifth, because everything we do here is to use our talents and gifts to serve others and why should football be any different? One of the things I'm most proud of is the wall mural in our offices that shows where all the missionaries on our team have served or are serving around the world. If you were to look at the wall, you may find a young man called to Mongolia. You may notice some who served in Russia and some in Australia and then Madagascar and then England and then—the list goes on. When members of the media see this impressive display, they usually become very interested. . . . They're amazed because these members of our football program are missionary/student/service-oriented/disciple people. It's an amazing thing to see their expression and impression of what this program is all about. They oftentimes can't comprehend it because it's so different.[3]

Values matter in college football. A recent *Sports Illustrated* online article indicated that serious crime among college football and basketball players is increasing and noted research suggesting that football players may be particularly culpable; most troubling are weapons-related arrests and cases of alleged sexual abuse against women. Author Jeff Benedict identified ten arrests in a single week during July 2010. "There's an undeniable problem," he said. "It starts with the type of players that some college coaches are willing to recruit. Until colleges and universities demand a higher standard, the problem will continue to get worse."[4]

Balanced priorities are also important because becoming a professional football player is simply not a realistic goal for most players. Fewer than 3 percent of all collegiate players advance to the NFL, and the average length of an NFL player's career is a mere three-and-a-half seasons, with injuries playing a significant role in the relative brevity of a professional football career.[5] Of those who get injured and are prescribed painkillers during their careers, nearly three-fourths misuse the drugs. When their careers in football are over, former pros are four times as likely as the general population to misuse prescription painkillers.[6]

Bronco notes that Green Bay Packer head coach Vince Lombardi reportedly once said, "Winning isn't everything, it's the *only* thing."[7] Bronco disagrees. He loves the game he coaches and works diligently to lead his coaches and players with a dogged determination to win every game they play, but for him, a win is ultimately more about a way to turn eyes toward heaven, to make space in hearts for experiences that are much more durable and fulfilling in a larger perspective.

Scan this QR code to see "Football Is Fifth" or go to http://bit.ly/NzK5QN

"I try to read the scriptures each day," writes Bronco, "but I haven't read anything so far that stresses the importance of football. I have read a lot about drawing nearer to the Savior, becoming of one heart and one mind, and knitting our hearts together with his, but not a single word about football." He adds,

> If you're looking for peace, if you're looking for happiness, if you're looking to find your way back to your Father in Heaven, it will be by looking outward, not inward, and by what you can do to help others. That's why I love coaching at BYU. The game is not compelling enough or important enough, but these young men are. The characters they build are. The good they do in the world by sharing their gifts and talents are, and if, by playing football and doing our best, we can help others see these most important things in life, then we've fulfilled our mission. I believe the most important thing is what we can do for others, through the game of football. If you've wondered why football comes fifth, that's the reason.[8]

STRATEGIES TO INFLUENCE

The Cougars' strategy is another design choice. Bronco had quickly recognized that the Cougars would differentiate themselves from the competition with a bold strategy to leverage the unique worldview, maturity, leadership experience, and disciplined work ethic of his faithful young players. We described this strategy in the previous chapter. Aside from the competitive NCAA football scene, though, there were many other important forces that would impact his team's success.

The world outside any organization imposes a constantly changing set of demands. It is no less true at BYU Football. Media coverage, BYU administrative requirements, academic policies, alumni engagement, and fan reactions are just some of the forces that pummel the team each year. The choice that all organizations can make to mitigate such dynamics is to reach out to their influencers, discovering and even anticipating their needs. The strategic approach should be to *proactively respond* to such pressures rather than to *haphazardly react.*

Everyone has expectations. Frustrations are almost always a result of a violation of expectations. One of Bronco's new roles as head coach was to manage the external environment by first, understanding its expectations, and second, accommodating or altering those expectations in one way or another.

This was all new to Bronco and quite different from being an assistant coach, but after discussing these ideas with Paul in the off-season, Bronco set up interviews with fourteen key individuals to get to know his on-campus influencers. Many of these folks were wary of BYU Football because of its rocky recent history, including scandalous trouble with a few of the former players. He describes the experience:

> I met with the chief of police and the director of housing. I met with the dean of students. I met with the chaplain and the vice president of student life. I met with the athletic director. I met with the janitor. I met with anyone that I could imagine who would have interaction with our players. Fourteen of them, and do you know, that was a long week. I'm not sure I heard one positive thing. They just vented. I would show up at an office, and they would unload on me. "When is BYU going to do it right? What are you going to do about it?" They had no problem telling me what they thought. Fourteen interviews. And so I had a very clear understanding of what their expectations were.

By conducting the interviews himself, though, Bronco was forming relationships that he hoped to develop over time into cooperative, constructive partnerships. He was beginning a dialogue with some of the program's greatest skeptics.

Bronco's most important strategy to influence these groups involved a change in football recruiting practices. As we explained before, commitments to the Honor Code would be secured early in the process in order to reduce the number of players who were likely to break it. Bronco felt that his best bet was to build trust that he would police his own house. He implemented a program called Band of Brothers, described in detail in the next chapter, which utilized weekly player reports to catch problems early before they could mushroom into Honor Code violations. Bronco felt that if he knew his players well enough, then if they appeared to be heading toward academic or behavioral dangers, he could counsel them individually and help them change their course long before a situation would rise to the level of the University Standards Office.

Bronco also turned toward reenergizing the engagement of football alumni in the program. At a kickoff alumni event in 2005, when new retro-styled uniforms were unveiled, 300 former players came to hear about Bronco's vision and had a chance to mix and mingle. Attendance at the annual event swelled to 1200 by 2010. These refranchised alumni agreed to participate in the new recruiting strategy, which we'll describe in more detail in chapter 6. They were to become the eyes and ears throughout the country who could identify potential recruits and alert BYU staff.

Bronco was once invited to speak at the Dean's Council. He took the opportunity to describe his commitment to BYU Football's

Scan this QR code to see "Strategies to Influence" or go to http://bit.ly/NzMHhC

flag-bearing responsibilities. He affirmed that if Cougar Football wasn't aligned with the institution's mission, it shouldn't exist. But if it was aligned, and if it could serve successfully as a beacon to the world, then indeed the very best players should be recruited. And these terrific players would want a chance to be admitted to and find support in BYU's colleges. Bronco continues to work with academic bodies on campus to partner for success at the stadium as well as in the classroom.

He reached out to athletic department partners to mutually agree about how they can serve each other and to establish indicators that measure success. This is ongoing work. In the business world such agreements are often called service level agreements, and they are an important tool in helping an entire enterprise meet its overarching purposes.

GOALS AND OBJECTIVES

The football team's 2005 goals and objectives were assembled from the commitments the players made at the bonfire the previous spring. "I did not give them their goals," says Bronco. "The players came up with their goals." They were statements team members had scrawled on flipcharts as the burning timber of the canyon bonfire crackled:

We will be accountable in all we do.
We will play with phenomenal effort.
We will finish.
We will be disciplined.
We will restore/remember/respect tradition.
We will have fun.
We will live the Honor Code and keep the rules.
We will be champions on and off the field.
We will win the Mountain West Conference championship.
We will go to a bowl game and win.

The next year, the team specified exactly what they wanted to achieve in three terse targets: 1) to be champions on and off the field, 2) to win the Mountain West Conference championship, and 3) to go to a bowl game and win. These three goals were not adjusted again until 2011, when the team became conference independent.

Effective goals indicate short-term progress toward achieving the desired outcomes. They are the yardstick for gauging the advance toward longer-term aspirations.

Leaders can identify and set these goals in partnership. They may need to revisit them periodically as well, as did Bronco's team. When BYU Football left the Mountain West Conference for independence, of course, their goals were adjusted to take that reality into account.

• • •

A new organization design was shaping up at BYU Football before season play in 2005 with Bronco as a new head coach. We've tracked through the set of choices that answer the questions "Why?" and "What?" regarding the team mission as well as its guiding principles, strategies, and short-term objectives.

Of course, the Cougar coaching staff was also deciding "How?" They made significant changes to their work routines and their organization structures (how they grouped people to do the work). Let's walk through some of these "How?" choices they made.

WORK PROCESSES

As a new head coach, Bronco knew how a football team operates, but he had something to learn about managing the fundamental work of the organization. He had never heard of *business processes.* Bronco got interested in business processes when he began to feel utterly overwhelmed by the sheer magnitude of work to do. Paul suggested he gather his staff and talk through some ways of getting a grip on the situation. So Bronco set aside a staff meeting and invited Paul for a little technical assistance.

First they learned that all organizations are made up of work processes. These are the value-creating flows in an organization. They are the very essence of the enterprise—its means of creating something of worth to customers (or fans)—so the essence of managing the enterprise is to manage its processes. A first step is to get them defined and prioritized and then to find the right folks to own each one.

So they began to identify their football program's core work, and it was not hard to do. They were just back from a round of spring recruiting and could immediately name "recruiting" as a core work flow. What else? "Game-plan development"—breaking down tapes, designing game plans, and performing follow-up analysis and review. "Game preparation"—the week's routine of running through drills, situational "blue zone" scenarios, trick plays, special teams routines, video tests, and walk-throughs. Bronco, fresh off speaking opportunities and recruiting visits where he'd been describing the team's new direction over and over, suggested that "setting strategy" is also a critical football program flow. The coaches named other types of work as well—special teams, spring practice, summer conditioning, and so on. Pretty soon they had a robust but limited list.

And then Paul asked, "Who owns each process?" If managing work processes is the essence of running an organization, then there needs to be a single owner for each process—someone who can watch over it to make sure the process is consistently delivering the expected output. Someone who can launch an improvement effort when it's time. Someone who will lose sleep over the process if it's not humming along pleasingly.

Who owns recruiting? Well, all the coaches had a part in it and had been flying across the country carrying out recruiting activities in their assigned regions. They all contributed to finding, evaluating, and visiting potential Cougars. But who *owns* recruiting? It was really quiet in the room. There wasn't an answer. No one had ever asked the question! Okay, then it must be Bronco.

Who owns practice? Well, all the coaches enthusiastically work with their teams and positions through spring, fall, and season practice. It's their favorite part of their job! But who *owns* this process? No one? Okay, then it must be Bronco.

Who owns game-plan development? Each coach covers his responsibilities in watching tape and designing game calls. It's the Xs and the Os, for crying out loud. Who *owns* it? Bronco.

The truth sunk in that in the absence of formally designated process owners, Bronco owned *all* of the program's work. Now of course, as head coach, the buck stops with him. No denying that. But if Bronco himself was in charge of making sure every flow was running smoothly, and if it was his job to periodically tweak, jigger, or revamp each one, then he indeed had a lot of work to do. No wonder he was feeling so burdened.

None of us can know how much this mantle of responsibility weighed on Bronco's shoulders, but it was clear that there was a logical way to help relieve him of much of it by divvying up the primary ownership for each work process. The football staff did that, and over the following years, each coach's job description was built to include what football program processes were his clear responsibility.

Identifying work processes and naming owners was an important step in the design of the Cougar organization, and the staff had it nailed as the 2005 season drew near. Efforts to map and manage work processes did not stop here, but we're just about to stop in our recounting for now because we want to save some choice details that unfolded in subsequent years. The goal was not just to name and assign those processes, after all, but to design processes *different* from those of other teams, or to do the same processes *differently* (remember Smooth Stone #1?). Many of the Cougars' best innovations were still in the future. Before we move on, though, we need to mention one difference that is quintessentially Bronco and undeniably formative of the team's culture: Bronco's kamikaze practice requirements.

Obviously, team practice is absolutely core to the work of playing and winning football games. The BYU Cougars under Bronco Mendenhall practice differently. His demands require an exceptional work ethic from everyone. When Bronco says "I don't intend to ask these kids to do anything different than I am willing to do," his promise extends to practice as well. He is in solidarity with them on the field, pushing them, driving them, and loving them toward the greatest effort they have ever given in their lives. He is literally running alongside them. He muscles them toward his ideal with a total and mutual investment in their physical, mental, and emotional exertion.

Nate Meikle has written about Bronco's involvement with him as punt returner. He remembers acutely his reluctance to take on the role for BYU because of the soul-crushing mental pressure on the punt returner during a game. "To drop a punt in high school or even in junior college is one thing," he says, "but to muff a punt in front of 64,000 fans is an entirely different matter." Thrown into tryouts his junior year by Bronco, he toyed with purposefully bungling the audition by dropping the ball. "'Then I'll never have to cost our team the game,' he thought to himself, 'especially a game televised on ESPN.'" He resisted the urge, realizing he couldn't do such a thing "with Coach Mendenhall standing right next to me," and ended up landing the job. He credits Bronco with his stellar performance over the next two years:

> I've never played for a coach who has been so involved in punt return, especially not the head coach. For every drill, he's standing right next to us, fully aware of the added pressure his presence places on us. I always gave the full effort

he required, but it was the perfect execution he demanded that was the real challenge. He expected me to catch every punt. Why did he trust me to do something I didn't trust myself to do? But I couldn't break that trust. I couldn't let him down. I had to catch it. I've never tried so hard, never focused so much, and most importantly, never expected so much of myself. How did he get me to do that? I think back to the team meeting when Coach chastised the entire team, saying, "You can keep testing me, but just know this: *I won't get tired!* If you think I'm going to change, I *won't*." If he won't get tired, if he won't change, I have to live up to his expectations every day. If I came through today, I can come through tomorrow. "One day at a time," I [would] tell myself, repeating one of Coach Mendenhall's mantras. "Every day your best. One day at a time."

In his senior year (2006), Nate made twenty-six punt returns for 307 yards, a conference high. He ranked twentieth nationally with an average of 11.8 yards per punt return.

What's particularly important here is that Bronco's players understand his insistence on perfection—his relentless pressure—to be neither cold nor inimical nor heartless, as such demands might be perceived if they came from a different soul. Rather, Bronco's ardent insistence on excellence is a blessing, an expression of his utmost goodwill for them, really an act of passionate allegiance.

"I think the players know that I really love them, and I would like to help them," he said in 2010, and he is right. "I'm completely interested and devoted to making sure they have their best chance to succeed, and I think they feel that."[9]

Bronco pours his heart and soul into the Cougars' practice process. His players return the favor.

TECHNOLOGIES AND PHYSICAL FACILITIES

The *technologies* used for performing core work and the *physical facilities* of an enterprise are design choices.

The technology for film study used by BYU Football itself is top notch. They themselves funded a new tape-editing system in 2010 that allows coaches to select and annotate footage for study with their teams or position groups.

In 2011, BYU Broadcasting opened a new 100,000-square-foot facility just a short distance from LaVell Edwards Stadium, turned the keys to Big Blue,[10] a state-of-the art, mobile HD production truck, and launched *Countdown to Kickoff*, an hour-long, live football pregame show delivering a network-quality broadcast of team analysis, in-depth features, and game breakdowns. This, plus live postgame shows and BYUtv's same-day rebroadcasts of Cougar ESPN games, left Cougar Football fans who receive BYUtv around the world feeling giddy.

These telecasts complement coverage by the "Radio Home of the Cougars," KSL Radio in Salt Lake City. Greg Wrubell's play-by-play is heard by upward of a quarter-million people in the Salt Lake City/Provo area alone. BYU fans tune in around Utah and throughout the nation via network affiliates and satellite radio (BYU Radio), and the games go out to the world via KSL apps and the Internet. BYU Football broadcasts on KSL garner the largest listening audiences in the market, surpassing those of University of Utah football and Utah Jazz broadcasts. Bronco's weekly radio show on KSL also draws a passionate audience to LaVell Edwards Stadium for the live midweek broadcast—an opportunity for Bronco to not only talk football but also to connect with fans while communicating his program's unique message.

The football team's physical facilities are also something special. They meet and condition in BYU's Student Athlete Building, which was new in 2004 along with an Indoor Practice Facility where they can drill and scrimmage, if they choose, protected from the worst of the punishing Rocky Mountain winters. When Bronco took the helm, the walls in the football halls of the new Student Athlete Building were slick with new, blank white paint. He and his staff were free to choose how to finish them off. What an excellent opportunity to align the team's surroundings with their purpose and objectives.

Bronco set out to use the walls of the Student Athlete Building as a medium on which to deliver information about the team's mission, history, aspirations, and culture. To present this information visually is important in a world where people increasingly rely on visual cues to gather information, a key message in *Seeing Is Believing* by Stewart Liff and Pamela A. Posey,[11] which was inspirational to Bronco. Pictures and graphics help organization members see their place in the bigger picture. They can give people a sense of belonging and relevance. When visual messages are aligned with the talk of organization leaders, the visible underscores the aural, and vice versa. Because skillful visual management keeps people focused on what is most important, it improves performance across the board.

To connect BYU players with the team's traditions and their short-term goals, Bronco had a Home of the Champions wall created that names every championship that's been won at BYU and gives the score, going way back to the first year of conference dominance in 1965 and, of course, including the 1984 national championship. "It gives you a deeper understanding of where BYU's been and where we want to go," says Matt Reynolds (offensive line 2007–11; team captain). "I always wanted my year to be on this wall," says Cameron Jensen. "That was a goal of ours." Did he succeed? If you don't remember or never knew, see chapter 6.

A wall for bowl history was also created, starting with the 1974 Fiesta Bowl matchup against Oklahoma State. How quickly did the Cougars under Bronco land themselves on this wall? Read on.

Missionary wall

"If you're a player walking through here every day, you want to be a part of it," says Cameron. "You want to be part of the history of BYU. Visually, it shows you that you can. All the hard work—it shows."

There's also an NFL wall that chronicles the BYU alumni who have gone on to play professionally. Each position meeting room showcases goals, photos of play situations and opponents, inspirational quotes, and other artifacts according to the position coach's preferences. The locker room announces the season goals on one wall. There's a white flag emblazoned with the navy "Y" oval hanging from a hallway ceiling. In honor of the BYU football team, it was flown over Iraq aboard a CH-47, which is a twin-engine, tandem rotor, heavy-lift helicopter. The flag was signed by servicemen. The BYU team flies it proudly to honor other flag bearers serving in a much higher-stakes capacity.

Perhaps most important is the Called to Serve display, which looms huge on the wall right where players emerge daily from the

Scan this QR code to see "Visual Management" or go to http://bit.ly/NA5yus

lockers to make their way to the team meeting room. It's a map of the world, and a headshot marks the location where each current Cougar served or is serving his mission. It unifies the team daily around their shared faith and connects them to their highest priorities.

The walls of the Cougar team meeting room have an entirely different appearance from the slick, professionally produced cyclorama of Cougar achievements and aspirations wrapping in and around the rest of the football department. Rough-hewn cardboard with amateur magic marker drawings are taped to every square inch of available vertical space within arm's reach.

What is this?

These are the products of a warrior-inspired rite of passage. Bronco's idea, of course.

As Bronco led players through fall camp team-building in 2007 and subsequently, he described the Spartans—in his words, "one of the most fierce and successful warrior cultures of all time." He drew attention to the armor used by Spartan infantrymen. In their tight phalanx formations, they held heavy circular shields—hoplons—to defend half of their own body, and half of the soldier to their left, carrying their spears upright on their right side and forming a strong barrier to the opponent. Bronco used the hoplon as a metaphor for protecting yourself and your teammates—a total collaboration. Bronco asked the team to depict the answers to several questions on a cardboard slab representing a shield. They were thought-provoking questions to help players express their priorities and affections and think through their hopes. In daily team meetings, the men would

Scan this QR code to see "Spartan Shields" or go to http://bit.ly/Ny61yD

take turns explaining their drawing to their teammates, and then the shield would be posted on the wall.

Is this "visual management" unique to the Cougars? Certainly other programs throughout the nation take advantage of their physical facilities by using them as a canvas for reinforcing program history, honors, and shared dreams. It's one of the best practices used in industry, too, for connecting people to performance and safety goals and can be a low-cost way to impact output results.[12] But certainly the Cougars do visual management differently from anywhere else, especially with their Called to Serve display and their cardboard shield-lined meeting room.

ORGANIZATION STRUCTURE

The structure is the way people are grouped to perform the work of the organization. The choices that organizations make about structure define boundaries—what groups work together to meet customer needs, innovate, monitor business processes, reduce wasted materials and effort, maintain and develop technical expertise, and communicate effectively.

The BYU football program's structure is separated into offensive and defensive teams. Each side, in turn, is organized into position teams: quarterbacks, linemen, running backs, tight ends, and wide receivers on the offensive side, and defensive linemen, inside linebackers, outside linebackers, and secondary on the defensive side.

This nearly universal football team structure has some big downsides. When players are grouped into two teams, offensive and defensive, that practice separately, they can lose sight of the real enemy and come to see their own teammates as opponents. Bronco had been the defensive coach and had seen a number of the offensive players leave the team when he took the helm. He wanted to minimize the differences between offensive and defensive players and to make sure that the whole team gelled as one. He wanted players to always recognize the opposing team as the common enemy, with Cougars at all positions strongly unified as one body.

What structural elements could Bronco create that would promote this unity and integrate his players both on and off the field?

"My experience was, the team was very divided," says Nate Meikle. "There were the walk-ons, who weren't really on the team, weren't part of anything. There was the offense and the defense. The offense did not like the defense. The defense did not like us. I shouldn't say 'us,' though. Although I was an offensive player, more importantly, I was a walk-on, and nobody cared about the walk-ons."

"I wouldn't say we actually really disliked the defense," says Jonny Harline (tight end 2004–06), "but I'd say it was competitive, and there was a rivalry between offense and defense—a bit of trash talk and stuff."

In the earliest months of Bronco's head-coaching role, his first action was to simply switch up winter weight-lifting groups. Previously, players from each team and even from each position lifted together. But Bronco and members of his staff spent long hours developing a new set of conditioning groups that were still well-matched in terms of ability, but that crossed team boundaries.

"I was a walk-on freshman," says Matt Bauman (linebacker 2004, 2007–09; team captain), referring to the days before Bronco was head coach, "so a lot of people didn't know who I was anyway."

But I ended up starting the last four or five games [in 2004], and I didn't feel like I knew anyone on the offense besides a very few. Some guys would be catching the ball or running for a touchdown, and I wouldn't even know who they were. That was partly because of the way things were designed. The offense and the defense lifted at different times. Pretty much we were never in the same meetings. We practiced on different fields; hardly ever practiced against each other, so it was just two different teams: the offense and defense. It was kind of hard to really get into cheering for these guys on a deeper level than just as a Cougar fan.

"When I came back from my mission, it was much different," adds Matt. By then, Bronco was in the lead role. "It was both the offense and defense lifting at the same time in the off-season."

"That was never done before," says Cameron Jensen. "I had my buddies, and I liked lifting with them." When Cameron heard that he would be lifting with offensive players, he was reluctant. "I didn't want to lift with Dan Coats! Who's Dan Coats?" says Cameron playfully. (Dan Coats, 2002–06, is the powerful former BYU tight end who went on to the pros with the Cincinnati Bengals). The defensive teammates he had been conditioning with were "guys I trusted, guys I played with. But after a couple of weeks, you learned to respect the other team. You saw how they worked, and that really changed the chemistry of the team. When you lift with somebody, you're working out, they're cheering for you, and you really get to respect those people."

Another similar method used to help bring players together was to switch up the way of assigning lockers.

"One thing that Coach did well, was he leveled the playing field for everybody, and he completely abolished the hierarchy that had evolved over the course of several years," says Nate, who walked on as a transfer student. "Before, it was the starters who'd get the best lockers, so people like me were stuck in the corner. I didn't even have a locker. My first year, I was throwing stuff in the corner."

"I mean, you couldn't go talk to somebody on the offense," says Scott Johnson. "In the locker room, we were split up—defense on one side, offense on the other. And there were people fighting in the locker room, and it was always defense against offense."

Bronco made the choice to assign lockers by seniority—first choice went to the seniors, second to the juniors, and on down to freshmen.

"Everyone was integrated and it became a team as a whole instead of individuals, or even sides," says Scott.

Cameron Jensen ended up a few slots over from John Beck. "That would never happen before, a middle linebacker and a quarterback. Before, you just lockered next to your linebacker friends. But I remember it was close enough that after practice, I'd go ask him what he saw about the defense, what we weren't doing and what we were doing. Our disguising got really good because of it. Just talking to him and asking what he'd seen that we could do better. There was more communication. Our proximity in the locker room helped with that."

And before things got too cozy, Bronco would initiate another switch-up. "We would have to move from our current locker to at least five spaces away," says David Nixon (linebacker 2003, 2006–08; team captain). "It was good because it mixed it up and let you become friends with other guys."

The universal team meeting was another new choice for the Cougars. But meeting daily as a whole team was not the only change: a hymn, a prayer, a spiritual thought, and an additional motivational thought were added to the agenda. "The spiritual thought was always excellent," says David. "Coach Mendenhall would end with his words and then we'd break. It kind of left you excited, pumped, ready to get out to the practice field. It was great to rejuvenate each practice and get you excited, refocused on what's important."

At first Bronco led and coordinated these meetings, but in

future years he turned some of that responsibility over to the position groups. It was their job to variously choose the hymn, assign the prayer, develop a spiritual thought, and present a motivational message.

"I looked forward to team meetings every day," says Cameron Jensen. "I looked forward to them, knowing it was not just going to be about football, that you were going to get something out of it about life, whether it was a quote, or whether it was a fellow player saying something inspiring or motivational."

Another structural choice Bronco made to help unify the team was to ask the players to choose a leadership council. Each position picked a representative, someone "to be their voice to me," explains Bronco. "If you haven't heard, a lot of players don't think I'm very approachable. They stay away from me, from my office. So there needed to be someone who could come and talk to me."

"You were able to get together with all these position leaders, kind of see what we needed to bring from each of the positions to help the team, and what concerns that position had," says Kelly Poppinga (linebacker 2005–07; team captain; defensive intern 2009; linebackers coach 2010–). "We could all work together to fix things and if there were any issues, the captains would then go and meet with Coach Mendenhall."

"We would meet with Coach Mendenhall weekly and go over things to better the team," says David Nixon. "Coach would ask about practice—how everyone was feeling on the team, whether we were tired or felt good. He would actually cut back. He trusted us; he knew that as leaders of the team, we weren't going to lead him astray and try to get out of extra work."

As time went on, the leadership council became a decision-making body as well. Bronco turned over certain responsibilities to them.

"We made a lot of decisions on the leadership council over the years," says Scott Johnson, "from summer workouts to practice structures to just activities. Things we wanted to see happen. We had a lot of ability to make decisions and affect things. I think that's good for a team to be able to feel as though they have a lot of input and their opinion matters, affects what happens on the field, and it's not just coming from the top down all the time."

For example, the leadership council was involved in deciding who should be rostered each year. "Coach allowed us to provide input," says Nate Meikle. "'What do you think about this guy; should he be in the 105?' We debated against each other and then he allowed us to make recommendations. Ultimately Coach had the final say, but where else do the players get to have input on who makes the team?"

Cameron Jensen explains that sometimes Bronco would come in to their meetings and give them a decision to make. "He'd say, 'You guys decide and let me know.' And he'd leave the office. It just helped me look at the program differently and take more ownership. We were making decisions, and then we'd take them to the team. So there wasn't all this complaining. It'd be like, '*We* chose. It wasn't the coach that chose. *We* chose.' It just created more ownership throughout the whole program."

As the years went by, Bronco entrusted the leadership council with increasingly weighty matters. "On the heavier end, sometimes there were guys who were getting into trouble," says Matt Bauman. "Coach Mendenhall obviously took that very seriously. There were a few times where we would sit in the leadership council and call some of these guys in and chat with them and see what was really going on."

Coach would have us in there so that peer-to-peer, we were the ones asking the questions. He was in there as well, but he would leave it up to us, so he didn't really say much.

Once, there were six guys we met with. We talked with all of them, dismissed them from the meeting, and then we talked about all of them for the next hour and a half or so. Everyone was just debating, talking about if it would be better for them to leave the program or stay, and if they stayed, how we could make it better so it wouldn't happen again.

What was the outcome of this serious situation? Matt explains: "A couple of guys left, a couple guys stayed, and we kind of put them in a situation with better influences around them, and it worked out."

The whole situation was not an easy one for the council. "It was controversial," says Matt. He continues:

There were guys who, sitting around the table, obviously didn't want anyone to leave. There were guys who said, "You know, they are not helping our program at all. They're not doing anything. We need to get rid of them." There were some guys who just felt really strongly that because BYU is such a religious school that the right thing to do would be to keep these guys and help them to try to get better. There were other guys who said, "You know what, they have had all the chances, this just isn't the right place for them." There was never really a consensus on that. But it was a good discussion, a lot of voices heard, a lot of opinions made, facts brought up, so it was a productive discussion that I think helped Coach Mendenhall make his final decision. It was ultimately his decision, but he didn't say anything; he wanted to hear our discussion for that hour and a half. Then he ended up making the final decision.

Mixing up conditioning groups, switching locker assignments, meeting daily with the full team, and establishing a council of team leaders are all design choices carefully put in place to overcome the downsides of the traditional football program structure. They had the intended effect of bringing team members in contact with each other who would be less likely to rub shoulders otherwise. How valuable is it to have your defensive team captain spontaneously asking your quarterback for feedback about the defensive performance? How valuable is it to convene the team daily to connect with the spiritual beliefs that they hold in common? To keep your finger on the pulse of the team through a council of players? Though the program's team-and-position structure helped the team *differentiate* on the basis of skill, and thereby maximize technical proficiency, less formal efforts such as shuffling lift groups and rotating locker assignments served in turn to *integrate* the team to foster cross-team learning, networking, and *esprit-de-corps*.

FULLY INVESTED: 2005 SEASON

The staff's efforts to align all the elements of the football program would continue at BYU in subsequent seasons, but what we've described so far brings us to the first season of play under Bronco Mendenhall.

In sum, Bronco spent the first year unifying the team and shaping them up. He established a new vision and direction for the program. He introduced fresh purpose and stringent rigor into the practice regimen. He worked players through symbolic team-building activities, such as the bonfire and the run to the Y. He mixed up lift groups and locker assignments and established new meeting routines with a spiritual component. He says he initiated "a very high standard of how we were going to work and why. I worked the tar out of them because they were entitled and soft and lazy and not mentally tough. Bringing them together and establishing our culture and the purpose for why we are playing, that was essential."

Come September 2005, the season started off painfully. During

Bronco's first game as head coach in the Cougars' own LaVell Edwards Stadium, the season opener against Boston College, a crowd of 58,000 resoundingly booed him when he chose to punt on a late fourth down rather than go for it. It was clear he was not yet entirely welcome in his new job. The Cougars lost that game, 20–3.

BYU battered Eastern Illinois the following week by a score of 45–10 for Bronco's first head-coaching win and first home victory, but the Cougars then lost the next two games—by one point in overtime against TCU in Provo, and by twenty-one points at San Diego State.

With the season record at 1–3, Bronco and his staff made two watershed technical adjustments. The Cougar defense had been running the singular 3–3–5 that Bronco had first developed with Rocky Long at the University of New Mexico, which relied on man-on-man coverage. After San Diego State, they implemented a 3–4 formation and zone coverage. "Bronco let go of his roots," says Nick Howell, who was an observer at the time but joined the Cougars in 2007 as a graduate assistant and eventually became the secondary and special teams coach.

"He was the 3–3–5 defensive guru," says Lance Reynolds, assistant head coach and tight ends coach. "He was a man-guy in coverage. But he grasped the uniqueness of BYU and turned to focus on how we could take advantage of our unique players, our unique recruiting situation, which also includes the limitations. Those things were big decisions for him."

At the same time, the offense switched from four wide receivers and one back to a tight-end, two-back set. "We decided to be better at running the football," says Lance. "We evolved to take more advantage of the tight ends and running backs in our scheme, and to make them more our chain-moving kind of guys. It comes back to being able to adapt to the people that you have and where you are the strongest." Though half-baked in the midseason, the scheme changes did much to better accommodate the particular talent the Cougars had going for them at that time.

Another change was made after the San Diego State game, which Bronco is much more likely to remember to tell you about—and passionately. He recalls:

> We started the season 1–3, and I was criticized. Some were saying they thought BYU made a mistake in hiring me. And they now had a record to prove it. Again, going back to the booing experience in the first game: I learned very specifically the conditional nature of my job. But it's okay. It is what it is. So we were 1–3 and the idea simply came, "We're not giving back enough." From what our mission was, we weren't in alignment. We weren't doing what we were supposed to do. We were going to football games, but so does everybody else. The other 119 Division 1A [Football Bowl Subdivision] schools travel on buses, travel on planes, show up to the game, play, and go home. We were just like them. And some were playing better than us. It was clear to me that we weren't doing it right.
>
> The decision came, being 1–3, at a 5:30 A.M. staff meeting. We were playing University of New Mexico that week—and I told the staff we were going to give a fireside* before every game. They collectively dropped their heads. Just like that. "How was that going to help?"

Bronco explains his thought process: "If you go back to the mission, if you go back to what we said we could do best, what were we doing about it? The answer was not enough." Hoping to give back

---

* A *fireside* is a special evening service for members of The Church of Jesus Christ of Latter-days Saints, or some subset, such as youth or unmarried adults. Firesides usually involve a guest speaker discussing a topic of particular interest to the group invited.

to the communities to which they traveled, Bronco had tried to arrange a fireside the previous week in San Diego. But the team had been turned down. Local Church leaders had been concerned that with all the high school football games that are played on Friday, no one would come. They'd seen BYU firesides before; they weren't interested. "I took no for an answer," says Bronco, "and we got pummeled. And our program was sorry."

So a fireside was scheduled in Albuquerque. "The players organized it," says Bronco. "Forty players volunteered to show up. It was new to them, too. They got on the bus, dressed in coats and ties. Showed up at the chapel. Two players spoke, there were two musical numbers from our team, and I gave the closing remarks." But only thirteen people attended the event. (Since the New Mexico game in 2005, an estimated 60,000 or more have attended BYU Football firesides.)

"Again, if you put it in relation to our mission, we are not at any other place. We're not trying to be anybody else. So in relation to our mission, it was right on. I knew that, and so I wasn't concerned about the game. We won [a 27–24 comeback victory]. But that wasn't the major accomplishment we had in that particular time period. It was a design element that we were supposed to do that now put us back in place."

After that, the Cougars turned around their win/loss ratio and earned their first bowl game appearance since 2001.

BYU went 6–5 in the regular season in 2005, tying for second place in the Mountain West Conference—an improvement on the three prior losing seasons. Sadly, the team lost in the Las Vegas Bowl

Scan this QR code to see "Firesides"
or go to http://bit.ly/Q6iP2p

BYU players singing at a fireside

to California, 35–28, playing against the likes of DeSean Jackson and Marshawn Lynch.

Bronco was by no means comfortable in his job and with the first season's results. He says, "2005 was more of survival. I was feeling my way, and I was just completely overwhelmed and trying to learn and hold on."

But you wouldn't expect a total team reversal to happen in just one year, now would you?

CHAPTER 6

Champions on the Field and Off

After transferring to BYU from Snow College, where I had played safety, it was really, really hard for me. I was struggling personally. I was stressed with school and football. I had been suffering badly since I had come home from my mission. I had never seen anyone for it—I just thought maybe my troubles would blow by. But they never had. Also, I didn't click with the defensive coordinator. We didn't see eye to eye. Knowing that I was a junior college transfer, I think a lot of the guys on the team thought I was supposed to be really good, but I didn't play very well. So my experience at BYU was sour my first semester. I went in to Coach Mendenhall the last day of spring in our exit interviews, and I told him I wasn't coming back. We started talking, and he asked why. I was very honest. I said that I didn't want to be here. Mentally, I was broken down. I didn't have any strength left, and I didn't think there was anything more I could do. I was giving football up, basically. I told him I was going to move home and go to school there.

He asked if I had prayed about it. I told him that I had. And I had prayed, but I knew what answer I wanted; I don't think I had prayed openheartedly. He said, "I think you need to pray again, and come back tomorrow and let me know what you think. I'm going to pray, too." So, I prayed, but I was still not very open to hear a response from God. The next day, he said, "So how do you feel?"

I said, "Exactly the same way. I'm not going to be here."

He said, "That's interesting because I received the opposite answer that you received, and I know you are supposed to be here."

So I left, disregarding what he told me. I was kind of upset because I wanted him to agree with me so I could leave on solid terms with him. I went back home to Ogden, Utah.

Every week that summer, Coach Mendenhall called me at least once. When he'd call me, it was never, "Hey, come back here and play football; we need you." It was more, "How're you doing; I want to make sure you're okay." He knew that I was struggling personally and didn't ever try to sway me to come back.

In early July, he called and said, "I'm in the area, and I'd love to stop and see you." He showed up at my house on his Harley. We had a really nice chat. He expressed his care for me and how he wanted me to be at BYU. He said, "I don't even care if you play football. I just know you're supposed to be at BYU." He said he couldn't guarantee that I would come back and it would feel better, but he said that he knew I was supposed to be there. He said, "You're gonna have the strength to deal with the issues that you may have to deal with."

After that I went on a vacation with my family, and I couldn't stop thinking about what he had said to me. I decided I was going to give it another run. Ever since then, it's been a different experience for me. Coach Mendenhall and I have had a really, really close relationship, and it was the best thing that's ever happened to me.

He pointed me toward a professional to get the help that I needed. I worked directly with her, and she would report to Coach Mendenhall and tell him how I was doing. I gave her permission to do that because sometimes it's hard to diagnose yourself and talk about your own personal needs. So Coach has always been really aware of my issue and has taken time to see how I am. He'll call me in occasionally to hear about my progress, or when he sees that I'm not doing so well, he'll immediately pull me into his office. I've received countless blessings from him, priesthood blessings in his office. It's been interesting, because I've since been able to help guys on the team that have struggled. At first I was a little ashamed of my struggles, but now I'm not. Coach compared it to a knee injury. If I had a knee injury, then I'd get help, and it's the same thing. It's a physical issue that I've really battled with. Coach definitely has helped me fight my way through.

Also, I met my wife here.

The reason I was supposed to be at BYU wasn't to play football. Coach Mendenhall knew it was for alternative reasons. Football's been a bonus.

This experience is something that's dear to me. I just have so much respect for him. It's hard for me personally when he's portrayed in an unfavorable light because people who do that don't know who he is, or what he stands for, or that he cares for a lost sheep, so to speak.

—Andrew Rich
BYU defensive back 2008–10

I F A COMPLETE TURNAROUND had eluded Bronco his first head coaching year and he was still far from settled into the lead role, he remained determined after that first season to continue to build on the new direction and to extend the alignment of design choices he and his staff members had espoused. They had gained experience as a group and would go forward.

They were building a football program. When something they had done appeared to be working, they jumped to make it even better. When something new and promising came into view, they embraced it and gave it a shot. Now we'll show the path the Cougars took to add to the design choices we described in the last chapter.

WORK PROCESSES PART II

In Bronco's first year, the coaching staff had identified all of their core work processes and found an owner for each one. They had concentrated on developing the recruiting and practice processes. In the coming years, they continued scrutinizing these processes, and they expanded their scope, searching for ways to make *all* their flows and regimens better.

One of the first process innovations came in 2006 with the off-season winter-conditioning routine. It had its genesis in "Fun Fridays," a regimen that Bronco and strength and conditioning coach Jay Omer had deployed the previous year.

"Every Friday they would just try to kill you," says Cameron Jensen. "Try to break your will. I mean, just the hardest, most difficult thing that they could think of. That's what we would do. Whether it was an obstacle course, racing around the stadium, thirty 200-yard sprints—it was just *so* difficult. I mean, you would dread Fridays."

Cameron adds: "It made you tough. We felt like we were machines, like we could accomplish anything." But Cameron notes a downside of these intensive voluntary challenges. "A lot of players wouldn't show up on Fridays. It was the least attended day."

In Bronco's estimation, the team had lost a number of close games the previous season because they had quailed in the face of onerous competitive pressure. So to intensify their exposure to stiff combat, the coaching staff in 2006 replaced Fun Fridays with a new phenomenon: the Supergames.

Leadership council members, pitted against each other, drafted their own teams. "You had to get an even team," explains Cameron. "Everybody had a list of the entire team broken up by position," says Nate Meikle. "Round one started, and everyone would choose a linebacker. Then everyone would choose a running back. And everybody would choose a safety." Supergames were held each Friday, and the team with the greatest cumulative score at the end of the off-season period got some "sweet" prizes. "It was still something challenging," says Nate "but they turned Fun Fridays into a competition."

They played water polo, soccer, flag football, dodge ball, ultimate Frisbee. They held track meets. The matches were impassioned. "There was almost an all-out brawl every single week," says Nate. "We were able to just keep it under control."

Teams also received points for total pounds lifted in the weight room. "That weight room was crazy, just because everybody was fighting for the last pound," remembers Cameron. "Previously on test day, whatever you'd get, it was no big deal," says Nate. "Whereas now, it was part of Supergames, so guys were really killing themselves. All of our test results just shot through the roof, because now you were not only fighting for your max, but you got points for your team for Supergames."

Says Cameron: "Peer-to-peer evaluation. There were guys sitting there saying, 'Hey, come on, get one more pound. That's what we need so we can have five more points.'"

Supergames have been played nearly every year since.

"It's cool what they have come up with to give us the opportunity to gain a competitive edge but doing it in a way where we also get the training that we need," says Brandon Bradley.

"These Supergames that we play," says Brian Logan, "they're intense. We're conditioning. I'm dead tired after these games. I sit there, and I'm like 'They're so smart!' We go 150 percent trying to win for our team, not knowing that we're killing ourselves. You just get so caught up in having fun and trying to win, and then you realize, 'I just ran for twenty minutes straight!'"

"It's all about competing," says David Nixon. "One thing I love about Coach Mendenhall is he wants to make sure that the fire of competition is always burning within us. That's why he develops a lot of these programs."

For summer workouts, another innovation increased Cougar advantage. "In the off-season, we do player-run practices," explains Andrew Rich (defensive back 2008–10; team captain), "where the older veterans go out, run practice, and do drills. They do all those things that we do when the coaches are there. It's really no different. This year [2010] we have a lot of young guys, and so it's been a real benefit to get out there and help those guys get up to speed, so when practice does roll around, they're not wondering what's going on."

The Cougars continued to innovate with their season practice regimen; they began to emphasize practice *efficiency* over practice *duration*. They developed the leanest practice possible.

In 2005 and 2006, practices were twenty-four periods long, at five minutes each period. That's a two or two-and-a-half-hour practice. Of those days, Scott Johnson says, "I remember consciously thinking sometimes, 'I might have to take this easy so I can give full effort on another part' that may have been more important in my mind." Even so, he says, "I remember I was running the whole practice and that wasn't just during specific drills, but it was from drill to drill. It was a run. I think that was one of Coach Mendenhall's favorite phrases. He'd kind of run behind you yelling, 'Now run! Now run!' I think he doesn't like being idle." Scott grins at the thought.

They'd beat each other up in full pads, or fire through walk-throughs, play after play after play after play, starting over from the beginning when even one guy screwed up.

"There got to be a point where guys were getting injured," says Jan Jorgensen (defensive line 2005–09; team captain). "I think Coach Mendenhall was trying to figure out how he could save our bodies, keep us from getting injured, and help us perform to the best of our abilities and still get just as much done." So in 2007, the coaching staff reduced practice to sixteen periods. That's about an hour and a half.

"We got very focused," says Jan. "They identified what was important, and we spent our time on those things, and that's all we did."

"With shorter practices, there wasn't a second where I was willing to take it easy at all," says Scott. "I was going to give it all I had because it was going to be over in just a little bit."

"The whole thing about practices is the tempo," says Matt Reynolds. "You go from one drill to the next, to the next, to the next. It's really efficient. There are plusses and minuses, obviously. Plusses: you get stuff done, and you're making sure that your time is used effectively. I really like that. But you know, on the other hand, you may not have as much time to correct things, and so a lot of our correction comes the next day during film study. For me, I really like the way that it works. I like to be able to get things done and then let it go, and then think about it the next day and fix it. I think Coach Mendenhall's focus on being efficient and effective at what we're doing has a positive effect on the team."

"During the season, having those shorter practices also saved your legs and saved your body for Saturday," says Jan. "I think a lot of times we were fresher and our bodies were in better shape than the team that we were playing because they'd just gone twenty-four periods every day, where we're out on the field less time, and our bodies were able to recoup and get ready for that game on Saturday."

Practices during the season and at camps still remained incredibly intensive, which is, of course, signature Bronco, even if practice times were shortened. As always, Bronco strives to make tough warriors out of his players, strong both physically and mentally.

"A lot of players who come to BYU are shocked by some of the things you have to do as far as workout goes," says Brandon Bradley. "Some people may see Coach Mendenhall's work ethic as a little, I guess, wild, crazy. So, to a lot of people, some things would seem a little extreme and a bit unnecessary. Like one of the things that we do before fall camp is run to the Y as fast as we can. I've seen a lot of players come here thinking, 'Who is this dude? Why are we doing this? It has nothing to do with football. It is extreme!'"

Brian Logan adds:

I remember when I came, I was thinking, "What are we running up a mountain for? Why?" I remember halfway through, I was jogging up, and I had to walk backward. I started cramping. That was the first time I had a concern, changing my mind toward BYU. Because I was like, "Why am I running up this mountain?" I think a lot of things Coach Mendenhall does are more for the mental aspect, to see how mentally tough you are. Not necessarily will this help you for football or will it be physical? It's more for mental strength.

My first camp, I could honestly say that was probably one of the hardest times in my life, and I've been through some things! I've been through some real legit things, and I honestly can say that was one of the hardest times of my life. I feel getting mentally stronger during camp does help you in the game, in the season. When I would get scored on, or if I made a bad play, or if I messed up, I'd be mentally strong to say, "Okay, I made a mistake; let's move on, and let's get better." I feel that that's what I did in some games. I could look back to the program trying to mentally break you down; you have to feel like it works.

Brandon Bradley and other guys told me, "Just make it through camp. The games are so much easier."

I'm thinking that there's no way the games are going to be easier than practice! You know, coming from what I've known all my life from junior college and high school. They were right! I get in the game, and I can breathe now. When you get in the game, it's so much easier. Because it's easier, you perform better.

So the Cougars were working their processes, sticking with things that were going well, making changes when something needed to be done a different way. We said earlier that the BYU coaching staff found an owner for each of their core work flows. Bronco saw that sharing process ownership with *players*—not just *coaches*—would be an additional way to give players an opportunity for leadership. Paul explained that engaging them in the work of the organization would increase their commitment to the team and ultimately impact game performance. The idea made sense to Bronco and the staff. This was, of course, a key aspect of Cougar Football strategy: leverage the unique capabilities of this team of experienced, returned-missionary leaders to do things differently and thus gain an advantage on the gridiron.

So in early 2006, a leadership council meeting was called and the player-leaders learned about work processes, too. They were presented with the list that the coaches had developed the previous year.

Then the players learned about *team development* and were introduced to five steps of ever-increasing independence that result in the emergence of an exceptionally high-performing team. What's important to know is that as teams begin to mature and excel they can and should take on more and more responsibility for managing their own work.

The leadership council was totally up for it, and members were either voted in or volunteered as the owners of various Cougar work processes, such as planning firesides, running the Band of Brothers program (see below), managing service opportunities, and coaching special teams.

What is that, you say? *Players* coaching special teams?

Yes. Special teams at BYU are coached by player-leaders (most years, but not all), with schematic assistance from a member of the coaching staff. Player-led special teams is a *structure* design choice.

STRUCTURE PART II

Remember from the last chapter that design choices about structure have to do with the way people are organized to perform the work of the organization. Organizing players to coach special teams is a decision about who will do the work of the organization, which in this case is special teams work.

The Cougars' 2005–06 punt returner tells the story by beginning with the bad news. "Our special teams had been horrendous the previous several years," says Nate Miekle. "I mean, 100th out of 118 teams in the country. Consistently around the 80-to-100 level. We developed a strategy for improvement that was to give the players ownership."

Nate is right; the idea was born when a gloomy Bronco commiserated with coauthor Paul about special teams. "I believe we're perfectly designed to get the results that we get," says Bronco. "We had to do something about our special teams."

"Who owns your special teams' performance?" asked Paul at the time. (You may remember him asking this kind of question before.)

"We all do," said Bronco.

Paul said, "Bronco. No. Who owns special teams?"

"I guess the special teams coach and I do," said Bronco.

Now special teams is like a suicide squad. You're giving your all. You're out in the open of everything. It's high risk. It's high effort. You're moving at top speed, and you're hitting your opponent full force.

"It's really almost the purest form of football, if you think about it," says Cameron Jensen, a former special teams player-coach. "It's kamikaze."

However, if you don't play on a special team, you have that game time to rest and recover. Even during practice, you have a respite if you're not involved in special teams.

So Paul said to Bronco, "Who *should* own it? Let's look at the design elements for a minute. Who coaches each one of those teams?"

Bronco said, "We do," meaning staff members.

Paul: "Who selects the players?"

Bronco: "We do."

Paul: "So who has ownership?"

The point, obviously, is that special teams performance would improve if the players felt more ownership.

Together Bronco and Paul batted about some ideas. What if the Cougars used the old school-yard method to select special-teams personnel? Players actually know who performs and who doesn't. They know who goes full bore and who leads out.

Bronco said, "I got it." Just like that. No more discussion needed.

"One day, Coach introduced the idea of special teams captains," says Nate. "It was born out of the Supergames. In the Supergames, Coach was able to see how competitive everybody got because we took ownership of the Supergames. So, as an extension of that, he said, 'Let's do the same thing with special teams.'" Bronco told the captains, according to Nate, "'It's your team. You're going to draft them, just like playground ball. You're going to pick who you want. You're going to manage the depth chart. It's your team. There will be one coach assigned to you to help with the schematics, but other than that, it's your deal.'"

Nate, who was elected the punt return captain, was "completely stressed out, 100 percent," he says. "I mean, returning punts is, I think, other than being quarterback, the most stressful thing in a football game because there can be such huge momentum swings if you drop a punt. The defense of the opposing team has just gained forty to fifty yards and your defense comes back on the field. So I was already extremely stressed out."

But he was not without ideas. He says:

> There were a couple of things I had noticed that special teams hadn't been doing well. One was holding players accountable. There was only a ten-minute block in practice per week to go over the previous week's special teams or punt return. Well, there were usually five plays. There are eleven players on those five plays. In a ten-minute meeting, it was not possible to critique all the players on every play. There were basically fifty-five things you had to watch for, so I realized that people weren't being held accountable. Coach Mendenhall's number one lesson, when he came to BYU, the very first principles that he brought were accountability, discipline, effort. Accountability, of course, first. I've never had a coach who held himself as accountable as Coach Mendenhall. If he said he was going to do something, he always did.
>
> Second, the thing that I really thought would be crucial

on punt return is self-selection. We learned from Paul that the people who self-select are the best employees or the best members of any group. And special teams prior to that had been just kind of a punishment. Nobody wanted to do it.

So I put up a sheet in the locker room and told the guys, "If you want to be on the punt return team, sign up; come talk to me." So that was the first thing I did. I did not want anybody who didn't want to be on it, so anybody who didn't sign up was already eliminated. I had forty or so guys sign up. Then, in consultation with Coach Higgins—but with basically my last word—we created a depth chart.

Nate developed a set of criteria for grading each player on each play.

I tried to make it so it wouldn't be subjective, because if it were subjective, I knew I would be dealing a lot more with personalities. What I said was if the punt returner catches the ball and everybody's assigned a man to block, then if you're between your man and the ball carrier when the ball carrier passes you, you've succeeded. If you're not between your man and the ball then you fail. My criteria as the punt returner was that I had to catch the ball and make one guy miss—because we had ten blockers—and get ten yards. That was the criteria, and it was very clearly identified.

Nate would analyze the plays Monday morning, grade the players, and find the five or six key plays that had gone well or players who had done a good job. "Paul would say, watch best practices, worst practices," says Nate. So during each practice, Nate would pass out the grades and then review only the limited set of best practices he had chosen Monday morning.

"I was responsible for one facet of the team," says Nate, "and I was basically the coach. At practice, I'm the guy. If someone's not doing it right, I'm getting mad at them. If someone's doing it right, I'm making sure the rest of the guys are learning the proper technique. I'm handling the personalities." Aside from much-appreciated schematic help and input on the depth chart from special teams coach Patrick Higgins, Nate truly led the punt-return team. The highest-scorers at spring camp became the starters going into fall camp, and likewise into season play.

Each special teams captain could run the team his own way. "It was my team," says Cameron Jensen, punt team captain. "I felt that completely." He chose his players, he showed the film, he gave pointers where needed. "The first eleven on my team got a shirt. It was a special shirt and if they failed their responsibility and didn't do it, they got to give up that shirt."

"It was an honor to be on those special teams," says Cameron. "A lot of starters played special teams, because they are the ones who the captains trusted and wanted to be on the teams. People would talk to me and ask, 'What can I do to be on the team?' It had become such a special thing. People were coming to *me*, not a coach. They were coming to *me* saying, 'What can I do?'"

"I thought, nowhere else in the country were there players who actually had input on what was going to happen on special teams," says Kelly Poppinga, who led the kickoff cover team and the punt team in successive years. "Coaches see things in a certain way and players see things in other ways. So it was kind of like bringing the two different views and putting them together. Nobody else was doing that, and it gave us an advantage. It's one of those things you can do at a place like this where guys are a little more mature. They have developed some leadership skills, you know, on their missions."

"We went from eighty-fifth in 2005 to twentieth in the nation," says Nate of the punt-return team's performance.[1] "We had been top ten to top fifteen all season long, then dropped to twenty.

Scan this QR code to see "Special Teams Player Coaching" or go to http://bit.ly/Ny4UPo

We finished well in the conference for the first time in a while. All four teams in 2006 finished either first or second in the conference, whereas the previous year, all had been either sixth or seventh in the conference." The punt team moved up in the national rankings from No. 100 the year before to No. 41 in net punting average while the punt-cover team improved from No. 79 to No. 67; the kickoff-return team moved up from No. 110 to No. 56 and the kickoff-cover team jumped from No. 90 in 2005 to No. 37 in 2006.

Besides special teams, two other processes that were headed up by players were the Band of Brothers program and the Thursday's Hero service program.

Band of Brothers

Bronco explains the beginnings of the Band of Brothers program, also called, at times, the Big Brother program, which was first launched in 2005:

> We'd had some players quit and leave the program, and I didn't want to see anybody else leave or fail. But how could we care for them all? I knew that I certainly couldn't do it for 123 players. I couldn't get to know them intimately enough and as fast as necessary and to know everything that was going on with them.

Bronco shared his dilemma with his father, who drew on his experience as a mission president to provide counsel. Paul Mendenhall, who led the New Zealand Auckland Mission for the Church from 1999 to 2002, described how missionaries reported to him as mission president: they wrote letters each week on behalf of each other.

LDS missionaries always travel and work in pairs (or less frequently, threesomes), called "companionships." These letters served as the most frequent form of communication between mature leaders at the mission home and young companionships acting with a great deal of independence in remote regions of the country. Bronco recognized this method of frequent, personal reporting as a best practice, with the added advantage that most of his players were well familiar with this system. "I thought, who better to know how to make sure these kids are doing okay and are on the right track than the Church that has dealt with the missionary program for a long time?" says Bronco.

So he seized the familiar concept of independent companionships caring for each other and incorporated it in the football program. "I remember trying to set up companionships first just by myself," he says. "It took a ton of work, and I think it was kind of maliciously obeyed by the team. It wasn't that they really grasped it and wanted to do it." But in time he shifted responsibility for the program first to quarterbacks coach Brandon Doman, and by 2006, leadership council members were establishing big-brother partnerships and structuring the reporting process.

Cameron Jensen explains that he and John Beck assigned the partnerships one season, but the next season the leadership council did it. "It was a thoughtful process," he says. "We tried to identify twenty or so of the at-risk players and match them up with a strong player who was also somebody whose personality would mesh well with their personality."

"Our big-brother letters were due Wednesday or Thursday," says Nate, "so every week we had to do our evaluation form—how our brother was doing academically, spiritually, athletically. At the end we could write anything we wanted to."

The day after letters were due, Bronco "put on the board the names of the people who hadn't turned in their big-brother form," explains Nate.

And if you were one of those names, "there were penalties," says Cameron. "You had to go run before practice or after practice."

Did Bronco really read all those letters?

He did. He still does. He says:

It takes maybe two or three hours to read through them. The specific instruction for each player is to report on his own physical and social well-being and that of his companion. That means, possibly, who they are dating and how they're doing that way. They also report on academic well-being and also spiritual well-being. That even includes church attendance. If they have a church assignment, it may include what they're teaching and things of that nature. So I'll hear about girlfriends, I'll hear about Church responsibilities, I'll hear about academic progress. And I'll hear about how they feel things are going on the field. A lot of times these kids won't be willing to say much if they're frustrated by not playing, but their partner will say, "You know, this has been really hard for him." And then I'll have a chance—a window—to talk to them.

There are usually six to eight letters that I set aside. Not that the companion will say what exactly is happening, but he will say something like, "You might want to talk to him." Or, "So-and-so could probably benefit from a visit." Other times they won't say that, but I'll just have a sense in the letters that I should get those six or eight in my office. Sure enough, there'll be something that is on the verge of happening or it is happening at the front end. We can correct it before it gets to the point where it is irreparable or has created more damage.

After big-brother partnerships were introduced, Bronco says, "It made our program a lot more cohesive." Cameron Jensen adds that "it helped get young players integrated into the program and make sure they did well in all aspects—on the football field, in the classroom, and spiritually as well. I would say, along with that, Coach Mendenhall was trying to identify problems before they happened, to nip them in the bud."

"Big-brother pairs are an essential part of our program," says David Nixon. "It really helps all the players connect with somebody and trust somebody. I think that the whole key to it is to develop trust between two players that if they were ever in a touchy spot or if they ever needed help, they could trust their teammate to come help them or bail them out of any type of situation. It is a great chance each week to sit down with the teammate of yours and find out how he is doing and if there is anything you can help him with. I remember there were many times when I'd see my little brother at a party or something. I'd check to see if he was doing all right, and he'd do the same with me."

"When I first got here," says Brandon Bradley, "my big brother was Bryan Kehl (linebacker 2002–07; team captain). He did a good job of bringing me in and showing me the ropes, helping me understand the program. So when I had my opportunity to be a big brother, I just tried to remember that when I got here, Bryan did this and this. I think one of the things I liked most about Bryan that I use as a big brother is that he never made me feel bad. He always talked to me in a teaching manner, in a manner that showed that he cared for my well-being, and that he was just trying to help. When I had my first opportunity to be a big brother, that's the kind of approach I took."

"In the end," adds David Nixon, "there isn't really any difference between a big brother and a little brother. You're just brothers, and you're both here to help each other out. It's a big checks-and-balances system. Everyone checking out for each other."

Matt Reynolds was assigned his real-life older brother, Dallas Reynolds (offensive line 2005–08; team captain). "Through the program there was a different part of our relationship. It strengthened the bridge between us because we were talking so often that, come Monday, when we had to write our letters, we knew what was going on in each other's lives. Even now that Dallas is off the team, if I go too long without talking to him, I have to call him because that part of our relationship is still there."

In some cases, the big-brother companionship has had a life-saving quality. "When I came here I was a returned missionary who had played at a junior college, so I was assigned immediately as an older brother to Jordan Pendleton [linebacker 2007–11]," says Andrew Rich. "When you're asking a guy about his life, you take an interest in things he's doing, and he takes an interest in what you're doing. That kind of instantly develops a different relationship than just a football friendship."

Andrew battled bitterly under the weight of football and personal issues during his first year on the team as he shared in the vignette that prefaces this chapter. "I'm sure Jordan wrote to Coach that I was struggling," says Andrew. "Maybe Coach talked to Jordan about helping me. I'm not sure. I was not secretive about it to Jordan, just because I needed help. I knew I needed help. It wasn't something I was trying to hide from Coach M."

With Bronco's assistance, Andrew's football troubles were eventually resolved, and he also met and became engaged to his future wife. Andrew remained close with Jordan through all this; they even roomed together. He was the only other player Andrew talked to about what was going on.

"The thing was, I never really shared my personal issues with my parents," says Andrew. "I've always had a hard time with that. I think Jordan and I were both kind of going through the same battles on the field. We're pretty different people, but that was one common thing for us. Our family lives were very similar. I don't know what would have happened if I hadn't had Jordan to relate to and make a joke about something that was really bothering me. But it really, really helped out that he knew what was going on. He still wears his dog tags with my name on it, and I still have his.

"That's what's great about BYU," adds Andrew. "The more mature players and even the younger players can identify and feel when something's not right. Here they care enough to talk to Coach about it. It's not being a snitch, or it's not, you know, throw one of your teammates under the bus. It's helping one of your teammates cope with an issue that's going on in his life."

We've noted that special teams and the Big Brother program are run by players. Andrew's accomplishments lead us to talk about one more process that the BYU staff identified as being important in their program: service. It's another type of work that is largely in the hands of the players, not the coaches.

Service

Throughout Bronco's efforts to help Andrew, he emphasized how important performing service was in helping Andrew find a way out of his predicament. "That was one of Coach's big things when I was struggling," says Andrew. "He stressed that if you serve other people, there is less time to think about yourself."

Bronco often assigns service work to players who are struggling, either to help them shrug off personal problems, or sometimes as a sort of penance for football, academic, or Honor Code issues. He encourages all of his players to be constantly seeking for ways to give to the community, in both visible and invisible ways.

Full-time volunteers Bob and Cindy Wakefield, a lively retired couple who coordinate service opportunities for BYU athletes, stand by to join players with requests that come in from the community. "Out of the 250 service projects we do a year," says Bob Wakefield, "the football team probably does 80 percent of them. That's for two reasons. One, everybody wants football players. They're the high profile sport. Number two, the football players know that they're expected to do service work. So when you ask a football player, you always get a yes."

"We don't do service for people to watch," says Bronco. "Yet, it is a delicate thing, because at BYU as an athlete, you're the flag bearer. Everything you do generates interest. The trick is how to do the service without the recognition, because we're not interested in the recognition."

What kinds of service work do the football players do?

They participate in the "Buff, Don't Puff" program to educate school children about the harmful effects tobacco and other drugs have on their bodies. They play ball with the Boys and Girls Clubs. They speak at youth conferences, fathers and sons outings, and Eagle Scout recognition banquets. They visit hospitals and clean up litter along highways. They sort food at food drives and put kits together at the Red Cross.

"Players will come up with projects and things that they get asked to do," says Jan Jorgensen. If they need help, "then it comes before the team and snap, just like that, we always get a lot of volunteers."

"If I wasn't a BYU football player," says Jordan Pendleton, "if I was just some random dude, walking up there at a school assembly and saying don't do drugs, I think the students would be like, 'Who is this?' They wouldn't really pay attention. But you know, since I play football at BYU, their eyes light up and they really enjoy us coming there. I went with guys on the basketball team, and there was a volleyball player. Just because we're athletes at BYU, it gives us an opportunity to be able to reach out to them a lot more. One time, we played all kinds of games with Boys and Girls Club kids. When we got ready to leave, they didn't want us to leave. It was really humbling. There was one kid I hung out with for like an hour and a half, and he said, 'You're the best friend I've ever had.' So it's really special."

Giving to others is an important way for football players to remember how much they have been given and how much they can give back. "Coach Mendenhall wants to make sure that we stay balanced," says David Nixon, "balanced in life. And that's the essential key, to always remain balanced because any time that you're out of whack, that you're not taking care of yourself in a certain area, it will definitely affect football itself. So you have to make sure that you remain balanced."

Serving others is so important to Bronco that he has used it as one of the primary modes of returning a wayward team member to full privileges.

"Coach Mendenhall prescribes a certain amount of time," says Cindy. "On occasion he has called us at home. 'Sister Wakefield, I have another student I'll be sending up to you. He'll need forty hours.'"

"He doesn't tell why," says Bob. "He just sends them to our office." "And we don't ask," says Cindy. She explains that most of these athletes "are anxious to show Bronco that they are serious and they are not going to be stepping out of line again."

Bob reveals some of his methods to expedite these service requirements. "I'm good friends with the head groundskeeper of the Provo Temple. I had a player laying sod there before the day was over. We have a standing arrangement with the food bank and the Red Cross to provide volunteers."

Football players sign up for most service projects in small groups, but once a week the entire team participates in a program they have come to call "Thursday's Hero." This grassroots effort has always been and continues to be player-led.

Thursday's Hero was initiated when players who knew of a seriously ill or struggling individual—often a child—invited the person (and their family) to team practice where they were honored and encouraged by the football team. By 2007, players had developed a routine for these visits. Matt Bauman, who was a process owner for the Thursday's Hero program, explains:

> Their whole family would be there, and they'd often just be in tears because they were so happy their little guy or little girl was excited and happy. We'd give them hats and jerseys, and we'd all sign a photo for them. We'd have them sign that big flag that we carry out before every game. We'd have them sign it as our hero and tell them they were part of our team because of the battles they were fighting. Some of them couldn't really even write, just kind of scribble on there. Coach Mendenhall would tell them, "Put whatever you want. You can draw a smiley face if you want; you know it still means you're a part of our team." They'd count to three, and we'd all dip in, and then we'd usually hold them up. We'd all yell, "Go Cougars!" really loud. It was just a really neat experience because these kids are going through a lot more than any of us, and they come and just have a great time, being with the team, being honored by the team. Some of the guys, mostly offensive guys, they know their names and they really like Harvey Unga and Max Hall and Dennis Pitta. Those team members would stick around after and play around with these kids. It's just a dream come true for them. Just a great way to give back and really touch a lot of lives.
>
> Sometimes, we'd correspond back and forth with them.

A Thursday's Hero meets the team

One little girl, Aubrey Frank, comes to mind [search for her on YouTube to see her as a Thursday's Hero]. She occasionally would send in a video before the game for the team. She was really hard to understand so her parents put subtitles underneath, but essentially, she'd give us an inspirational, motivational pep talk. Actually, it was really, really inspiring, because of who she was, this young girl who could barely speak. She just loved BYU, and she was always happy. Coach would show the videos to us on Thursday or Friday. I enjoyed that. Coach was trying to keep in touch with each of them.

This weekly opportunity for team members and challenged or terminally ill fans to share their love and goodwill on the practice field was initiated and developed by the young men themselves. It was another way of bringing the team members together while allowing them to express some of their most cherished values of serving, loving, and helping.

Scan this QR code to see "Thursday's Heroes" or go to http://bit.ly/LsxJbD

Combined with other, more technically oriented exercises, the Band of Brothers and Thursday's Heroes programs were yielding a unique football program and would soon deliver a different set of results. Before we review these results, let's explore the rest of the critical design choices made by the Cougars.

MEASURES

In the last chapter, when we were exploring design choices about the goals and objectives of the BYU football program, we named three short-term targets for each season through 2010:

1. To be champions on and off the field
2. To win the Mountain West conference
3. To go to a bowl game and win

As early as Bronco's first spring as head coach, he and his staff sought to pinpoint the game performance measures most closely correlated with winning. Building on some early research by the team under former head coach Gary Crowton, they studied twenty years of Cougar football and then college football as a whole to uncover the top ten statistics that indicate success. They aimed with laser-precision at finding the absolutely most crucial metrics.

Bronco hearkens back to early LDS history to explain the sifting process, recalling the early Mormon pioneers' arduous flight by handcart and covered wagon across the plains to the isolated Salt Lake Valley where they hoped to finally live free of religious persecution:

Think of the pioneers going over the mountains in their wagons. Not everything made it over. The pianos were left behind many times. Sounded good, looked good. It would be nice to have it in your house. But not everything can make it. So we're just looking for the essentials. We went through all the studies and came up with the top ten statistics. But knowing that we couldn't focus on ten things, we focused on three. So the idea was, if you can measure anything, what will determine that we win games?

Bronco named those precious three essentials "the three pillars."

"Every Monday, Coach Mendenhall would discuss the three pillars, whether we reached our goals for that particular game," says Andrew Rich.

"It was the first thing he'd show after a game," says Cameron Jensen.

"We would talk about it in team meeting and then we also would talk about it in defensive meeting," says Jordan Pendleton. "That was where it got the most attention."

Player faith in this slim set of objectives is firm. Andrew Rich says, "It's really interesting. If we reach our goals, we never lose. They actually are solid in predicting wins and losses."

From David Nixon: "It was an easy evaluation after the game—if the result wasn't in our favor—to go back to our three pillars and see what it was that prevented us from winning."

These measures set the team's sights on the same target. "What it does is, going into the game, you know what our goal is," says Matt Reynolds. "You know what we're trying to accomplish or trying to avoid on defense. I think that's where it has the most influence: going in, you know what everybody else is thinking."

Even during a game, these statistics drive player behavior. "I thought about them a lot," says Jan Jorgensen. "We always knew exactly where we were."

"When the offense is struggling," says Jordan Pendleton, "it motivates our defense to make the play and put our offense in a good situation."

Likewise, "if we see that the defense is struggling," says Matt Reynolds, "then that just means we, the offense, have got to do everything we can to keep scoring."

Certainly, other college football programs carefully watch their own sets of key statistics. Cameron Jensen suggests that what may be different at BYU is the acute focus on the three pillars by players as well as coaches: "I think it is unique just how much it's talked about on the team. I remember during games, talking about it. Or when the second-string guys would go in, it meant a lot to the first-string that the second-string guys were also focused on those goals."

"Every other statistic beyond our three pillars, they are interesting and they are relevant, just not as relevant as those," says Bronco. "So they go off the wagon. The wheels can't pull them. The oxen are tired, they're hungry, so we're keeping the flour and something to make fire and just whatever the essentials are. The rest is going to be left out there on the plains. And it's nice if somebody can use it. We would if we had more time. We don't have time. These three pillars are what we have time for. And it's one of the reasons that we've won so many games. We don't really focus on or care about much else."

Before moving on, we should note one key stat that has less directly to do with football performance: grade point average. Bronco has set a team goal of a 3.0 GPA. "The coaches don't like it," says Bronco, "and the players sometimes don't. But we're capable." And Bronco believes that the program consistently achieves the highest GPA of any Division 1 football program in the country because of this emphasis. The team has a tough time reaching it each year

Scan this QR code to see "Three Pillars" or go to http://bit.ly/Mt1StE

but consistently falls within a couple of tenths or sometimes just a couple of hundredths of the target.

To provide a little more incentive, the staff has at times organized an "academic championship series" or let the team form themselves into virtual "academic houses," or groups of players who have a similar balance of GPA histories who are then challenged as a group to deliver an overall 3.0 average.

PERFORMANCE MANAGEMENT

Another design choice the Cougars put in place is the system for managing performance—for giving feedback to players and holding them accountable. As students, of course, players are graded, and their grades show up on their report cards. Scholarship players can lose their scholarship if either academic or game performance slacks off. Conversely, if a walk-on player proves his worth, he can be awarded a scholarship not originally anticipated.

If academic work is not current at any time during the year, or if there is a question about the player's commitment to the Honor Code, Bronco manages player performance by holding them out of practices and games until the necessary correction is made—even if the player is a star athlete. We've already told about the Wakefields' role in hooking up behavioral malefactors with the necessary service work to redeem themselves in Bronco's eyes. Sometimes, though, just sitting out a day or two of practice is enough to do the trick.

But players don't just *receive* feedback about their performance. They are also involved in formally *giving* feedback to their coaches. This is sometimes called 360-degree feedback, when leaders receive information from team members about their strengths and weaknesses. A student athlete survey is collected from all BYU players each year that gathers comprehensive information about their experience with the athletic department. Respondents rate such statements as:

- Cares about me as an individual
- Develops winning strategies
- Creates a rewarding practice and playing environment
- Respects and encourages my spiritual life

"It was great that we could evaluate the training staff, the academic staff, the weightlifting staff," says Cameron Jensen. "From middle school, to high school, to junior college," adds Nate Meikle, "I never had an option to offer feedback and give my side of the story. Coaching is so one-sided. They're always telling you what to do, and you never get to voice your opinion. So it was awesome to be able to say what we thought, and to know we were going to be heard."

"Feedback is a gift," Paul told Bronco. So Bronco, once an avoider of unnecessary student interaction, now scrutinizes the results of the student athlete survey annually. He is chagrined to find that of all his scores, his lowest continues to be the responses to "is easy to approach and talk with." He tries to get that number to creep up a bit each year. He talks over both his own and all the coaches' results with them in staff meetings.

"I knew that Coach Mendenhall would take into account any type of advice or any type of constructive criticism that the players might give the coaches," says David Nixon. "I felt as though there were definitely changes made here and there according to what some of those survey results said. The players talked about the surveys and what they had written, and I think there were changes made from it. I saw results. Because it was all anonymous, I thought it was a great way to be honest and frank. Every day they're ranking us and criticizing us. Not that we're trying to get back at them, but I thought it was a great opportunity for them to be evaluated by their players. I took it seriously."

These 360-degree surveys, along with firm consequences for academic malaise and Honor Code violations, contribute to the signature characteristics of the Cougar Football performance management system.

REWARDS

An organization's reward-oriented design choices include its pay and benefits structure along with incentives, celebrations, informal rewards, and recognitions.

BYU, no different from most college football programs, offers scholarships to top athletes. But, notably, Bronco talks about scholarships being granted on a year-by-year basis. In other words, a player can't feel that once he nails a scholarship, it's his for the duration of his college career. "If you aren't doing well or you're not giving the effort you need to give," says Andrew Rich, "Coach has no qualms about taking you off the scholarship and making you pay for school. You came here to go to school and play, and if you're not doing it, then sorry. He's so walk-on driven," adds Andrew, who started as a walk-on but was awarded a scholarship after his sophomore year. "It gives a chance for us as walk-ons. It motivates everyone to work."

BYU is on a semester system with additional short spring and summer terms, and the scholarship for the spring and summer terms is not a given, either. "For someone to get a scholarship for spring to be able to take spring classes, you have to get either a 3.0 or better or improve your GPA from the previous semester," explains Andrew.

Less formal rewards are part of the Cougar system, too, most notably for academic performance. The staff offers an off-season GPA banquet each year with an extraordinary menu and an almost Oprah-like giveaway of cool gear. "You have to qualify for it," says Cameron Jensen. "Coach rubs it in, too." He reads the menu to the whole team: filet mignon, the works. He describes the gifts. "'Only a handful of you are invited,'" he'll say, chuckles Cameron. "Every chance he gets, he tries to rub it in to the people who don't qualify, to motivate them to qualify next time."

Another example of a Cougar motivator: helmet stickers are given for success with the three pillars. Players can get up to four stickers per game: one for each pillar, and then an additional sticker if all three pillars are met. An additional "head coach" sticker is given for extraordinary play or effort.

Food, gear, and stickers are not the only incentives that Bronco puts to work. "Just getting Coach's approval was a big deal," says Nate Meikle. "He would show clips to the whole team of guys working hard. So if a guy's diving for a ball in the indoor practice facility on the turf, he'd show that and say, 'This is what this program is about.' Just getting his approval was important, but that was also a way to be recognized in front of your whole team."

RENEWAL

An oft-neglected type of design choice has to do with an organization's methods of encouraging and formalizing ongoing learning. These types of choices describe how an organization constantly assesses and improves all of its other choices. It is the system of continuous improvement, of organizational learning, of cyclical adaptation to changes in the competitive environment.

Renewal at BYU Football happens on an ongoing basis. The staff sifts through the team's most important work processes to discuss how they can be changed and enhanced. For example, the recruiting process is scrutinized each spring in conjunction with the recruiting season. Even the leadership council periodically evaluates its success as contributors to or leaders of the work. Members of the council set goals to reach higher and do better.

Of course, rituals such as the run to the Y are symbolic events that help teach new players about what it means to be a Cougar as well as to reconnect returning players with the team's spirit and mission. Such events are among the most important ways the team can bring itself back to fundamentals and ensure that it remains headed in the direction it has set for itself.

RAISE THE BAR: 2006–2009

Now that we've thoroughly studied the design of the BYU football program, we're ready to remember (or if you weren't following at the time, to report) the success of the Cougars' hard work.

Reset to the 2006 season, Bronco's second as the Cougar head coach. The staff and the leadership council had intentionally and systematically crafted design choices that they hoped would deliver on the team's promise: to be flag bearers for BYU and to play football at the highest level. They had put in place routines and structures that they hoped would create a culture of accountability, discipline, and effort. They had been guided by their values: tradition, spirit, and honor. They had set their goals: to be champions on and off the field, to top the Mountain West Conference, and to go to a bowl game and win. They had established a full range of practices for recruiting, working out, serving, meeting, leading, providing incentives, rewarding performance, and improving—practices that they believed as a whole were different from any other football program and that would work together to give them an upside competitively.

They believed they had a great program, a great team, and were ready to break through.

BYU opened the season unranked at Arizona and lost 16–13 on a last-second field goal off the toe of Nick Folk, later to kick for the New York Jets. The Cougars handily won their next game at home against Tulsa, 49–24. At 1–1 on the season, BYU visited Boston College, a team led by future Atlanta Falcons QB Matt Ryan. The Eagles were then ranked twenty-third nationally, coming off a win over No. 18 Clemson the week before, and the BYU–B.C. game would be nationally televised on ESPN2. The Cougars took an early 7–0 lead and led throughout the first half, taking a one-point cushion into halftime. A back-and-forth second half resulted in a 23-all regulation deadlock followed by two overtime periods, with Boston College eventually earning a 30–23 victory. BYU's spirited effort had been undone by three turnovers and three missed field goals, but some players were satisfied with the competitive nature of the setback. That attitude received a slap-down from their coach, with Bronco admonishing those players for feeling too proud of themselves. Nate Meikle says:

> Coming back from the game, a lot of us felt pretty good about it. We played on national television and played against a good team and really had them on the ropes at their place. That Monday afternoon meeting, Coach just came in and said, "I hope you guys don't feel good about that. That's not a moral victory. That's not a victory. You guys lost. And we're only as good as our last game. And we're not better than Boston College. I don't want you guys to think you're better than them." He basically just told us, "You're not any better than what you've done, and you're 1–2 right now." And for us that was a good lesson on accountability. It made us more hungry. You know, if you accept moral victories, you're content. You can become content in losing. Coach can tell you the brutal facts, but he's not a negative person. He's a very optimistic coach, a very optimistic person. But his strength is being straight-up with you.

The straight-up lesson apparently sunk in; the Cougars did not lose another game that season. The week after the Boston College defeat, BYU blanked Utah State, 38–0, in Provo. The following week, the Cougars again played on national television and beat No. 17 TCU on its own turf, 31–17, ending the Horned Frogs' thirteen-game winning streak. It was the first time since 1999 that BYU had conquered a ranked team.

"They were a good team," says Jonny Harline. "Everyone was talking about how good their defense was and how fast they were. But we pretty much dominated them. I remember in the locker room, after the game, everyone was just pumped up and just going nuts. That's when everyone started to believe we were a really good team. I remember even telling my wife—my fiancée at the time—I had never had this particular feeling before, but I said to her, 'I think we're going to win the rest of our games.'"

The ensuing victories were all secured by large margins (47–17 versus San Diego State; 52–7 versus UNLV; 33–14 at Air Force; 24–3 at Colorado State; 55–7 versus Wyoming; and 42–17 versus New Mexico), setting up the regular season's final contest: the Utah game.

The 2006 regular season finale has since been called one of the greatest games in the history of the BYU–Utah rivalry, a "church vs. state" matchup between the institutionally owned BYU and the state-owned University of Utah—two schools located forty-five miles apart from each other in territory settled by Mormon pioneers. Played annually since 1922 (with the exception of three seasons during World War II), it is simply one of the most hotly contested series in college football.

Having lost to Utah for four years running, BYU went into Thanksgiving Friday in Salt Lake City heavily favored to win. An early 14–0 lead quickly evaporated, and BYU found itself trailing 24–14 entering the fourth quarter. Retaking the lead with thirteen consecutive points in the final stanza, BYU saw the Utes answer with a nine-play, eighty-three-yard drive that gave the home team a 31–27 advantage with only a minute and nineteen seconds remaining. Starting at its own twenty-five-yard line, with quarterback John Beck commanding the team, BYU covered sixty-four yards in nine plays, leaving the Cougars at the Utah eleven-yard line with only three seconds on the clock. BYU's biggest game of the year had come down to one final snap.

In a play that would become a permanent fixture in Cougar lore, Beck tantalized fans by shuffling left, safe, pointing, waiting for a receiver, and then reversing to his right when pressured by a Ute defender. Finally, with zeroes showing on the clock, he threw across his body and connected with wide-open tight end Jonny Harline, who caught the ball on his knees in the end zone. Some BYU fans dubbed the play "the answered prayer."

"I get asked all the time about that Utah game and when did I see Jonny and how did it feel," writes John Beck. He recalls:

That one play was definitely a great moment and one I will always remember, but to be honest it was a culmination of many things, of years of work, that made that game and that play so special to me. In that game there was a group of guys on our team, on both sides of the ball who had been through so much adversity. Through all the adversity we never lost the belief that we could do it. The road to get to that opportunity was a difficult road to travel. The thing that made it so special was that everyone was prepared. Everyone wanted it so bad because we wanted to overcome the hardships that we had been through and just go out there and win it . . . and we did![2]

With this victory, the Cougars went 8–0 in the Mountain West Conference, their first unbeaten conference record since 2001, and ended regulation season play ranked twentieth nationally, ahead of both Boston College and TCU.

The Cougars had realized one of their victory goals: a conference championship. The next objective: a win over Oregon in the Las Vegas Bowl.

By now the players knew the principle that you get the results that you're designed to get, so they were convinced that to avoid a second consecutive bowl-game loss, they'd need to be sure to do something differently. They had some ideas about what to change, and by now they knew they didn't have to be afraid to let their head coach in on what they were thinking.

Cameron Jensen explains that when you go to a bowl game, the team's routine can be destroyed. "You're going to dinners with the other team; you're going to shows. As leaders, we decided that we needed to remind people about why we were down there. We said, 'Let's remember we're here to win.' As leadership council members, we were determined to make sure no one was losing track, making sure to keep everyone focused and keeping things as much the same as we would throughout a usual week. I remember saying, 'We don't care about all the bowl activities.' We talked about how we'll remember the game more than we will anything else. We players met and said, 'This is what we need to do differently.'" So the players decided to ask their coach if they could stick to routine as much as possible, if they could engage in those kinds of activities that were familiar and important to them, that stood for who they were much more than some of the other pastimes available in Las Vegas. Bronco says:

> The leadership council set up a meeting with me. There were ten of them. They came in and they said, "Coach, we didn't do it right last year." You know you can't get that kind of feedback unless you provide platforms of ownership. So now the players are telling the head coach, "We didn't do it right last year." I could have been offended. I've been before. They said, "We didn't do it right."
>
> I said, "What do you mean?"
>
> They said, "Last year we traveled on Sunday and our players wandered up and down the strip Sunday night like they were tourists." This is the players talking to me,

now. They said, "We thought we represented something different."

The year before, they had had a community service project that the Las Vegas Bowl set up, but it was scheduled during practice, so only our injured players could go. They said, "We're not interested in that any more. This is who we are. This is what we'd like to do."

So then they tell me, "Since we're traveling on Sunday, we'll go right from the airport to the first chapel and do a fireside on Sunday night."

I said, "Well, we play on Thursday."

And they said, "Yeah, we're going to do it on Wednesday night, too" in order to continue the tradition of holding a fireside the night before a game. So they were telling me Sunday and Wednesday, two firesides. "And besides," they said, "we're going to organize two service projects while we're there."

I said, "We're only there three days."

They said, "Coach, the game's not relevant. We're there to represent who we are."

So fifty players go to a Boys and Girls Club for kids whose parents aren't at home right after school. I walk in there and the players are on the floor, gingerbread frosting in their hair, gumdrops stuck—and the whole room is just vibrant with this interaction between role models and kids.

I leave from there to drive across town to this old hotel where high school students who don't have either parent are staying to try to finish high school. I walk into the bathroom and [quarterback] John Beck—this is Tuesday night, we play Thursday—John Beck has a paint roller in the bathroom, painting. The players set it up.

We get in the bus to leave and this young man comes

down from the second floor waving his arms. He's got a book in his hand. The bus stops, the air shocks go down, the doors open, and Gary Lovely [linebacker 2004–06] walks by me. He sits down on the curb with this kid, and he's got a trigonometry book. The bus and the team sit there for about half an hour, and he helps the kid. He found out somehow during the community service that the kid needed help in math. And he tutors him for half an hour on the curb, while we are there to play the game.

The Cougars overwhelmed Oregon 38–8. It was BYU's first bowl-game victory since 1996. Fans poured over the railings and swarmed the field as the game ended, and coauthor Paul was among them. His memories of that triumph are dear. Jubilant in the throng on the field, Paul amazingly caught Bronco's eye as he hopped on the awards platform. Grinning at each other, they pumped their fists in the air, silently celebrating the victory and season that culminated two years of hard work and intense organization design activity.

"You might think the 38–8 victory over Oregon—pounding them, and it wasn't even that close—you might think that was the most important thing," says Bronco. Without question, it was important. To go undefeated at home that season in LaVell Edwards Stadium, the most dominant home team in BYU Football history and in the entire nation that year, winning games by an average 35.16 points per game. To be a conference champion. To win a bowl game. To finally be recognized once more nationally, landing fifteenth in the final national rankings. To complete the first of four consecutive seasons of double-digit victories for the Cougars. It was important.

Scan this QR code to see "Bowl Game Service" or go to http://bit.ly/NA5aw6

But it was not the *most* important thing. The most important thing was his own players, helping with trig homework and making gingerbread houses by their own preference and from their own shared sense of tradition, spirit, and honor.

In 2007, BYU clinched another perfect record at home and an undefeated conference season, going 11–2 overall and beating UCLA in the Las Vegas Bowl, 17–16. In the post-season contest, Eathyn Manumaleuna blocked the Bruins' last-second field goal attempt, preserving the Cougars' one-point edge and the victory. The team finished No. 14 to end the season. Notably, this was the year that Max Hall took over as quarterback from three-year starter John Beck, and freshman Harvey Unga stepped in for all-time leading rusher Curtis Brown. Max would become the all-time winningest BYU quarterback and Harvey would surpass Curtis to gain the top slot in BYU career rushing stats.

In 2008, Bronco promoted secondary coach Jaime Hill to defensive coordinator, a job Bronco had retained since becoming head coach, but he reserved defensive play-calling duties for himself. He was at last relaxing into the role of head coach. Jaime knew the defensive schemes well, and Bronco was learning to ease the intense pressure on himself and hoped to claim more territory in his life for his family. His little sons were growing up, and he wanted to give them more of his attention. He also hoped that by moving to a less hands-on role he could devote his attention to overall team functions such as building the team and counseling individual players. A few years later, Bronco would reclaim the defensive coordinator role, but this move in 2008 signaled that he was finally becoming more comfortable with his head-coaching responsibilities.

The 2008 team yet again went unbeaten at home, the first BYU team to achieve this feat in three consecutive seasons. The Cougars' 6–2 regular season ledger landed them a third-place conference finish, behind No. 24 TCU and No. 7 Utah. BYU earned a fourth consecutive bowl bid, but fell 31–21 to Arizona in the Las Vegas Bowl, finishing with a 10–3 record and final national ranking of 21. In 2009, BYU once again reached the eleven-win pinnacle achieved by the 2006 and 2007 teams. Bronco gave full defensive play-calling duties to Jaime Hill that year, backing off even further from technical hands-on duties, still working to restore a more normal family life. The year started off with a bang when BYU upset No. 3 ranked Oklahoma, 14–13, in the Dallas Cowboys' gleaming new stadium. An early-season loss to Florida State and a midseason setback against eventual conference champion TCU were the only blemishes on BYU's slate. The Cougars defeated Oregon State 44–20 in the Las Vegas Bowl to finish the season 11–2 (3–1 against ranked opponents), and ended the campaign ranked twelfth nationally, the highest BYU finish since 1996.

Bronco became the only coach in BYU Football history to take his first five teams to a bowl game. The Cougars' overall record for those five years was 49–15—the best of any first-time head coach nationally over those five seasons and a win-loss mark topped by only eleven other programs. Four straight seasons with ten or more wins also represented a first-time accomplishment at BYU.

From 2006 through 2009, the Cougars went 43–9, a record surpassed by only four teams nationally—Boise State, Florida, Texas, and Ohio State. Only Boise State, Ohio State, Texas, and Virginia Tech recorded as many double-digit win seasons during the same time frame, and BYU was one of only six programs nationally to be ranked in both major polls at the end of all four seasons.

You get what you design for. Sustained success was what the Cougars were after, and it's what they got.

CHAPTER 7

Work Not Equal

We players had interviews with Coach Mendenhall all the time. It was in those interviews that you could really tell he cared about your life and if you were doing well in school. He would ask, "How's your life doing? How's your wife? How's your family?" It was great.

My senior year, my wife was diagnosed with Crohn's disease at twenty-one years old. About halfway through the season, she was having a really hard time. I had been accepted into a master's program and was preparing for that. I had all these classes, all these things due, all these tests and projects. It all just hit me one day. Coach Mendenhall could tell at practice that day that I wasn't right. I was making a lot of mental errors and screwing up different plays, or I wasn't covering the right guy. Things like that. So he pulled me into his office, sat me down, and asked me what was going on. I told him everything. He said, "I'll just give you a little advice about what you need to do." I was thinking that he was going to tell me about studying more film or something like that. He said, "I'm going to tell you something that helped my wife and me when we had some struggles.

You need to pray every single morning together. I leave the house usually five o'clock in the morning during the season. Even though she's probably half asleep, we still pray every morning." He also said, "Every month you need to fast together and have a common reason for why you're fasting." He also said that we should read our scriptures together every single day. He said, "If you do those three things, I promise you you're going to feel better about yourself."

My wife and I started doing those things, and we haven't stopped. It's had a huge impact on my life and on our relationship as a couple.

No other coach would give you that advice.

—KELLY POPPINGA
BYU OUTSIDE LINEBACKER 2005–07;
CURRENT BYU OUTSIDE LINEBACKERS COACH

BRONCO HAS a lot of jobs to do all of the time. Most of all, he loves to personally counsel players in his office. He must coordinate recruiting efforts. He loves to coach defense. He monitors games from the sidelines. He approves and extends scholarships to talented athletes committed to an upright lifestyle. He crafts practice regimens and character-building experiences that contribute to the formation of a disciplined culture of young men eager to do their best. It's in his interest to coordinate with the training staff, academic office, and equipment room. There's Junior Day and high school summer camps. Bronco is often asked to speak in the community. There's publicity and marketing for the team.

All work is not created equal. Some of the work that Bronco takes on directly generates an advantage on the playing field, such as developing schemes that capitalize on his players' strengths and carrying out well-organized practice sessions. Some of his work does not directly impact game performance, but it's still important, such as overseeing facility enhancements and speaking to the boosters.

This is true in all organizations. Some of the work that people carry out has a marketplace upside, such as developing innovative products and delivering excellent customer service. Some work that they do does not, but it's still important, such as administering benefits and maintaining information systems. And if leaders aren't careful, some work that people do can actually create a competitive *disadvantage*. If they fail to report their earnings accurately, they may lose investor enthusiasm or even find themselves in legal trouble. In short, the work that people do differs in its *relative strategic impact*.

Smooth Stone #3

 Organizations are made up of business processes, and not all processes are created equal.

If you are a leader, you need to know what work has the greatest strategic impact for at least one crucial reason: you have limited resources. When you are making decisions about how to fund, staff, and improve the processes and projects in your business, you are naturally restricted in the number of people, the sophistication of the technology, and otherwise the amount of money you can throw at a problem or opportunity. Every "yes" you say necessarily means "no" to something else. You can say "yes" more confidently if you are clear about the relative strategic impact of the work that is winning the thumbs-up.

So with this in mind, the BYU staff went beyond identifying their work processes, which are the same set of flows that might define the work of any number of football teams. Since, as we have emphasized, BYU was trying to define how they would be different, they sought to define how their execution of each of these processes would create competitive distinctiveness. They needed to decide what work, if done differently, would have the greatest strategic impact.

So one afternoon at Park City, with their unique mission in mind, the coaches classified all their work by its strategic potential. They used these definitions:

Competitive work *creates* sustainable competitive advantage and distinctiveness (it creates differentiation in the marketplace).

Competitive-enabling work *enables* or *facilitates* competitive work but does not itself directly create competitive advantage.

Essential work neither creates advantage nor facilitates the work that does, but it must be done well for the organization to continue to operate.

Compliance work is done to manage legal risk to the organization.

Nonessential work no longer adds value to the organization and should be eliminated.

This is a powerful activity because once leaders know what work has the greatest upside in the marketplace (or on the gridiron) they can lavish resources in that direction. Essential work should never be neglected—it is still important, after all—but the focus can be on performing this work as efficiently as possible so as to keep resources freed up for competitive work.

When the Cougar coaches categorized the strategic impact of their work processes, they kept their end purpose in mind. "Everything we do as far as competitive work is to put a finished product on the football field," says Brandon Doman, offensive coordinator and quarterbacks coach. "We talk a lot about all kinds of other things, but at the end of the day, we've got to walk out there and win football games. Otherwise the product isn't going to deliver the message that we want it to deliver."

LIFEBLOOD

Above all, "*recruiting* is the lifeblood of our competitive advantage," says Bronco.

Therefore, recruiting was the first work process that the Cougar staff attacked. "This is how it started," says Lance Reynolds, assistant head coach and tight ends coach. "Bronco came into a meeting with the staff and said, 'How should we recruit? What makes us special? What makes us different? Where's our niche? Where's our competitive advantage?'" He goes on:

> We decided we were not going to be a traditional recruiter. We were going to switch to a different kind of system that focuses more on who we are. Finding the right fit and getting good players at the same time. Bronco was open to outside-the-box ideas, and he had the courage to make changes. We started to offer people earlier, we started to evaluate the fit of the player with our program, who they were, where they were. That seems like a no-brainer, but there's a certain kind of system that had been used over the years, not just here, but everywhere. To discard some of those ideas and change is a big deal.

Now, recruiting at BYU is unlike anywhere else in the country. The criteria used to select candidates are different and the strategy for attracting them to the school is different.

The year before Bronco became head coach, the database of potential recruits included a thousand high school athletes. The next year, that pool shrank to only thirty-four. Why?

"Different mission," says Bronco. "Different criteria. Different screening." What other institution that plays Division 1 football explicitly nurtures religious values? There are a few. But who also sets such competitive academic admission standards? And what other university has a character-building honor code as strict as BYU's? What other football program sends its freshmen off on missions, just as they are gaining the skill, bulk, and knowledge to really serve the team?

"Everything we do, every process that we create, is guided by our values: tradition, spirit, and honor," says Brandon. So the staff adopted a new policy: *fit first*. It was more important for the ultimate goal of winning to find young men who could be successful in the total BYU environment than to seek out the best athletes and persuade them to change their behavior and relocate to the Rockies.

"If we recruit a kid who we know up front can't make it, we've done that kid a disservice," says Patrick Hickman, the high school relations coordinator. "We've wasted his time, and we've wasted a scholarship, and we've hurt ourselves as well. Everybody loses when somebody doesn't make it at BYU. If he's not a good fit, he'll either be dissatisfied his first year and want to leave, or he'll do something that will make him ineligible to attend BYU. He can't help us on the field, and we can't help him have a great experience and prepare himself for the next stage in his life."

Finding talented athletes who are up for the BYU environment was not the only challenge. Bronco and his staff were familiar with a study commissioned by Robert Kraft, the owner of the New England Patriots. The study found that only three to five plays per game really separate football dynasties from average teams. Although the researchers had expected that exceptional talent would be the factor that made the difference in those few plays, they discovered instead that the advantage went to the team with the most accurate execution of the planned play. "Not about talent," says Bronco. "Conscientiousness. Work ethic. Team players. If talent is what you want, most of the time you get an entitled person with that. 'What can you do for me?' At least that's what the Patriots found. They decided 'B' talent is where they're going to find conscientiousness, team players, and work ethic." So BYU Football requires these attributes as much as clean living and a faithful outlook.

The coaches define "fit" by the criteria we introduced in chapter 4. A recruit must:

1. Demonstrate the talent of a Division 1 football player
2. Obtain an ecclesiastical endorsement
3. Have earned a 3.0–3.3 GPA, depending on his ACT score
4. Evidence a farmer-like work ethic
5. Have a passion for BYU

First, the candidate must be capable of playing *NCAA Division 1 football.* The coaches recruit from all fifty states plus Samoa, Tonga, and Canada, but to focus their efforts, they target the ten states with the largest LDS populations. BYU coaches assigned to those areas— area coordinators—talk to coaches, gather film, and receive referrals. A vast alumni network provides information about talented players across the United States. Each coach reviews film coming from the regions that they are assigned. They refer promising footage to the coach who coordinates recruiting (the process owner; Paul Tidwell through 2010, now Joe DuPaix), who then sifts through those submissions, and then all the coaches review the top performers together. Whenever possible, the coaches prefer to see their recruits at a high school summer camp on campus. So the evaluation process is extensive.

Second, the candidate must have an *ecclesiastical endorsement.* Each area coordinator starts exploring a candidate's character by asking the same five questions required by BYU Admissions on a formal ecclesiastical endorsement:

1. Is the student in full fellowship with his congregation?
2. Does the student live a chaste and virtuous life, including

avoidance of pornography, abstinence from sexual relations outside of marriage, and abstinence from homosexual conduct?

3. Does the student abstain from the use of alcoholic beverages, tobacco, coffee, tea, and other harmful substances?

4. Does the student demonstrate appropriate and consistent church activity?

5. Is the student honest?

Later, an ecclesiastical leader must ask these questions of recruits. If the candidate is LDS, his bishop and stake president must vouch for his character and ability to live by the Honor Code. If he is not LDS, then the leader of the local congregation he has been attending will be asked to provide the reference, or else a leader at his school. "I've called Catholic priests before," says Paul Tidwell, recruiting coordinator until 2011. "I've called ministers of other faiths and talked to them. I've talked to counselors, high school coaches, athletic directors—people who are close to the young man." The coordinators are asking about the likelihood that recruits will thrive in an environment such as BYU. If the referrer doesn't know much about BYU, "we educate them the first opportunity that we have. We don't try to sugarcoat anything. We don't try to glaze over it. We just hit them right from the very beginning and say, 'This is what the recruit would be getting into.'"

When Brian Logan, a member of another faith who transferred from a California junior college, was told about the Honor Code, he didn't flinch. "Coming from a strong Christian background—I've been going to church since I was five, and my mom works for my pastor back home—it wasn't a big deal. Stuff like that is not really going to affect me."

Conversely, some LDS athletes have been turned *off* to other schools when they chose to make recruiting trips to those schools. When Andrew Rich visited the University of Texas at El Paso and the University of California, "both times my hosts went to parties and drank. I was the only sober person basically. On my Cal trip I walked from the party to the hotel because I didn't want to be there. It wasn't the coaches; the coaches were great. But the quality of people associated with Brigham Young, I wanted that. I wanted to be in that lifestyle."

"Growing up around here, I thought every school was like BYU," says Matt Reynolds, who was top-ranked (the second-ranked high school offensive guard in the nation and among the nation's top-100 high school players) and heavily recruited out of high school. "I figured for the most part, college was just college. It wasn't until I took a trip down to a different school that I realized that life at other places is totally different." He adds:

My host was LDS himself, and instead of trying to show me what I wanted to see, he showed me how college life at that university would be. He took me where all the other recruits were going to be that night. It was a party. In fact, we had to go to two different parties because cops came to one of them. Parties in Provo are kind of like family home evening with some music. People just kind of get together and talk, maybe play some board games, maybe dance. Down there it was completely different. It was wall-to-wall with people, and everybody had a beer in both hands and was dancing all over each other. I just sat in the corner with this person who was the designated driver for her group and talked to her until we left. She was the only sober one who could hold a normal conversation.

I'm not going to lie. Part of my decision had to do with social life. I wanted to be social and have fun, but that's not how I wanted to do it. That's when I realized what I wanted from a university and from an education. That for me was

159

when I really said, "Where am I going to get the type of education and social life and football that I'm looking for?"

"Football itself only lasts four months out of the year," adds David Nixon. "You have to live the other eight months of the year just as a normal student. So I really wanted to take in the whole environment of the school."

Third, a prospective recruit must have garnered a *3.0–3.3 grade point average* (depending on their ACT score) in high school. BYU calculates an estimated grade point average that projects what the student's college GPA will be; the number is based on an algorithm that combines the student's high school GPA and ACT score. "That's the highest bar in the country that I know of," says Bronco. If a recruit has been unable or unwilling to perform at that level or close to that level so far in his life, he's much less likely to survive the rigorous academic climate at BYU, even with the help of close academic advising.

Fourth, the Cougar staff is looking for a strong *farmer-like work ethic.* Bronco is going to be driving them relentlessly. The best predictor of future behavior is past behavior. Is the individual up to the ordeal? When Cameron Jensen first spoke to then-defensive coordinator Bronco, "I loved the fact that he said we played with 'fanatical' effort. He said, 'If you don't want to play this way, then don't come.' I always wanted to be part of a team that gave more effort than others, because those are the people I like to be around."

BYU coaches look for players such as Cameron who savor an intense experience. They can gauge that by evidence of hard work in their past. For example, they look for young men who have graduated from "seminary"—a daily high school scripture study class for LDS kids that in most of the country is offered only in the early morning hours before regular classes begin. Having maintained part-time or summer employment is another evidence of a strong work ethic.

Finally, the recruit must demonstrate his *devotion to BYU* and what it stands for. So from the beginning, the coaches talk to them about the mission of the program. In the final interview with the head coach before their scholarship offer, Bronco has them read the words of Church presidents Gordon B. Hinckley and Thomas S. Monson, as we described in chapter 4. "What we offer them is not just a scholarship to come and play football," says Paul Tidwell. "It means a lot more to the type of young men who come here. They are passionate to be at BYU."

The first year this new recruiting process was implemented, the staff had twenty-four scholarships to offer to a pool of thirty-four qualified candidates. Such a selective screening process is not a limitation according to Bronco. "It's a strength. It's efficient."

Of the recipients of those twenty-four scholarships, twenty-one had committed before the recruiting season had even begun. "Somebody asked me, 'Who do you think you are, Texas?'" says Bronco, because at the time only the University of Texas had signed more athletes. "I said, 'No. We're BYU.' If I find a young man who is ecclesiastically endorsed, has at least a 3.0 GPA, and is a Division 1 player—why would I let someone else have him?"

The BYU coaches have mapped out their recruiting process step-by-step, with boxes and arrows in workflow format. It begins at BYU's elementary and junior high school summer youth football camps, building "brand loyalty." High school camps group the freshmen and sophomores separately from the juniors and seniors so the coaches can get a better look *at the younger group.* BYU begins recruiting when students are sophomores. By the time many recruits are seniors, they have been eyed for most of their high school careers.

Jordan Pendleton, a three-year starter on his high school team who was named the *Salt Lake Tribune* and *Deseret Morning News*

5-A Most Valuable Player and the best overall athlete in the state by the *Deseret Morning News*, says that BYU "offered me so early that I couldn't really resist. It was way before my senior year. I'm thinking, if I commit, they're going to commit to me. If I get hurt or if anything happens, they're still going to fulfill their commitment. I can just play my senior year, and I won't have to worry about getting a scholarship. I can just go and be me and just have fun.'"

In order to identify candidates outside the purview of summer camp intelligence, BYU asks football alumni to be their eyes and ears. Former students and fans feed referrals to the Cougars regularly.

But the Cougars rarely award a scholarship without meeting the candidate at BYU, particularly if the athlete is not LDS. "We try not to offer a young man until we've actually met him, visited with him, brought him on campus," says Paul Tidwell. He goes on:

> You can tell them on the phone, you can write it in letters, and they can read it on the Internet, but until they actually get here, actually see the area and the campus, and actually hear it from the position coach's mouth and the head coach's mouth, they don't fully comprehend what BYU is all about.
>
> Parents are a huge factor for us. If we can get a young man here on campus with his parent—mom or dad or both—that's a huge plus for us.

Shane Cragun, who accompanied his son Davis to a Junior Day in 2011, tells how Bronco familiarized these top recruits with the BYU Honor Code and other expected standards of behavior. He had the volunteers from the group read through a list one at a time, and after discussing each point, said emphatically, "If you can't live this, please don't come to BYU. *Please*, I beg of you. We don't want people here who can't live these standards and be excited about it."

He reiterated the message for each of several points: "If you can't abide by this, please don't come here."

Shane explains that Bronco told the boys, "'We're trying to give you enough information and enough experiences here at Junior Day that you can either select in or select out. So if you don't want to be a part of this, that is not a problem, because we will get enough.'" Shane says:

> Davis just thought it was very cool. According to what Davis said, and he talked to some other people, they thought it was awesome that Bronco did that. These were the best of the best. They were from all over the entire country. Some of these guys were being recruited by USC, and UCLA, and Georgia. Clearly it was unlike anything that any of the other coaches at other universities would do. Who says, "Please don't come here"? You just don't say that, because you want that boy. Rather than having a top-ten list of guidelines, or rules, that are even stricter than the Honor Code, the other coaches would have a list of the top-ten reasons why their college is the best fit for you.

"I didn't understand the value of a mission statement nor really the impact it could have until I put it to work in our recruiting process," says Bronco.

> The players who come to Utah from outside the state have a huge adjustment to make. Come to Provo, and turn the knob that increases the degree of adjustment required. Come to BYU's campus and turn the knob all the way. Then represent the institution as a member of a visible athletic team. Have that spotlight following you around, and you're a flag bearer whether you like it or not. So I'm looking for those

young men who view it as an opportunity, not a burden. I want them saying, "Let me carry the flag; let me be the one."

I let the mission choose the man. They come because of the mission. They come because of the values. That aids not only our retention levels, but it engenders a competitive spirit that's unmatched. The mission chooses them, not me.

"For your company," Bronco adds pointedly for the benefit of leaders everywhere, "if it is about you, the company itself won't ever have the success necessary. You ought to work independently. If it is about the mission, that's the greatest unifying factor there is. For us, we're looking for young people who want to be a part of a team and a mission."

In late January 2006, BYU Football hosted an on-campus visit for the next year's recruiting class as they do every year. It was two days packed with events intended to share information with the recruits about what BYU has to offer as well as learn from them how much a BYU education would mean to them. Coauthor Paul met with Bronco early that week and was eager to hear about the schedule Bronco had put together reflecting the new recruiting approach. He made the rather awkward discovery—awkward, that is, if you know the importance of alignment—that a buffet breakfast had been scheduled for Sunday morning and that no church services had been planned. "We'll distribute a list of local meeting times and locations," Bronco explained.

The Sunday in question was a "fast Sunday." These special Sundays are generally scheduled on the first Sunday of each month. Church members refrain from eating or drinking for two meals and, with increased spiritual awareness, volunteer to share heartfelt, often emotional "testimonies" about their basic beliefs during their main meeting. By scheduling a breakfast on Sunday, the Cougar staff had interrupted this practice. By dismissing recruits and their families without a morning service, they hazarded sending the message that church was not as important as football activities. Paul mentioned the possibility of changing the schedule to incorporate worship, but Bronco felt that the morning was simply too packed to fit in church at BYU. Paul prodded a little, but Bronco retreated into silence. Paul left that day unsure what was on his friend's mind.

Bronco e-mailed Paul the next day to say that he'd had a change of heart and scheduled a worship service after all. And then, late Sunday morning, Paul got a call from a very excited head football coach telling him how well the meeting had gone. BYU President Cecil O. Samuelson Jr. had been there along with strength and conditioning coach Jay Omer, who led the meeting as current bishop (volunteer pastor) of a student congregation on campus. Offensive coaches Robert Anae and Lance Reynolds blessed the sacrament (the Lord's supper) and players on the team passed it to the recruits and their families. The speakers that day included a couple of players, President Samuelson, and Bronco himself.

As Bronco sat at the front of the football team meeting room in the Student Athlete Building, he scanned the faces of the participants. Tears ran in streams down some of the parents' cheeks. They were moved by the words of the speakers and the knowledge (Bronco hoped) that they would be placing their sons in the good hands of faithful university leaders, coaches, and upper classmen.

These families and their sons were right for the mission.

COMPETITIVE WORK

The BYU recruiting process is not the only process that provides the Cougars competitive advantage on the field. The coaches have identified other processes that are important differentiators, such as game-plan development and execution. They have mapped out these processes, established routines and procedures, and devoted periodic attention to adjusting them so that they are constantly improving.

One of the Cougars' differentiators is the efficiency with which they do their competitive work. BYU certainly has one of the most streamlined weekly routines in the nation because the coaching staff doesn't stay late on weeknights and meets only six days a week during the season. Says Bronco:

> Would that not be hypocritical if we had a choice—and I do have a choice because I'm the head coach—and we chose to work Sundays? But we don't work Sundays. We leave every day after practice at 6:30 because isn't family more important than football? Our coaches go home to their families. We practice less than almost every program in the country because our kids are interested in doing well in school, doing well in the community, and doing well at home.
>
> The idea is, how can you do more in less time at a higher level than anybody else? Certainly the critics will come out and say we're not working hard enough. But we're working as efficiently or more so than any other program in the country. We will not put cots in our office and sleep at the office and disregard our families and see them for a half an hour maybe on a Thursday once a week. It won't happen.
>
> As a leader, you have to make choices for those in your care that reflect your priorities. If there is a mismatch there, it's hypocritical, and you're not being trustworthy, in my opinion.

The team has developed a system of practice "tempos" to quickly communicate the degree of physical effort required while running a

Scan this QR code to see "Making Choices That Align with Values" or go to http://bit.ly/LsyUI5

given play. For example, "run-thru tempo" requires sharp mental focus without touch, while "thud tempo" moves at game speed but restricts players from taking other players to the ground. Tempos such as this are not unique but Bronco believes that BYU practices, in addition to being shorter, involve less contact. "Knowing we're not the fastest team, if we can be fresher and more assignment-sound and more efficient than our opponents, then the advantage starts shifting to us," he says.

The coaches also agree on what work *enables* but does not directly create a competitive upside, such as the work of coordinating fall and spring camps and conditioning workouts.

They also know what work is *essential work* or *compliance work.* These are activities that must be done but that don't create a distinct advantage on the gridiron. Because this type of work tends to expand and consume all of the time available, Bronco has learned to rely on Duane Busby, the football operations director, or his assistant head coach Lance Reynolds, to expertly dispatch the important work that can too easily divert Bronco from the more strategic aspects of defensive coordination and head coaching. "I think it is really hard sometimes to identify and make sure that you're focusing your time and energy on the competitive work," says Brandon Doman.

When you come to terms with the reality that you could use your time in a way that better maximizes the potential for wins, it nevertheless is not always easy to say no to some lower-priority requests. For instance, Bronco spoke to church and community groups over 150 times his first head-coaching year. "I'm talking about speaking at firesides, to businesses, to the Cougar Club, and more," he says. "How can you speak that many times and not be giving up something else?" Within a few years, he had narrowed down his engagements dramatically. For him to agree to speak, he now requires that a large number of people are present or that the event is televised so that his efforts reach more people in less time.

These opportunities are important, and Bronco doesn't want to give them up. But they do not directly contribute to wins.

"My job is to make sure I have scheme design and program development and player development and a recruiting process to bring the right players here and use them right," says Bronco. "What's our competitive work? That becomes clearer to me every year in relation to my role, because what was my competitive work in 2005 is not my competitive work now."

• • •

As BYU's on-field performance improved under Bronco, so did that of its conference rivals. The Cougars went 2–1 against both TCU and Utah from 2005 through 2007, but 1–3 against those same programs in the ensuing four seasons.

During those latter years, Bronco says, opponents studied BYU vigorously. "They were investing more time in us than we were in them. They put more emphasis on targeting us, and there was some predictability being established in our program. TCU has a BYU football helmet in their workout room. We became their off-season work."

"We were ahead of the curve with those guys for a little while, and the brutal fact is that they passed us up," says Brandon Doman. The race for dominance propelled all three teams into the final top twenty-five national rankings in 2008 and 2009, though only TCU was able to hold its spot in both national polls in 2010 and 2011 (Utah claimed a spot only in the final 2010 coaches' poll and BYU only in the final 2011 coaches' poll.)

As we mentioned in the last chapter, BYU went 11–2 during 2006 and again in 2007. Those were heady years as the team institutionalized its signature set of strategies and design choices. A slight dip in performance and a major dip in Bronco's energy in 2008 set the stage for some new innovations, which we will detail later on. On the strength of those innovations, the Cougars then earned another 11–2 mark in 2009.

Comparatively speaking, the bottom fell out in 2010. The Cougars' 1–4 start was their worst in thirty-seven years; the four-game losing skid that followed a season-opening win was the program's first such streak in seventeen seasons. But after a mid-season shake-up to the coaching staff, which included Bronco's reclaiming the role of defensive coordinator, the Cougars rallied for a 7–6 finish, including a New Mexico Bowl game victory against UTEP. Bronco decided to go with a rotation of two quarterbacks for the first few games of the season, a bad choice in hindsight. The rotation plan ended when sophomore quarterback Riley Nelson suffered a season-ending injury in the third game of the season, putting highly touted true freshman Jake Heaps in the starter's role for the remainder of the campaign. After losing three of his first four starts, Heaps gradually settled in, going 5–1 in his final six starts and setting every BYU freshman quarterback record, including passing yards, touchdowns, and wins.

Yet, Heaps's youth and inexperience were emblematic of the growing pains suffered by the 2010 team, as roughly forty of the sixty-five players on the traveling team were true freshmen, redshirt freshmen, or sophomores. BYU's impending departure from the Mountain West Conference and entry into football independence (effective in 2011) made it imperative that the team be in "rebuilding mode" for no longer than a single season, so valuable lessons would need to be learned amidst the struggles of 2010. More about all that in the remaining chapters.

Meanwhile, the two quarterbacks who started for BYU during Bronco's first five years—John Beck and Max Hall—were working out their careers in the NFL: John with the Miami Dolphins, Baltimore Ravens, and Washington Redskins, and Max with the Arizona Cardinals. In the next chapter, we visit "Quarterback U" to take a look at the BYU system that is turning out top quality quarterbacks once again.

CHAPTER 8

Knowledge

At the end of the day, no matter what we say or what we do
or how great the environment we create, we have to walk
out on the grass and teach these guys how to play football
and produce a football team. If we can't, if we're not masters
of the learning process and if we can't transfer that football
knowledge to them, it doesn't matter how great of a guy you
are. You've got to be able to coach football.

—Brandon Doman
BYU quarterback, 1998–2001;
current BYU offensive coordinator
and quarterbacks coach

I N THE MID-1970s, quarterbacks Gary Sheide and Gifford Nielsen
put BYU's passing attack on the map. The succeeding four quarterbacks—Marc Wilson, Jim McMahon, Steve Young, and Robbie
Bosco—broke 103 NCAA records among them. Jim McMahon was
the first Cougar to win the Davey O'Brien Award as the nation's best
quarterback, Steve Young the second. Robbie Bosco led the Cougars
to their 1984 national championship. All but Gifford Nielsen won
the Sammy Baugh Trophy given to the nation's top college passer; all

six were drafted into the National Football League. Two of them—more than any other school—led their NFL teams to Super Bowl championships (Jim McMahon and Steve Young). Nielsen, Wilson, McMahon, and Young have all been inducted into the College Football Hall of Fame.

Cementing BYU's fame as a quarterback factory, Ty Detmer broke sixty-four NCAA records on his own in the late 1980s and early 1990s. He earned the Heisman trophy along with two Davey O'Brien Awards and another Sammy Baugh Trophy and proceeded to play fourteen seasons in the NFL. He eventually became BYU's fifth quarterback to be inducted into the College Football Hall of Fame, making BYU second only to Notre Dame.

Steve Sarkisian set three NCAA records in the 1990s and led the Cougars to the first fourteen-win season in NCAA Division 1 history. He was the seventh Cougar quarterback to receive the Sammy Baugh Trophy; BYU has had nearly twice as many Sammy Baugh Trophy winners as any other college. Brandon Doman landed the starting job eleven games into LaVell Edwards's final season in 2000; he then led BYU on a fourteen-game win streak. "The Domanator" became a Heisman trophy candidate in 2001 and was later drafted by the San Francisco 49ers.

By the time Bronco became head coach, John Beck was under center. He was discouraged and disheartened after two miserable losing seasons as a starter. But Bronco's background was defense, so he went hunting for a quarterbacks coach who could restore BYU's storied quarterback-training apparatus.

Brandon remembers his interview:

When I sat down in front of Bronco, the very first thing he said was, "We have a quarterback in the system right now who has been emotionally and physically battered and bruised. The coach has been fired, and the quarterback has been blamed in part. He didn't perform up to par. The fans have been tough on him, and the media's been really tough on him. He's been emotional in front of the camera. So, if you were to get this job, in your first meeting with him, what would you say? What would you do?

Brandon was surprised by this line of questioning. He had been preparing to answer football questions. But Bronco was asking him a psychological, emotional question that had nothing to do with Xs and Os at all.

"I wouldn't say anything to him," was Brandon's response. "I would put him in my car and drive him down to the local store and buy some war paint. I'd paint his face like we were getting ready to go to war." Brandon adds:

> I didn't know Coach Mendenhall at all. I had no idea that every year he studies a different warrior culture and that later, when I showed up at the building in Provo, there'd be warrior culture symbols everywhere. If there's one thing that's important it him, it's the art of going to war. Ha! I don't study war cultures—or didn't up until coming to BYU's program.

Needless to say, Brandon was invited to join the BYU staff. He gave up his NFL career, bidding the 49ers a fond farewell after three seasons, and was at work in Provo in just a few weeks.

Brandon's task was to build a new generation of stellar offensive leaders at BYU. The venerable history of Cougar quarterback excellence made Smooth Stone #4, which has everything to do with obtaining and diffusing organization knowledge, a most important weapon. Smooth Stone #4 is that knowledge is the purest form of competitive advantage.

Smooth Stone #4

Knowledge is the purest form of competitive advantage.

What we mean by this is that even when the conditions under which an organization competes are constantly changing, it will nevertheless thrive if the people who make up the organization know how to create new ideas and solutions to problems, how to reach out to others to collaborate in doing so, and how to share what they learn across the landscape of their organization.

BYU Football's annual personnel turnover runs about 40 percent. Coaches know that when a player is recruited, it may not be until after his two-year mission that he enrolls at BYU. Young men initially not interested in leaving for service as a missionary change their minds suddenly; recruits committed to other schools have a change of heart in the mission field and transfer to BYU after all. Walk-ons come from junior colleges. Injuries bench a starter for all or part of a season. The BYU roster experiences an unpredictable flux that keeps coaches and players alike constantly improvising with the talent on hand.

The knowledge challenge is enormous. Players must rapidly and soundly absorb the BYU schemes and identity if they are to execute plays on the field that will win games. Coaches must become expert at cultivating new knowledge in players and finding ways to transfer that knowledge to new recruits and walk-ons when missions or injuries or graduation take starters off the field. When they are able to do this well, fans are thrilled to see the program build momentum from year to year rather than burst like a popped balloon when more important achievements such as matriculation and church service claim their football veterans.

The very visible role of the quarterback is just one position where this drama plays out each year. As a new coach in 2005,

Brandon Doman had the responsibility of creating a system that could cultivate quarterback knowledge and ensure its preservation, innovation, and continuation from season to season, starter to starter, for another few decades of quarterback excellence.

"It's an interesting place to try to be a quarterback because of all the expectations of you as a player," says Brandon, who as a former Cougar signal-caller speaks from experience.

> You're no different than Coach Mendenhall as the head coach in that you're not just representing a football program, you're representing much more than that. These fans of ours revere these quarterbacks and place high expectations on them on and off the football field. So do the players. They expect the quarterback to be their leader, and they have to trust him. There must be truth in his purpose and willpower in his character.

The process of cultivating and sharing knowledge in an organization is often called *knowledge management*. Smooth Stone #4 is a tool for leaders for managing the most critical knowledge in an organization.

ORGANIZATION KNOWLEDGE

BYU coaches discuss several types of knowledge. Some knowledge is *explicit* or *codifiable*—easy to explain and thus to share, such as football schemes; whereas some is *tacit* or *noncodifiable*—hard to describe to someone else or to teach in a systematic sort of way—such as how a linebacker reads an offense on the line of scrimmage. Some knowledge comes from study and contemplation. We'll call it "*know-that*." It's facts and values, such as the opposing team's preseason ranking or a belief in the importance of service. Some comes from experience—"*know-how*"—the skilled execution of difficult tasks such as recognizing and avoiding a blindside blitz while finding an open receiver. You can read more about these types of knowledge in section 2.

The full array of knowledge types needs to be cultivated in young football recruits. Brandon took up the challenge by first identifying and discussing all types of quarterback knowledge. He capitalized on an Alumni Day to invite several former quarterbacks into the position room to get their help.

"We opened up the discussion," says Brandon. "I said, 'Let's separate our knowledge about being a quarterback into codifiable and noncodifiable know-that and know-how.' That was pretty easy. We could go through the codifiable know-thats and know-hows for the quarterback and then into the noncodifiable know-thats and know-hows for a quarterback. We did that with alumni quarterbacks and our current quarterbacks in the room."

They drew a four square on the white board and filled its cells (see chart on following page).

They decided that quarterback "know-that" includes explicit facts such as the rules of the game and team playbook as well as implicit leadership qualities and confidence levels. Quarterback "know-how" that is explicit includes the routines quarterbacks are trained to execute before and after a snap, while tacit "know-how" involves such knowledge as how to get the ball off under pressure.

Once these four categories of knowledge were on the table, Brandon began to think about ways of helping his quarterbacks learn them. For Brandon, teaching the codifiable knowledge was the easier task. It was the other side of the chart that posed the greater challenge. "Sometimes, in football, we use the word *intangibles*," says Brandon. "We wanted to find out, can you train somebody to acquire those intangibles—noncodifiable knowledge—as a quarterback? Some people would argue that no, you can't."

The good news is that the learning of intangible knowledge can

Cougar Quarterback Four-box Knowledge Model

	Codifiable	Tacit
Know That	**Facts** • Formations • Rules • Plays • Steps (drops) • Game situations • Clock situations • Progressions • Defensive fronts • Defensive coverages • Protections	**Beliefs** • Familiar with diversity of teammates • Knowing different attributes for building team chemistry • Read keys for quick throws and progression reads • Decision-making • Recognizing man vs. zone • Confidence • Leadership • Cadence change-up
Know How	**Routines** • Throwing motion • Lead with your heels on drops • Ball handling • Read coverages • Grip a football • Take drops • Footwork for drop back and play action • Run different pass routes • Pitch a football • Delivery of a throw • Take a snap	**Expertise** • Throw football under blitz pressure • Throw football under bad weather conditions • Build team chemistry as a team leader • Communicate to peers • Doing pre- and post-snap reads and adjustments • Feeling a blindside blitzer • Anticipate throwing a ball before its break • Read zone blitz • Timing with throws • Touch on the throws • Consistency • Precision and execution

be accelerated, but the methods are different from those for teaching explicit knowledge.

ORGANIZATION LEARNING METHODS

Brandon set out to design a complex of quarterback training experiences to help his players gain each type of knowledge. He recalls:

The alumni quarterbacks talked about a quarterback having eyes behind his head. How does he know that someone is behind him so that he can step up and make the throw?

The reality is he knows that because actually there are certain things he can recognize prior to the snap of the ball that allow him to anticipate a blitz. The answer we came to is, yeah, you can actually train a guy in the noncodifiable "know-hows" and "know-thats." If you actually are able to do that, that's how you become great. That's how the great quarterbacks become great. So if you want to be great, those are the certain things that you're going to have to be able to do.

The first step is to learn as much as possible that is explicit. "You can't learn tacit knowledge unless you qualify first in the codifiable," says Brandon. "But as soon as you qualify in the codifiable knowledge, now you can transfer into the noncodifiable."

After two years as a starting quarterback, John Beck knew plenty about the explicit facts and figures of football. He had all the team plays down pat, he was well-versed in NCAA rules, and he had studied defensive fronts endlessly.

Codifiable "know-that": check.

A good way to absorb "know-how" is by watching. Good thing John was already a football film junkie with hours of film-room time under his belt.

And he was lucky to have a coach such as Brandon, who had learned the professional ropes under the tutelage of the same 49ers coaches who had worked with Steve Young, among them Greg Knapp, now of the Oakland Raiders. A rigorous "protocol" had been developed in San Francisco to help quarterbacks learn the offense— to guide them through a sequence of actions, reads, and decisions during a play. This protocol had been written down and perfected. It prescribed a series of assessments and gestures made by the quarterback, a stylized choreography that moved him beat-by-beat through the moments before and after the snap of the ball. The protocol assigned tag words to strings of these actions for ease of discussion.

Brandon brought this protocol to BYU and taught it to John, Arizona State transfer Max Hall, and the other quarterbacks. "It takes them through a very systematic, line-by-line process. It's almost robotic. I don't want these guys to be robots—I want them to play intuitively—but it gives them a checklist to follow. It is a very codified manner in which we teach these guys." It's a routine—and running through structured routines is one of the best ways to develop action-based knowledge.

Codifiable "know-how": check.

Next in importance, in Brandon's estimation, was John's confidence level. As a belief, confidence is tacit "know-that." Brandon reflected:

> As I look back at my first season with John, he had been a two-year starter but had been brutalized by fans, by the experience of a coach being let go. He was the quarterback, and so I think he blamed himself. He just didn't have the confidence that you'd like a young man to have. He sure as heck didn't have the same confidence that he originally had as a young kid coming out of high school where he won every game. Now how were we to help him regain that confidence?

Bronco and Brandon developed a practice philosophy that they believed would lead to calm, poised assurance in their players, including their quarterback. The core of their belief is that confidence is built through simple, daily successes. Brandon says:

> That's a program-wide philosophy. The way we create our structure and our strategy creates an environment for that quarterback to succeed. At the end of the day, that's something I think we do well here, probably better than anybody else in the country. We create an environment; we have a

strategy in place, that on a day-to-day basis, we're presenting opportunities for that kid to succeed. Now the rest of the team has its successes along the way, but if we come out of a practice and we haven't created an environment to allow our quarterback to be successful, or to learn and gain those simple successes along the way, we failed that day as a program because, really, as goes the quarterback so goes your team.

To develop a quarterback's belief in himself as a winning quarterback who leads a winning team, having confidence that he will throw the ball to the right receiver and that the ball will be caught— the BYU strategy is to let that young man show himself that he repeatedly succeeds, day in and day out, in the familiar setting of the practice field so that the same scenario is familiar again in front of a roaring crowd in LaVell Edwards Stadium or far away on the road. They let him get used to his own ability to perform.

Tacit "know-that": check.

Finally comes the most important type of knowledge: tacit "know-how." Expertise, effortless and instinctive, is the hardest type of knowledge to train and to acquire. For quarterbacks, football expertise is being able to decide, act, and react well on the field in unpredictable, novel situations. It's one thing to drill routines and plays each day on the practice field; it's another to stand in a stadium filled with upward of 64,000 screaming fans and 300-pound linemen coming at you while discovering that not one of your wide receivers is clear of tight man-to-man coverage.

At BYU Football, the bedlam of game day is known as "the fog of war." It's the same thing that Jonah Lehrer calls "the savage chaos of the game," where "every play is a mixture of careful planning and risky improvisation." A quarterback's responsibility in the midst of this savage chaos is such an exquisite example of split-second decision-making that Lehrer begins his book *How We Decide* with a play-by-play of the last minute and twenty-one seconds of the 2002 Super Bowl. Lehrer describes how Tom Brady, the former second-string quarterback of the underdog New England Patriots, is a model of poise and efficiency. With the score tied, he leads the Patriots in moving the ball forty-seven yards in sixty-nine seconds. A forty-eight-yard field goal seals "the greatest upset in NFL history."[1]

The Cougar coaches seek to develop the same kind of poise under pressure in their players. The ability to make sound decisions in the face of great adversity is most possible when the adversity has a familiar quality—when it looks like something players have seen before and requires actions that they have done before. The more accustomed the player is to a situation, the more likely he will be able to react instinctively, without consciously thinking. Without deliberating.

A well-trained quarterback has experienced so many repetitions of gamelike scenarios that he can viscerally recognize whether he is safe from the blitz. He knows instinctively if a pass will turn out favorably. He has internalized this knowledge in such a way that it comes to him as an emotion, a feeling. Acting spontaneously on a feeling requires less time than deliberating over a set of choices.

As wide receiver coach Ben Cahoon says, "The less thinking we do out there, the more ingrained guys are in the offense. The less thinking they do, the faster they play. We need to maximize all the speed we can. . . . It's just doing it enough that you're not thinking about it."[2]

All this explains why a quarterback can act so quickly. If he had to consciously evaluate all of his passing alternatives, he would never have time to choose among them before he was sacked. "Even quarterbacks are mystified by their talents," says Lehrer, and then quotes Brady: "'I don't know how I know where to pass. . . . There are no firm rules. You just feel like you're going to the right place. . . . And that's where I throw it.'"[3]

As a coach, Brandon's job is to help young players develop skills that they will eventually be unable to explain. "It's muscle memory," says Brandon. "At whatever distance, their muscles must know exactly how far to throw that thing. At the end of the day, that's what we're trying to train."

How do they do it?

They use a number of strategies. Chief among them are repetition, gamelike practice, and mentoring.

Repetition

To ensure that a quarterback can fluently make a pre-snap assessment of the field and automatically time his drops (backward steps) and gathers (small forward motions in preparation for the throw) as needed for the play, the protocols must be rehearsed over and over. "If they have put enough repetition into it, they can go through the protocol checklist almost instantly," says Brandon.

> When I say "Red 96" to a QB, the whole protocol for that play should just snap in his head, mentally in his mind and, with repetition, in his body. We should have repped Red 96 with quarterbacks alone a hundred times. Then we bring in the running backs and we do that a hundred times. Then we bring in the tight ends, and we do that a hundred times. Bring in the receivers and you do that a hundred times, and now the whole group's there.
>
> By the time this young man actually walks out on the grass against one of our opponents and we call Red 96, that whole protocol is intuitive. I want these guys to play with intuition. I want them to know the protocol. I want them to know exactly where to look, what they're trying to read

in the defense. But I don't want them to think one second about what he's doing on the play, how many steps he's taking, how many hitches forward. I want his body to take him through it.

In the way that I was trained, you can actually take your mind through the play. Imagine a QB dropping back and looking to his right for a receiver fifteen yards down the field. If he's not deep enough behind the line—if he's ready to throw the ball before the receiver ever gets to the fifteen yards, and he's standing in the pocket or behind the line waiting for this guy to run the route—then he's going to get sacked. So there should be a particular length of drop that he takes and then maybe the play's going to require two gathers before he throws that route, because the timing of that route is critical. If he gets through the timing of the drop and for some reason the receiver is not there, he's got to move on. For some reason, something happened. The quarterback's footwork was timed to throw it to that guy, but he's not there. Or say the key defender, the narrow vision defender, did something that's caused the quarterback at the top of the drop to go elsewhere. Now his body will also take him through the needed decision-making. He's trained it so many times that his legs are actually going to take him to the next guy in the progression. If he's not there, then his body has already taken him to the next guy, and his eyes are going to follow.

Research has consistently shown that 10,000 hours of practice are required for true expertise—that's about ten years of serious study. Mindless repetitions of important skills is not enough; practice must deliberately aim to improve errors. Repetition without reflection does not necessarily generate improvement. For example, just because you spend a large part of your day typing doesn't mean that you are steadily becoming any faster or more accurate. Improvement only comes with an intentional effort to target weaknesses and get better.[4] That's why film study is so important to football players and other athletes—watching their performance helps them to identify and analyze weaknesses and to develop practice strategies for targeting those weaknesses.

BYU Football, of course, can only design its program to add to the number of practice hours a young recruit has already put in throughout his lifetime. But it certainly can maximize the volume of reps for a given play and with the particular personnel playing that season.

For example, John Beck's 2004 performance within the opponent's twenty-yard line—BYU's "blue zone"—was shaky. The looming possibility of a touchdown seemed to undo him and the offense. So improvement efforts the following season were focused on blue-zone repetitions. Practice began in the blue zone and ended in the blue zone. The goal was to make this territory the most comfortable and familiar terrain on the field in order to amplify John's confidence.

It worked. While the team scored touchdowns in only 61 percent of blue-zone forays in 2004, the 2005 stat rose to 72 percent and dipped only slightly to 70 percent in 2006.

Gamelike Practice

To develop and lodge reliable post-snap instincts in a quarterback that trigger success even in the fog of war, coaches must ensure that a young quarterback passes the football not just in contrived technical drills, but in hundreds of repetitions of gamelike situations.

The more that young man experiences the bedlam of the college football field—in practice or on game day—the more effortless become his visions and drops and the stronger becomes his emotional memory about what responses are required in which types of situations. "You have to train the same as you play," Brandon says. "So if you're going to go out to practice, it ought to look just like a game, the best you can make it look."

"Everything that I've studied in relation to being a coach and now being a coordinator," he adds, "is to put players through as much simulation as possible. That's how the military trains its soldiers and generals and all the different people who go into battle: as many simulations as possible. How do we create that in practice? How do we set up the strategy of the day so that the quarterback is gaining very tactical experience for that day, rather than just going out there and working solely on the mastery of the technique—position mastery? Defensive line coach Steve Kaufusi says:

> When we design practices, we try to create chaos. The kids get frustrated and tired. That's the whole reason why we do that, to push them out of their element, to push them out of their comfort zone. We train kids to handle chaos. We ask them, "How do you solve this situation without losing your mind and throwing a tantrum, or throwing in the towel and giving up?" We try to put the kids in the most difficult situations to see how they respond. The more we do that, the more they get comfortable with sorting things out and taking a deep breath. Be calm in time of war, in time of need. Be focused straight on the task at hand despite all the noise around you. If you do that, the theory is that the game itself becomes easier for you. The chaos that you've been put through in practice is going to be so much more than the game situation. Then the game should be a breeze to you.

Roaring fans, controversy over bad calls, and goading opponents can all cloud up the conditions on the field. To simulate these irritants, the Cougar coaching staff has gone so far as to pipe crowd noise into the practice arena. They have developed scoring systems to intensify the competition between the scout team and the starters and then used that same system to unfairly penalize the starters as sometimes happens in a game. "It's very difficult to create in practice what it's like with 64,000 fans screaming and you're playing from behind with a minute-and-a-half left to go against Utah," says Bronco. "But you can bring out a lot on the practice field, and we make it as chaotic as we can. Then I show the result in front of the whole team the next day."

Staying poised in the fog of war is a coaching imperative as well. "In our work, you can sit down and make the plans for the game," says Lance Reynolds, assistant head coach and tight ends coach, "but then when you are actually in a game, emotions run high, similar to war. Obviously our lives aren't on the line, but the communications difficulties and the emotions that arise are similar. That's why you see teams in emotional times sometimes make the dumbest decisions. Not just us, but even the NFL."

The coaches at BYU have sought to improve on two fronts: first, their communication, and second, their advance planning.

To improve their communication, the staff discusses what information needs to be relayed, who is responsible for giving it, and whether or not it is being received. They also analyze the coach-player lines of communication. They don headphones during practice, sometimes even perch on the practice field balcony to imitate the distance between the play-caller in the booth and the team on the field. They also record the vocal stream of a game to help coaches recognize if they have contributed to any occasional . . . er . . . tiffs or other indiscretions. Bronco doesn't require his coaches to listen to it, but for some of those who have, it's been enlightening.

As a new coach, Kelly Poppinga was once at home grading film after one of the games. The audio stream was playing. "My wife was right there, and she was like, 'What's the deal?'"

Kelly tuned into his voice and thought, "Wow! I sound like an idiot!"

> I'm on the headset talking to Coach Mendenhall. I'm yelling and screaming stuff when things are happening, because things are so fast paced. When the offense has the ball, then Coach switches his headset to the offense. Not having him listening, I ended up being more opinionated on things.

Kelly says he completely changed from that experience. "I became a lot more calm. It helped me actually be able to focus on things a lot better and not worry so much or get so riled up. The emotion of everything kind of went away." Kelly mentioned the insight to Bronco. "He said, 'Yep. You've got to be able to manage the fog of war.'"

To improve its game-time decision making, the coaching staff creates firm plans for stressful situations in advance. When there's 1:35 left in the fourth and they have used two time outs, how far down the field will they go before using the third? What will they do in a third-down-and-fifteen situation? What will they do when they have the ball with four minutes to go and they're trying to kill the clock? The coaches imagine these scenarios in their staff meetings and then expose their players to them later on the field.

"It's almost as if you've gone to war with a crusty old veteran, and he's already been there," says Lance. "Say you're at Utah Beach and the enemy is shooting machine guns. If the veteran has been there, you can look at him and you know you're okay." Running the team through these scenarios is a way of creating crusty old veterans. "It helps them with confidence," says Lance. "It helps them with their composure, helps them make fewer mistakes. I mean, you lose more games making mistakes than you ever do any other way."

Targeted gamelike practice paid off big in John Beck's last regular-season outing of his senior year, a game against rival Utah in Salt Lake City. Despite blue-zone reps and other tactics, "there were certain hurdles that John had never overcome until that very last football game," says Brandon. In the Cougars' last drive, with the clock ticking relentlessly away, John patiently shuffled back and forth away from pressure for nearly ten seconds, waiting for an open receiver. In these final moments, he demonstrated the poise that he and Brandon had worked so hard to infuse into his muscles and sinews during hours of small successes, repetition, gamelike play, film evaluations, and other activities carefully crafted to maximize his acquisition of wisdom. Jonny Harline's dash across the end zone, John's pass to Jonny, and Jonny's reception on his knees were the blessed outcome of a pointed knowledge management endeavor.

"How John was able to actually make that play seemed irrational and kind of magical for everybody," says Brandon. "He'll forever be remembered as making this magical play. We had done a lot of things in practice and as a program to generate momentum toward such a moment. We had tried to place him in as many chaotic, stressful situations as possible so he was prepared for that eventual moment. We always say when preparation meets opportunity, it equals success."

"That one play was definitely a great moment and one I will always remember," John said, "but to be honest it was a culmination of many things, of years of work, that made that game and that play so special to me."[5]

John went on to lead the Cougars to a 38–8 victory over Oregon in the 2006 Las Vegas Bowl. It was the Cougars' first bowl win in ten years and Bronco's first as head coach.

John was picked in the second round of the 2007 NFL Draft by the Miami Dolphins.

Mentoring

A third method of developing know-how is through mentoring.

It's a good thing that the Cougar quarterback alumni remain dedicated fans.

"Those guys reach out!" says Brandon. "We have the best mentors in the country in just our former players."

Former Cougar quarterbacks have provided an open-door policy for the current quarterbacks, sharing their cell phone numbers and encouraging a call any time.

Often the alum himself will initiate the contact. "When I was a player here, I'd get phone calls from those guys," says Brandon. "My coach was Robbie Bosco, but occasionally, I'd get calls from Steve Young. He'd say, 'Hey, why did you do this?' and 'What was that for?'"

They continue to help him now that he's a coach as well. Brandon welcomes it.

> The one thing I've learned as a coach is that I certainly don't know everything. But I want to learn. If I am offended, or my ego gets in the way of my learning or of getting better at this profession, then that'll be the downfall of my coaching career. These guys have played at the highest levels, they know BYU, and they understand what it means to be a BYU QB. They were inside a very similar system that we run offensively. They can relate to our players in a real, unique way, so I would take every ounce of guidance and information that these guys have, even if it has to do with the coaching or the technical side of things. I may not like it or I may not believe the same thing they believe. But for the most part, 95 percent of everything that we talk about, we're on the same page. I'll usually make a change if they point

out something that we could be doing better. I might spend some time looking at it, and I'll make the change.

Brandon has worked with both Gifford Nielson and Ty Detmer in relation to mechanics and footwork. While Max Hall was still quarterback, for example, Brandon consulted with Gifford about footwork and some of the drops. He says:

I knew that the coach who had coached him years ago at BYU, a guy by the name of Doug Scovil, was the master teacher of QBs and this BYU offense. He was the mastermind behind it thirty-five years ago. Gifford had the opportunity to play for him, and so I wanted to just get a feel for what Doug Scovil was like and how he coached. I wanted to know what made him so great and how he built a quarterback's confidence and what technical things, what fundamental things, did he do.

These guys watch on TV or they're here in the stadium, and they see the details of the quarterback's performance. So I wanted to know what he thought. Gifford felt we could do a few things differently with Max's footwork. I'd been doing it in a way that I'd been trained in the NFL, and I thought it was the right way to do it. I thought, inside what we're trying to do, I'm going to make that little tweak that he mentioned and see if it works. So I tried it myself before I ever taught it to my QBs. I actually went out to try the footwork myself. I started liking it. So I started working through it with Max. It was leading into his senior year, and it ended up being a really, really good change. I think it helped him be a more effective quarterback.

On another occasion, when Brandon was working with Max Hall's backup Riley Nelson—then a new transfer from Utah

State—he and Riley both became discouraged when the left-handed Riley consistently had problems receiving the snap from the center.

"I'm coaching him," says Brandon, "I'm telling him all these different things. He'd try this, try that. He kept struggling." Then on the way home from work one evening, it occurred to Brandon that all left-handed quarterbacks might have the same problem.

"We happen to know a left-handed pro quarterback," he says. "So I called him that night and left him the message."

Steve Young called him back immediately. He had had exactly the same problem as Riley in his days as an NFL rookie. Steve told Brandon, "A left-handed person has to learn how to be a right-handed person most of his life. So he's going to have to take a snap like a right-handed person."

"When he told me that," Brandon says, "I knew exactly what he was talking about. He just basically said that it doesn't work for a left-handed quarterback to take a snap from a right-handed center. 'The functionality doesn't work,' said Steve. 'And I never knew that until I got in the NFL.'"

"I kept dropping snaps," Steve told Brandon. "I'm in the NFL! I can't drop snaps! I'm in the NFL! One day I just thought, 'I'm going to try and take the snap right-handed and see how that works.' Because the coaches were basically saying, 'Well, Steve, if you can't get the snap, you can't play. You know, you've got to get the snap!'"

"It was the same way I was feeling about Riley," says Brandon. "I had told him, 'Riley, you can't play if you can't get a snap.'"

Brandon took Steve's counsel to Riley, and they worked out the new mechanics. It was an easy, smooth fix. "He hasn't had a snap problem since," says Brandon.

It wasn't long after this that the team was engaged in preparing for its 2009 season-opener against Oklahoma. Though BYU stood at No. 20 in the preseason rankings, Oklahoma was No. 3, so the Cougars were the underdog by all accounts. To top it off, the game was to be the inaugural college contest in the brand-new, massive, state-of-the-art Dallas Cowboys Stadium. At this point, Max was a three-year starter up against a young defense. But with such high stakes, Brandon was looking for anything extra that could give his quarterbacks an edge.

So he called Steve Young again and arranged to surprise the quarterbacks the week before the game by inviting him to offer some tips over the speakerphone.

Steve shared his thoughts about how a quarterback should approach that game. He gave us some real tangible experiences that he'd had. He talked about Joe Montana and some of the things he'd witnessed Joe Montana do and gave some great insight to Max. It was prophetic, because it ended up happening exactly as Steve said it was going to happen in the game.

He basically said that the only way to win that game would be to be in it at the end of the game. He said, "You've got to have a chance to beat them at the end of the game. You're not going to just go blow these guys out, so you've got to be in a position to make that last drive to win the game. And when you're in that last drive of the game, it can't be treated as anything other than just a normal drive. If you treat the last drive of a football game as if it's the last drive of a football game, then you are going to be unsuccessful, because you won't be able to manage your emotions or make clear decisions. Let the defense worry about it being the last drive of the game. You go make the drive happen as if it's a normal drive and just execute the football plays. Eventually that Oklahoma defense, it's going to be the one that is going to make the mistake. When it makes the mistake and you don't make the mistake, you'll make that final throw to win that football game."

So when we got into that last drive, sure enough, we got down to the final maybe two or three plays of that game, and they made some mistakes defensively that got us in a position to score the touchdown. They ended up triple teaming Dennis Pitta, who had caught the previous three catches in a row. They left McKay Jacobson uncovered. We made the throw for the touchdown. It wasn't even a hard throw! It was just an easy throw. So it was just Max Hall making a normal routine decision that he had made over and over again. We didn't have to make a spectacular throw or a spectacular catch; it was just a little loft up over the top.

Max had been tutored well.

After McKay's touchdown with just 3:03 remaining and a successful conversion by Mitch Payne, the Cougar defense held the Sooners off in their final drive. The sellout crowd of more than 75,000 watched the Cougars win that game 14–13, their first victory over a top-three ranked team since the 1990 victory against No. 1 Miami. It was a high-profile upset of the kind BYU fans relish.

A little long-distance mentoring from Steve Young had done its part to prepare Max for a likely scenario that panned out almost exactly as Steve had anticipated. Max's college career was capped with a 44–20 win over No. 16 Oregon State in the Las Vegas Bowl, giving BYU an 11–2 record and a No. 12 final ranking.

Max went on to sign and play with the Arizona Cardinals as a free agent.

At the start of the next season, eight former BYU All-American quarterbacks visited campus for Y Quarterback Weekend, an event to raise money for quarterback scholarships. Brandon arranged for the alumni to visit the quarterback room. Unsuspecting, the current year's quarterbacks—including Riley Nelson, Jake Heaps, and James Lark—were gathered for a regularly scheduled meeting when legends Virgil Carter, Gifford Nielsen, Mark Wilson, Jim McMahon, Steve Young, Robbie Bosco, and Ty Detmer knocked on the door and sauntered in. Brandon says:

> Our players were just awestruck. They were probably just like any young kids seeing their idols—seeing these superstars—guys they have looked up to for so long. For me, I was just as awestruck and starstruck as anybody. To see, you know, Jim McMahon, whom I had never met, a guy I'd looked up to for a long time. These are College Hall of Famers, Super Bowl MVPs, NFL MVPs, Heisman Trophy winners, and national champions. The pedigree here is about as good as it gets. So for these kids to be able to see these guys and to feel like a part of that fraternity was pretty cool.
>
> I introduced each one of them individually. I told them that we were grateful that they were there and that we understood the sacrifice, the time that they'd taken to come. We also wanted them to know how much we looked up to them and revered them for who they were. We hoped that they would take some time to speak to us. I said that our quarterbacks may or may not have some questions, but I just kind of turned the time over to them.
>
> They just kind of launched out. They're all pretty outgoing, successful, motivated guys who like to talk. Their advice was all mental, philosophical: how to go about being a quarterback, how to handle your team, how to lead, how to handle critical game situations. Just sound advice about how to handle yourself as a QB. Our quarterbacks ended up grabbing some footballs for signatures.

The BYU quarterback fraternity is framed around ongoing, good-spirited, multi-faceted mentoring that helps young players master the game faster and gives alumni a chance to give back to their alma mater.

WISDOM IN 2010 AND 2011

"Wisdom," says Brandon, "is the application of knowledge. We talk about it all the time. We talk about gaining as much experience as you can." He adds:

The expectations are high for BYU quarterbacks. They are just a part of a culture in which quarterbacks excel. Even when our quarterbacks are young and some of them are new, the culture and the environment are such that we're having a higher rate of simple successes at a faster rate than we've ever had, because the culture's in place. These kids are exceeding in those difficult situations at a much faster rate now than we were. It's not even close. Hopefully we're at a point right now that the next quarterback fills the shoes of the former guys. We'll go play without much hesitation and have a ton of confidence and move forward.

Confidence, though, can be both deceptive and elusive.

For the first three games of 2010, the Cougars ran a dual-quarterback system. Riley Nelson, who had been a *Parade* All-American quarterback in high school and an eight-game freshman starter at Utah State before his transfer to BYU, had been joined during spring practice by the highly touted true freshman Jake Heaps, the nation's No. 1-ranked quarterback recruit, as a leading contender for the starting spot. The two players' stats throughout preseason preparations were so nearly equivalent as to be useless in differentiating a clear starter.

"We ended up not quite knowing which quarterback was going

to give us the best chance to be successful," says Brandon, "so we alternated them in the opening game against Washington. We ended up winning that game." And that, says Brandon, may have been the worst thing that could have happened because it gave them confidence that a two-quarterback offense could really be viable. "We launched into the next few games trying to go down that road, but neither one of these guys really got enough volume to give them a chance to be successful."

Of course, the decision to play both of them flew in the face of one of the Cougars' foremost learning principles, which is to maximize repetitions. Both practice plays and game drives were split between the two leaders. At any rate, designated starter Riley sustained a season-ending shoulder injury in the third game of the season at Florida State. When Jake stepped solely into the leadership spot, he felt at a great disadvantage to other college quarterbacks. "After Riley got hurt, then Jake ended up getting all the repetitions," says Brandon. "By the time he got done with the season, he had started getting sufficient volume. When preparation meets opportunity, that equals success. In the early season, the preparation wasn't there yet. The opportunities were there, but the preparation wasn't there, so we weren't being successful. Once the preparation caught up to the opportunity we started having some pretty good success with the QB."

The fact that Jake went on that season to break every Cougar freshman quarterback record speaks to the number of reps Jake had performed *before* BYU as well. With three state high school championships on his resume as the starting quarterback at Skyline High in Washington, with more than 9,000 passing yards, 114 touchdowns, and only 14 interceptions, Jake was hardly a novice, even if the Cougar offense was new to him. Jake's high school career was preceded by hours of intense personal practice and two dozen weekends yearly at a quarterback academy run by his high school coach

Greg Barton, who also tutored eventual Heisman trophy recipients and NFL starters.

"[Jake] thought about footwork and technique constantly," said *The Seattle Times* about Jake's preparation before high school. "After a training session, he couldn't wait to tell his parents about the new skill he learned. And when he couldn't perform a drill exactly right, he'd get in the car crying. His parents would catch him practicing that drill in front of a mirror."[6]

The coaches came to believe that Jake Heaps's pro-style drop-back passing style was the new identity of the BYU offense. They let Jake know that he would retain the starting job for the next season. Great news for Jake, but awful news for Riley. "I was of the mindset that no matter what [Riley] did, I had already seen what Jake could do, and I believed he was our future," says Bronco.[7]

Bronco even approached Riley about changing positions to free safety. "Riley is a great athlete and a great competitor and has tremendous leadership skills," Bronco says, and he wanted those traits on the field. "That might have made him angry," says Bronco. Riley was "bold and blunt" in insisting on staying where he was.

If he was angry at first, Riley seemed to settle into his lot. "'I realized I needed to stay the course, and so much can change from play to play,' Riley explained in retrospect. 'I came to grips that if I didn't play another down, it didn't . . . lessen my value as a person. I knew if I worked as hard as I could, that I could sleep good at night, and if I didn't play, it wasn't in the cards.'"[8]

Meanwhile, expectations for Jake and the team soared for the 2011 season. Fifteen starters were returning, including all but one of the offense. Jake worked to increase his strength and put on fifteen pounds. He even appeared on the regional cover of the Athlon Sports 2011 preseason *College Football* magazine.

But in BYU's first four games of the season, though the team eked out two wins—one a gratifying 14–13 victory over Ole Miss—the two losses had a particular sting. One was at No. 24 Texas, the only ranked team BYU was scheduled to face, and the other was an embarrassing 54–10 home-field blowout at the hands of archrival Utah. And to be sure, the whole offensive staff—a new offensive coach and two new position coaches—were put through their paces in the tough early season.

"During my first six years as a BYU coach," says Brandon, "I was learning and growing as a position coach. During those six years, I developed lots of thoughts and opinions about what we could do as an offense." When he was given the opportunity to be offensive coordinator, he tried to implement far too many of those ideas. He planned to trade the spread-type offense that BYU had been running in recent years for a new pro-style system with roots in the West Coast offense traditionally run at BYU. If they could establish a solid running game, they could then invoke play-action and keep defenses on their toes, winning big yardage through deep passes and relying on Jake's powerful, accurate arm.

But there were risks. Brandon had new offensive position coaches and a quarterback with limited college experience who had taken snaps shotgun-style in high school rather than under center as called for by the new offense. "We were just too overzealous." To develop all those new schemes and drill their execution adequately was just too much. The Cougars had trouble establishing their run game. Big yardage through the air didn't happen. There were too many interceptions. Third-down conversions were elusive. The team's eagerly anticipated Saturday performance seemed uninspired.

As the season progressed, the offensive staff found the humility to accept the reality and adjust their approach. Brandon says, "It would have been easy to say, 'No, we're right. We did it right. We've just got to stay the course.' But it was very clear that if we hung in there we were going to die. Change or die."

The low point was the third game of the season—the loss to

Utah. "At halftime I believed the game would come down to the last play or so," says Bronco. "As the turnovers continued to mount, as the field position continued to be in Utah's favor, and as we pushed harder and harder, our execution became worse."

"We turned the ball over seven times in that game," says Brandon. "We played miserably bad. We did not score a point in the second half. It was poor coaching and poor execution. Something between the coaches and the players didn't transfer."

"It was very painful to watch," says Bronco. He goes on:

> I had to acknowledge that our team at that point wasn't prepared to play as effectively, as efficiently, as cleanly, and as soundly as I thought they had been. The feedback that I was getting, as hard as it was, was essential to moving forward. It was very difficult. I took full responsibility, because I believe that players play as they're prepared to play.
>
> After the game, I looked inward first. Holly and I spent a long time together assessing our position as leaders of the program and what we might do to help the situation.

In an unprecedented action, Bronco phoned all of his staff and asked them to bring their families to the football offices on Sunday afternoon. "There were probably many that believed I was getting ready to resign in front of them and wanted their families together for that. I don't think any of them knew what to expect, nor did we tell them. We just asked them to be there."

But what Bronco was worried about was the impact the bitter loss to Utah would have on his staff's families. Since that game is in-state, neighbors and congregation members and community members become more vocal and more bold—sometimes not the best version of themselves in preparation for the game or afterward, based on who wins. "I knew that the other wives might be hurting, children might be hurting. I thought that coaches were probably worried about their jobs, possibly what it would mean for their families. To leave people wondering and worrying and feeling anxious was not what I wanted to portray in our organization. I would rather have clarity." Reflecting on the situation, Bronco says:

I do believe in transparency. To have my family on display in front of the staff—because there's no one that it was more difficult on than us—and for them so see us linked arm in arm and unified but also hurting, but determined to move forward, I think was something that was necessary for them to see. We wanted to let our program know that nobody's isolated, nobody's alone, and we intend to rely on one another. We had coaches who were brand new to the staff, and we thought it would be very helpful for them to hear how we intended to approach this loss.

Our approach was very simple—to learn from the mistakes but to recommit to our goals, values, and direction so our team and our program could improve. I wanted to be sure that everyone knew our direction, our reasoning, and what lay ahead. And then I asked for their commitment to do that. It was unanimously supported by wives and kids and husbands. I wanted to leave there as one united body.

People needed to hear from leadership that there is a consistency that even a game like that can't alter or cause to waver.

The next day the Cougar offensive staff regrouped. "We had to simplify the plan significantly," says Brandon, "and try to find ways to increase the repetitions."

But simplifying schemes and adjusting practice routines were not enough. Two games later, at home versus Utah State, when BYU seemed headed for a third loss in five games, Brandon made the call that brought Riley Nelson off the bench like a high-fiving phoenix from the ashes. He took over midway through the third quarter of a game BYU trailed, rallying his team for a win against the school at which he had begun his college career.

Riley saved the day with his talent for making plays against the odds, a skill that did not become apparent until he was enveloped in the heat of the battle. "He pushes forward," said one analyst, "moving, dodging, sliding, twirling, and eluding before somehow pushing the ball downfield."[9] His last year of adversity had paid off—confidence and poise exuded from him. It was just what the Cougars needed.

Not one to cower in fear of making mistakes, Riley made some big ones. But they were not his undoing. Sometimes he exploded in rage. Sometimes he assumed an attitude of plucky belligerence. For instance, in a late-season game against nationally respected TCU, a dangerous pass contributed to a tipped-ball interception in the end zone. About that pass, Riley says:

> I'm sorry, but I made a play and my guy got two hands on it and he got hit early and it wasn't called. Whatever. That's football. That's what happens. I'm not going to worry about it. My decision-making and my execution and the sharpness with which I execute the pass game will keep getting better. That's something I am conscious of and something I am focusing on. But I'm going to be me. If I try to be someone else, my play will be very poor. And I'm not going to let that happen.[10]

Later in the same game, Riley reached over the goal line while being tackled, securing a two-point conversion. He was so jubilant that he bounced up and high-fived the goal line official who was signaling the conversion with upraised hands. ESPN caught the action, and commentators Joe Tessitore and Rod Gilmore chuckled about it. The clip was posted on YouTube and nearly went viral before it was removed for copyright infringement.

"Loved it. Loved it," said Bronco. "When you get an idea of being in the moment, that's pretty much it. I've never seen that before. I would love that to kind of be a symbol of BYU Football—you're having so much fun that you're finding someone to celebrate with."[11] Even if it's one of the game officials.

Though the offense's performance was not enough to defeat TCU, Riley was soundly in the zone. He had energized the offense. His unexpected second chance was "like Christmas for him," says Bronco. "He was really excited to play football, and that was a contagious frame of mind. Riley got us the energy and execution with this chip-on-the-shoulder mentality of I don't care what other people think."[12] His enthusiasm was infectious to his team and to BYU fans.

Riley's inspiring ability to play with utter abandon had not come without experience and reflection. Between the 2010 and 2011 seasons, Riley says, "I stopped trying to be perfect. . . . I stopped trying to make the perfect play or make the perfect read. I stopped trying to put the ball in the perfect spot every time and let my playmakers make plays. . . . I put so much pressure on myself last year. I was so worried about what everyone was saying and labels they put on me, I was so worried about whatever everybody else was saying it was affecting my performance on the field."[13]

Emblematic of Riley's new, more relaxed attitude was the long, flowing hair he sported in the game against the Aggies. He had kept his hair short after his mission, falling well within the standards for male hair length at BYU. But over the summer and into the fall he had let it get long enough to brush his collar and thus the boundaries of the Honor Code.

In Provo, some fans expect the very visible quarterback to be impeccable in his fidelity to the school's standards of dress and grooming. Other fans had enormous fun with the lapse. A Facebook page titled "YES, we love you, Riley Nelson! Now, get a haircut" popped up the weekend of the Utah State game. Another fan posted a must-see clip called "Ode to Riley's Hair" on YouTube which received over 12,000 hits in just two days.[14]

Riley quickly got a haircut the day after the game and apologized the next week. "I was just being a lazy, dumb college student," he said,[15] but his two younger brothers vouched for him, explaining that the three athletes had playfully decided together to let their hair grow for the sake of its legendary physical power (think Samson). "He was growing it out with us," his brother D.J., a high school quarterback, told the press with a smile.[16]

Riley's goofy socks, bared abs—which a rolled-up jersey exposed during fall camp—and his long hair elicited chuckles on the Internet. But "grit" became the word most often invoked to describe his dual-threat, tenacious playing style. "One of Riley's strengths," says Houston Reynolds (offensive lineman 2009–) "is that when things get a little shaky, he can make things happen with his feet. . . . As an offensive lineman, that has contributed because you know when things get ugly, even when blocks get missed or assignments get missed, or things get messed up, you know that he's back there fighting and there's a chance he's making something happen on the other side of the field that you don't know about. You fight a little harder and you fight a little longer knowing it might be your block that gets the first down when he decides to run."[17]

In 2011, the Cougars earned nine regular-season victories, landing a berth in the Armed Forces Bowl against Tulsa. On a sunny day in Dallas, the Cougar defense gave up a touchdown to the Golden Hurricane on the first drive of the game, but held Tulsa to 272 total yards of offense; only 37 were rushing yards, compared to Tulsa's per game average of over 200 yards on the ground. Kyle Van Noy (linebacker 2010–) made ten tackles, including five tackles for loss, two sacks, one forced fumble, and one quarterback hurry.

Special teams stepped up to contribute as well. Punter Riley Stephensen (kicker, punter 2009–) placed seven of his eight punts inside the Tulsa twenty-yard line. Justin Sorensen (kicker 2008, 2011–) made all of his placement kicks and recorded a kickoff touchback. JD Falslev (wide receiver 2009–) returned three punts for forty-four yards, including a twenty-two-yard effort that set up BYU's game-winning drive. Late in the second quarter, Reed Hornung (deep snapper 2010–) hit the Tulsa punt returner and forced a fumble, which was recovered by David Foote (running back 2006, 2009–12) at the Tulsa seventeen-yard line. On the next play, offensive lineman Matt Reynolds, helmetless, retreated to the backfield to protect a scrambling Riley. Matt's block gave his quarterback the time needed to find Cody Hoffman for a tide-turning touchdown; at the half, BYU trailed 14–10 but was back in the game.

A third quarter touchdown toss from Riley to Cody gave BYU a 17–14 cushion heading into the game's final fifteen minutes, but a Tulsa touchdown early in the fourth quarter had BYU trailing 21–17. With less than three minutes to play, facing a fourth and nine with no timeouts, Riley scrambled fourteen yards for a first down to keep the drive alive. Seven plays later, the Cougars had advanced to the two-yard line, but only eleven seconds remained on the clock. The coaches were jumping up and down on the sidelines and calling for a spike to stop the clock. Riley saw the Tulsa defenders anticipating the same, standing and relaxing their guard.

Now this is where the late-night film study, which had once seemed indolent to his mom, paid off. He remembered seeing Dan Marino fake a spike in the last moments of a 1994 Miami Dolphins victory against the New York Jets. The Cougars had just such a play in their playbook known as "Red Alert," though they hadn't practiced it in some months. Riley audibled the change. "I kind of felt it inside," he said in postgame interviews. "I felt it was a high-reward, low-risk play. It was on me."[18] Riley and Cody both played the fake—Cody squaring and relaxing his stance and Riley aiming his false throw in the opposite direction. When Riley turned to Cody, the Tulsa cornerback had overcompensated. Riley caught Cody's eye and threw the ball. The pass was completed for the game-winning touchdown—Cody's third touchdown catch of the day.

"To have a quarterback in that situation fake spike it on his own and throw a touchdown and be on the same page with the receiver—" says Bronco, "that's the kind of magic of the guys I get to coach."[19]

"I look like the hero," said Riley after the game. "But it very easily could have been the other way around and I would have been the goat—and I have been the goat before. That's kind of what happens when you are the quarterback."[20]

BYU had claimed its third straight bowl win, a school record, and also claimed its fifth ten-win season and fifth bowl win in Bronco's seven years as head coach. The final *USA Today* Coaches' Poll ranked BYU at No. 25.

The Cougars had come a long way since that awful loss to Utah early in the season, which Bronco says ended up being a good learning experience for the team and for fans. "The sun actually does come up" after a loss to Utah, he says. "We still won ten football games, we finished in the top twenty-five, and we won another bowl game. All these things happened after what many at the time thought was possibly the end of the world as we know it."

The Cougars maintained an elite spot as one of the current most-winning college football programs in the country—sixty-six wins in seven years, which is more victories than all but fourteen teams in the nation, and the fifth most ten-win seasons in that time frame.

LOSING A QUARTERBACK

"I would much rather have had Jake stay," Bronco said after it was announced that Jake Heaps would be transferring from BYU. "I wanted him to stay. I love him as a young man, and he has such great football skill." Nevertheless, Jake was not thriving at BYU. Brandon said, "It was hard to see him go after spending three years being involved with his life and recruiting him. . . . I'll be rooting for him, but it was sad to see him go."[21]

Jake needed a new playing field where he could make a fresh start. He transferred to the University of Kansas under new head coach Charlie Weis. His departure left many fans mournful and stumped about what had happened with one of the most prized recruits BYU had ever signed.

It was a perfect storm: a battle between two closely matched offensive leaders, a coaching staff shake-up, a new offensive scheme, and a schedule both years weighted in difficulty toward the beginning of the season—so many factors to disrupt the nurture of a promising but inexperienced young quarterback.

Brandon and Bronco agree that they should have redshirted Jake in his first year. "Wisdom is the application of knowledge and especially application in the fog of war," says Brandon, who adds:

> Jake did not have enough volume of simple successes before he was playing against very good opponents in very difficult environments. The demands and the expectations had risen too high.
>
> Riley just had more experience quite honestly—more volume of years and thus of wisdom. He probably had more football plays on the football field between his freshman year at Utah State to being a redshirt to suffering injuries to watching Max Hall play to watching the ups and downs of Jake's career.

It requires 10,000 hours of deliberate work to become a master. If you do deliberate work with a master, you can increase your learning speed. Jake never got to do work with a master who was his peer. He was never trained by a starting quarterback.

A true quarterback factory has starting quarterback after starting quarterback after starting quarterback in the program. The next guy in line gets to learn from the previous starting quarterback. He's doing work with the position coach and the current starter who has hopefully become a master of that position. Jake never got that experience.

On the other hand, Riley indeed was mentored by Max Hall. In his year as Max's backup, Riley had plenty of opportunity to watch him carefully and question him about his technique and his decisions.

Now, Riley is himself taking on the role of mentor with a robust array of quarterback depth. "Our young quarterbacks are looking really good, especially having someone like Riley teaching them," says defensive back Mike Hague (2006, 2009–12) after rookie Taysom Hill escaped out of the pocket in a spring scrimmage. "Riley is one of the greatest examples of perseverance, commitment, and knowledge. He's passing that on to these young guys," adds Mike.[22] "They are eager to learn," says James Lark (quarterback 2006, 2009–12), Riley's backup. They ask a lot of questions, he confirmed. "I was the same way with John Beck and Max Hall. I'm happy to help these guys."[23]

THE FUTURE OF
BYU'S QUARTERBACK FACTORY

The vantage point in 2012 promises a succession of expert quarterbacks as Brandon has described. He's already setting rookies in place, even before their missions, to learn from veterans Riley and James.

"There are a lot of quarterbacks we're managing," says Brandon Doman. "It's rare to have this many quarterbacks on scholarship, but we're losing three of them after this year, so I want these young guys to see how the guys who have been in the program do things. I don't want them here next season without the experience of learning from those guys, so that's why we have so many quarterbacks."[24]

BYU's offense is at a historical juncture. Offensive preparations for the 2012 season are built around bringing the pro-style West Coast-based offense Brandon began to implement in 2011 into clearer focus. Of what will happen, Brandon says:

> I don't know if we truly had an identity ever in 2011. When we ended the season, our identity was "Try Hard Because of Riley Nelson." I don't know if there was anything that we were doing that was as good or better than anybody in the country. That's not good. That's just average football.
>
> There's a tier of teams that do the critical things better than anybody else in the country. At BYU, we know that there are particular things we can do as well as or better than anybody else. There are some things in the BYU offense that I know our staff knows. We've lived it. We know it. We've been around it for years. We've had experience with it. It drips from the walls. We're not going to be anybody different. That's who we're going to be. We'll complement it with things that will enhance it.

Brandon says that he will mold the Cougar attack to be "the most efficient progression-based system in the country."[25] By "progression-based," he's referring to the Cougar quarterback protocol that we discussed earlier. BYU will be seeking mobile quarterbacks for this job, guys who can deliver a 65 percent completion percentage, a high third-down conversion rate, and close to 300 yards passing per game.

That's asking a lot of an offensive leader, but it's not out of line with what's been on display at BYU for more than thirty-five years. The Cougars' signature practice system is designed to develop this kind of capability. "That's who we are and that's the culture that we're trying to maintain," says Brandon.[26] "We probably practice in full pads less than anyone else in the country," says Bronco. "We probably practice in shorter periods than any others. Our focus is still on volume and the tempo of practice. We're adding increased volume and honing our unique practice structure to get an even more precise and efficient result."

Riley himself has been known for his moxie but not so much for his strong nor accurate arm. As he studied his 2011 film, he could see that his reads were correct but his feet and mechanics needed improvement. He and Brandon worked on cementing proper technique and proper form. By spring camp, Brandon could say that Riley's completion percentage and efficiency were as good as John Beck and Max Hall's. "He's right there with them. I think he can do this offense. He can do some things those guys couldn't do and he can certainly do those things as well inside this offense."[27] Riley's talent as a running threat will embellish the developing BYU offense with more play action, naked bootlegs, and sprint outs in 2012.[28]

If all goes well, this old-style/new-style attack will launch BYU's offense toward years of offensive excellence.

CHAPTER 9

Diffusion

I think my favorite moment playing at BYU was after the 2006 Utah game. We'd just beaten Utah. But it wasn't so much the John Beck to Jonny Harline play. It was after everything was over. Coach Mendenhall actually called on me to say the prayer in the locker room. He would come in and say what he had to say, and then we'd always end with a prayer. I had the opportunity to say that prayer. To me it was a very special moment, because it kind of tied it all in together. We'd just all had this incredible victory. We'd just won the conference title; we'd just beaten our rivals with a big play. Having the opportunity as a freshman to be called on by Coach Mendenhall to say the prayer after that game, just to be there and thank the Lord for everything—to me it was a culmination of what this program is for me, of all the effort and everything that we accomplished, Having the opportunity to bring the Spirit into it and bring the Lord into what we did—I think that was probably my most special moment here at BYU.

—JAN JORGENSEN
BYU DEFENSIVE LINE 2005–09; TEAM CAPTAIN

B RONCO IS KNOWN to be an avid reader. His interests range from warrior cultures to business practices to scripture—as we have seen. But if Bronco closed his books each night and left everything he read on his bedside table, he himself might be enriched, but his organization would not benefit at all. Even if he came to work each day and enthusiastically described to his colleagues the insights he was savoring, if he was yet unable to help them learn and apply promising ideas, his study would remain unavailable to the organization.

The last chapter focused largely on knowledge acquisition. If we were to stop here, we'd run the risk that many groups and organizations do. We'd have spent all our knowledge management energy *finding* new knowledge. But we would have forgotten about another component of effective knowledge management: knowledge *diffusion.*

The story we shared in chapter 8 about Gifford Nielsen's tips on footwork is a simple example of diffusion where knowledge flowed from a veteran pro quarterback to a quarterbacks coach to a young college player. In organizations, even with social media, the spread of certain types of knowledge across firm organization boundaries can be far less facile.

For example, by the time Brandon had become offensive coordinator, he was overflowing with ideas to implement. But teaching the new scheme system to his new staff members—with everything else they needed to learn as first-time BYU coaches—as well as to his offensive players was very difficult. After the 2011 loss against Utah, Brandon scaled back to a scope that was more feasible.

In college football, it is essential that the transfer of knowledge to rookies happens as efficiently as possible, and it is ideal to find a way to preserve the knowledge developed by graduating seniors, rather than lose it forever when players move on to the NFL or to careers in business, medicine, or other areas. Passing wisdom from coach to players, from alumni to players, from team to team, and even to other organizations outside of BYU are just some of the diffusion and application opportunities presented to the Cougars.

ORGANIZATION-TO-ORGANIZATION DIFFUSION

Bronco always says that BYU Football is a learning organization. He regularly organizes learning opportunities of all kinds, not just for himself but also for the whole staff. Many of them are far beyond the usual purview of football strategy and technique.

Just before fall camp in 2009, for instance, the Cougar staff rented Harleys and headed north on a five-hour ride to Jackson, Wyoming. Jackson is a rustic mountain village nestled in the shadow of the spectacular Teton Range. It's crowded in August with summer tourists who have come to raft on the Snake River and hike the slopes of the Grand Teton, but the mountain air is cool and the scenery awe-inspiring. It is a perfect place to unwind from the pressures of the gridiron game and spend some time incubating new ideas. One of the topics on this learning trip was *learning* itself.

Bronco had arranged for a pair of innovators to make the short trek from BYU–Idaho in Rexburg across the Tetons to Jackson Hole. Clark Gilbert and Henry J. Eyring had been recently engaged in groundbreaking work about teaching excellence and came to share their findings with the Cougar coaching staff.

They taught Bronco and his team that when students are actively involved in teaching each other, "their ability to retain, apply, and synthesize their learning increases." But this does not mean, of course, that there is no role for the teacher (or the coach). Rather, the teacher needs to see himself or herself as "the engineer, the designer, the architect of the learning experience; not just the sage on the stage telling people what he or she thinks they need to know."[1]

Using *peer instruction* involves several important practices, explained Gilbert and Eyring. First of all, teachers must encourage student preparation before class (or before team meetings, in the case of BYU Football). They also taught the Cougars that teachers can draw upon a repertoire of tools to craft a participatory classroom experience. They can direct a discussion Socratic-style, asking questions as a way of navigating participants toward a predefined learning outcome. They can turn students loose to engage each other on the topic. They can arrange students into groups to solve a problem or analyze a case. They can even rotate students through the responsibility of leading the class themselves. What's important is that teachers (or coaches, in our case) design the interactions, select the problems to engage, and facilitate group work. They must remain highly engaged, their role elevated from that of a traditional teacher, their capabilities in play both as a content expert and learning process expert. Finally, teachers (coaches) should closely observe, prompt, and, if needed, redirect student interactions in order to ensure that the discussion is profitable and that effective learning is taking place.

This whole Jackson scene is an interesting example of knowledge diffusion. Here were two Harvard guys, working out west at BYU–Idaho where the intercollegiate athletics program had been totally disbanded (and not without controversy), talking to the football coaches from a sister university about innovative pedagogical methods.

Is the most crucial football knowledge technical know-how about strategy and skill? Is a football coach's facility with Xs and Os his most important competency? Or his knowledge of position mastery? Or must he also be an expert designer of learning experiences? When you watch your favorite team succumb to defeat in a big game, are you thinking about how the coaches and players botched it technically, or are you also wondering what learning events are going on behind the scenes—either failures in learning that may have resulted in the loss, or successes in learning that will incorporate the loss into a bigger picture of life lessons and character-building adventures?

COACH-TO-PLAYER DIFFUSION: PEER-TO-PEER LEARNING

The Cougar coaches took their new thoughts about peer instruction home from Wyoming, augmented them with more new ideas from additional experts, publications, and other sources, and found ways to apply them at BYU. Of course, many of them already used some forms of peer instruction—most expert teachers do. Bronco and other coaches had been architecting innovative peer-learning methods for years.

For instance, when Bronco was at UNM, he coached the kickoff return team. As we said before, players often eschew special teams because of the extra work—many players would rather their assignments be limited to their offensive or defensive positions. "But this kickoff team was a coveted position," says Nick Speegle, "because you got to run down for Coach Mendenhall. Not everybody got to do that."

To ensure that his players were well prepared—one of the conditions for successful peer instruction—Bronco submitted his kickoff return team members to a regular position catechism. He'd line them up with the first team in front, the second team in back. He'd point at each position on the first team, and they were to repeat their job and assignment and position in the lineup. "If you were, say, number five, your job was to run straight down, line up on the goal post, angle in—there was a whole series of things you had to say for each spot," says Nick. Then Bronco would point at each player on the second team and have them repeat the exercise. Next, both teams had to say the information at the same time in a chorus of baritone voices. Last, he'd have the teams and positions speak in sequence, one after the other, in a round that resolved ultimately into song. It was a veritable football fugue.

"It was just hilarious," says Nick. "You would start serious, and then you would realize how ridiculous it was. Then we'd just start cracking up. And Coach Mendenhall would be cracking up, too. It was awesome. We were singing our assignment to the tune of 'Row-Row-Row Your Boat'!"

This singing exercise helped prepare team members for practice. It's an example of a creative way of getting learners to ready themselves ahead of time—and by having players repeat their assignments several times, Bronco was cementing their studies in their minds. Players obviously must grasp their assignments cognitively before they can execute them physically. Good preparation is essential for successful peer instruction because students can hardly discuss and explore concepts with which they are not already acquainted.

Cougar coaches strive to incorporate student-to-student interaction when it comes to reviewing film and teaching plays. "Coaches are famous for wanting to stand up and let players know exactly everything we know," says offensive line coach Mark Weber. "The worst thing that coaches do, in my opinion," adds running backs coach Joe DuPaix, "is go into a meeting room and just turn on the tape and let it run and talk about the plays as it runs. Just go on for an hour while kids are falling asleep." Great coaches and teachers everywhere know this scenario is a learning disaster. "What's important to me is that kids learn," says Mark. "I've got to try to orchestrate that. More of my time has gone to orchestrating the best way for them to learn, rather than me trying to tell them everything I know."

Joe DuPaix uses a common peer-to-peer technique, which is to invite students periodically to take a place in the front of the classroom and teach a concept themselves. "They're the coach," says Joe. "They have the room. When a player has to stand at the dry-erase board and draw up a play against a certain defense, a certain protection against a certain front, that individual is learning more than he would if he were just sitting in his chair." Peer instruction such as this also gives Joe a chance to "see if my teaching is actually getting through." It ratchets up the energy of the whole classroom. "It changes the attention of the rest of the players in the room. 'Oh, wow, Brian Kariya [running back 2005, 2008–2011] is teaching us today!'" When Coach Kariya is up there on the board, says Joe, "it becomes more fun for them. The players are learning a little bit more because their mental edge just got enhanced."

A state-of-the art video editing system at BYU facilitates efficient film study. Early in the day, coaches review both wide and tight shots of the prior day's practice and edit them down to the clips most applicable to their positions. They create diagrams and make comments to be viewed in the system along with the clips. When they meet with their teams, they are at liberty to use these clips however they want. Mark often asks his linemen to first watch them without taking notes, then he gives them a couple of minutes to rapidly write down everything they can remember. They all then discuss what they picked up. Or he'll create huddles around the room, assigning upperclassmen to lead a discussion in each huddle about the material in the clip. "There will be conversations going on all over the room. It takes longer to go through the film, but I'd rather they learn fifteen plays really well than fall asleep listening to me talking all the time."

"Bronco encourages us to always be learning," says Mark. "He provides the education about better ways to teach the kids. We don't have much time because of the whole program's philosophy of family first, and going home after practice, and not working on Sundays. So you have to be more efficient. It's forced me to learn the very best way to teach."

With coaches providing comments on the film and being available in the room to monitor presentations and discussions, they can ensure that the most important topics are covered. But as we mentioned in chapter 6, during summer months when NCAA rules prohibit coaches from running practices, upperclassmen step up to organize workouts and film study. Then the quality of the learning experience is truly up to players. "The outside linebacker guys come to me," explains Kelly Poppinga. "We make a calendar and post a calendar. I give them all the position drills that I have. I say, 'You guys take out what you think you guys need or what the younger guys need to work on.'" He provides some direction about what to emphasize, and they go from there. "They sit down with the younger guys and watch film with them. They get up on the board with them. They go and have walk-throughs with them. They do it all on their own."

"The summer before my senior year," says David Nixon, who was a player alongside Kelly, "I was in charge of coordinating, along with Max Hall, our 7-on-7 workouts and texting everyone, making sure everyone was there. I really tried to take ownership, knowing it was up to us to hold these guys accountable."

POSITION-TO-POSITION DIFFUSION: A COMMUNITY CLASSROOM

What about the Cougars' efforts to transmit knowledge not just among players sharing the same position, but across the whole offensive or defensive teams?

In mid-season 2010, Bronco was searching for ways to increase team unity. The 2010 season, as you will recall, started off with a win against Washington, which was followed by four losses, the longest BYU losing streak in seventeen years. After resuming his job as the defensive coordinator following game number five, Bronco immediately eliminated staff specialization such as run-game coach, pass coach, and third-down coach. Instead of breaking down the game individually and coming back to report, the whole group watched the previous week's game together and collaborated on the call sheet. They debated and tested and wrangled until they had reached consensus on a more limited game plan. Essentially, they changed their focus to the big picture, and as a result their play-calling was greatly enhanced.

"It helped create ownership and establish trust and gain speed," says Bronco. "All the coaches could see why we were calling what we were calling, what play was supposed to help." The number of calls they planned for each game was reduced, but the purpose of each call became clearer. Only the plays that looked good in practice and that made sense to everybody landed on the final call sheet.

The team won their following game, 24–21, against San Diego State. As the team prepared the next week for TCU in Fort Worth, Bronco stumbled across a promising new idea for structuring defensive team meetings. The hotel conference room where they met was arranged with four screens. Bronco watched as a coach from one position called over to another position about a certain play, and suddenly a conversation was live between the two groups. Bronco says, "The thought came: there are no barriers here. They are all in the same room. What if we came back home and set up four screens and basically all the position meetings went on at the same time in the same room? At any one time, a coach could yell to another coach, 'Hey, what are you guys doing here? What do you think?' I could stop all four meetings at the same time and say, 'Look at this play.'"

When the coaches got back to BYU that is exactly what they did. "The silo effect that happens when the teams are divided in different rooms went completely away," says Bronco. "The teaching standard was raised and the energy was raised and the collaboration was raised. It was almost like the stock exchange. There were people pointing and shouting and looking at this play and that play. There was no way possible for you not to be engaged in what we were doing. That became a contagious learning environment. Sometimes, people would stop and move chairs and act as though they were blockers. It was a very unique learning environment in terms of facilitating collaboration."

"Bronco can stand in the middle," says Steve Kaufusi. "He can actually talk to everybody at the same time. Or he can watch a clip or two here and talk, and then all he has to do is turn his body." He might confirm something that one coach is saying, then turn to another position and add to a point made by another coach or a player. "If there's a change, he can put everybody on the stop and just make that announcement right there," instead of waiting until the next day.

"It just brought the defense back together again and made us feel like a whole group instead of us in separate rooms and separated by position," says Kelly. "Now we were all together and we were learning the same thing, and we knew that one coach or another group of players wasn't learning different things. We were all together on the same page."

The defensive side couldn't gather like this every day because their defensive room was not properly arranged nor equipped for the groups to accomplish their work without sometimes inconveniencing each other. But the new approach worked so well that after the season ended, minor construction was commissioned to modify facilities to accommodate the new ultra-collaborative approach.

TEAM-TO-TEAM DIFFUSION: LINKING MECHANISMS

As far as moving knowledge back and forth between the offensive and defensive teams, daily team meetings help but are far from adequate. We've already discussed other design elements of the Cougar football program that move knowledge between teams: the leadership council comprised of representatives from each position, locker rotations, and weight-room switch-ups. Just being in closer proximity with guys from the other side of the ball facilitates knowledge sharing, as when linebacker Cameron Jensen and quarterback John Beck kicked around ideas in the locker room about how the defense could better disguise their coverages.

DISCOVERY AND DIFFUSION

In this chapter we've made the claim that knowledge *diffusion* is just as important in an organization as knowledge *discovery.* Yet this aspect of total knowledge management often gets short shrift. On the positive side, in many organizations, social media is enhancing the ease with which people can share information across boundaries or come together online to collaborate on new ways of applying knowledge (see section 2).

The Cougars have made a point of putting design elements in place to facilitate knowledge sharing. For them it's been about scheduling learning events to bring new knowledge into the organization, designing facilities that draw people together, and setting up mechanisms such as the leadership council that link people across different sides of the ball. The coaching staff's approach to knowledge management is, of course, never stagnant. Techniques that are very successful one year may be inappropriate the next, given the changing needs and abilities of players and coaches. But the idea is to always be fostering an enhanced free-flow of ideas across the whole organization, which also has the effect of helping people feel more united—one of the topics of our next chapter.

As we shall see in chapter 11, one of the staff's overarching goals is to develop leaders who will have a positive impact on families, communities, and the world. As players, graduate assistants, and even coaches move on from BYU, one of the best tests of success in this area will be the extent to which ideas that have worked well for the Cougars are applied in and adapted to the unique requirements of other settings—in other football programs, in business careers, and in community groups and homes.

Barry Lamb, a thirty-three-year defensive coaching veteran who left in 2010 for health-related reasons after sixteen seasons with the Cougars, is now the assistant head coach at Tulane. He joined a program with a new head coach, eager hopes for a turnaround, and ambitious plans for a brand new stadium. He talks about making his knowledge available to the new Tulane staff by first confessing his initial reluctance when Bronco himself was a new head coach:

> I have to be truthful. I was not all in at certain times because I really didn't understand where Bronco was going. But I let myself go. We all let ourselves go and open up a little bit. That really shook us up because coaches are used to doing things that have proven to be the right things. We all caught his vision and became fully invested. Some of the things we did were completely different from anything else any football staff I've ever been on has done, and I've been at seven schools. The principles we based our BYU program on were correct principles. They worked in our organization.
>
> In some way, I'm trying to duplicate that here at Tulane. Coach Mendenhall wants us to be mentors. He wants us to help along young people coming up in the profession. The head coach here, Curtis Johnson, has never been a head coach before and has been out of the college game for about six years, coaching with the New Orleans Saints. We talk about a lot of things that Coach Mendenhall and Paul taught. Of course, we're applying them in a different way because it's a different school. This is a private school, but it is not a faith-based university. But we're using a lot of the same principles. I use them every day. We use the same words that we used at BYU. On the back of all of

our business cards—from the head coach on down to the graduate assistants—it says "Raise the Bar." The T-shirts that all the kids wear every day say, "Raise the Bar." I use the five smooth stones—I don't call them that—but I use them every week certainly, if not every day. Our head coach talks in those terms. It is really interesting going through the process being the teacher instead of the student. I am trying to pass on some of the things I learned at BYU to our new staff here at Tulane. It's going to be an interesting experience seeing how long it takes us to get this program going.

I was fortunate to have been there when Paul and Bronco got together and changed everything. It was fun to go through, and I am glad I paid attention. It was a magic moment in everybody's coaching life who was involved in it, and I think we knew it was a magic moment—what we were going through and what we were learning. I wouldn't have missed it for the world.

Diffusion is at its best when ideas spread, but with adaptation to make them better and more suited to each new application. You can turn to section 2 for more ideas about how to put the five smooth stones to work for you.

CHAPTER 10

Fully Invested

The first time I met Bronco I was on the top of Sundance Ski Resort's back mountain, having just completed the team's "Eco-Challenge." I was eighteen; young, in shape (so I thought), but Coach Mendenhall had just beaten me to the top by over an hour. As I made the final summit, Coach Mendenhall reached down and pulled me up the final few feet. I literally looked up to him then, and I would continue to "look up to him" for the rest of my football career at BYU.

He asked me to participate in some crazy safety drills during fall camp or winter conditioning, but I never complained or questioned his motives because I knew that he wouldn't ask something of me that he wasn't capable of doing himself. Sometimes, practice could feel like I was in the middle of a frantic train wreck.

During the first week of my freshman year, I sprinted from place to place not having any idea where I was going or what was going on. In one particular drill, we had to tackle three consecutive standing tackling dummies positioned twenty-five yards away at a full sprint. Looking back, these drills were helping us learn the "reckless abandon" ethic that

Coach would so often preach. The last tackling dummy in that drill had a football on top that I had to knock down, pick up, and then dive over another bag into the end zone with (perhaps a drill that sixth graders would love, but a tough one on the artificial turf in 100-degree weather).

I will never forget being a freshman, walk-on defensive back, participating in that drill for the first time. As I started sprinting to the first bag, I felt a presence to my right. I took a quick peek and found that it was Bronco Mendenhall doing the drill with me, almost as fast as me. I picked up my pace to not be outdone. This is a simple example of the respect that Coach Mendenhall garners from his players.[1]

—SCOTT JOHNSON
BYU DEFENSIVE BACK 2006–09; TEAM CAPTAIN

FOR THE 2010 HOME GAME against San Diego State, Bronco put aside his polo-style staff uniform in favor of a T-shirt with the slogan "Band of Brothers" printed on the back. Since then, he has worn a T-shirt with that message every game day. So have many of the BYU defensive players, who wear the T-shirts under their jerseys.

Band of Brothers, as we have seen, was the name of a buddy system internal to the football program designed to monitor the well-being of players and to smooth the entry of new recruits and transfers. It was also a theme of the 2006 season, when Bronco's efforts in his second year of head coaching were still very much about bringing the offense and defense together as a unified group and recharging the team after several disappointing seasons. That year the Cougars posted an 11–2 record, their first double-digit win season in five years.

Over the ensuing three seasons, BYU bookended a pair of 11–2 campaigns around a 10–3 effort, but in 2010, by the time Bronco donned his T-shirt at game time, the Cougars' hopes of double-digit wins had already vanished. Though BYU had recorded a win in the season opener with Washington, the four-game losing streak that followed was the first such streak since 1993 and gave BYU its worst five-game start since 1973. Did the new system put in place by Bronco and detailed in this book have an answer for the challenges the team faced that year? Bronco's T-shirt was part of an effort to bring that system to the rescue of the young and inexperienced 2010 crew.

By the next season—2011—Cougar football had gone independent and was partnered with ESPN. (See chapter 11 for more on football independence.) Some fans, observing Bronco's new look on national TV, found the T-shirt a bit of an embarrassment. They expressed themselves on the message boards. "On national TV, can't he go with a nice golf shirt, white or blue with trim?" asked commentator Dick Harmon as he set out to explain the method to Bronco's madness. To his own question, "Is Bronco dressing down?" Harmon gave the answer, "Mendenhall often does things that are symbolic."[2] Bronco's T-shirt was laden with meaning and message for the Cougars on the field.

Enter Smooth Stone #5, "Effective Leaders Capture Hearts and Minds." Bronco has always captured hearts and minds, wherever he has coached. Smooth Stone #5 was like an old friend to him, and in 2010 he pulled it once again from his shepherd's bag of weapons, this time to use it against the mighty Goliaths of inexperience and adversity.

Smooth Stone #5

Effective leaders capture hearts and minds.

To have captured hearts and minds is to have effectively directed the attention of a group of people toward a worthy cause and to have gathered their energies and efforts in service of that cause. To be successful, hearts and hands must be given freely and gladly, without force or coercion. Minds enter the flow zone—a state of total commitment and pure enjoyment of the work itself, for the benefit of the cause, and out of love for the people alongside and for whom they labor.[3]

People give their hearts and minds when they are *ignited* by a transcendent purpose, *involved* in problem-solving in service of that purpose, *united* closely with others in the journey, and periodically *revived* by organization rituals or respites of their own devising to keep the energy alive. This chapter shows how BYU Football has crafted their organization to elicit whole-hearted dedication to their unique purpose.

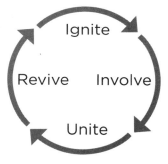

IGNITE

What best rouses a human heart to strive with its fullest effort and reach its greatest capability is a purpose beyond itself.

To understand this, it is important first to recognize that people ultimately derive the greatest satisfaction from endeavors that are compelling because of their intrinsic worth. In other words, when people value and enjoy what they are doing because of the activity itself—not because of rewards that are external to the activity, such as wealth, fame, or good looks—they feel happier and perform better.

Of course, people can find intrinsic pleasures at work even if the mission of the organization does not resonate with them personally.

Every day throughout the world, many people find that they enjoy work not necessarily because it brings profits to shareholders or satisfaction to customers but because they like the challenge of mastering their task or interacting with their peers to solve problems.

But an enterprise guided by a noble cause has an exciting capacity to ignite the interest of investors, employees, and even customers. It creates energy because people want to be part of a worthwhile mission, and investors and employees feel blessed when they actually get paid for doing something worthwhile. Even when people have differing personal reasons for coming to work, everyone can coalesce around a fundamentally noble mission, whether that mission is to protect households through alarm system products or provide surgical services to the underprivileged in Kolkata.

"I don't think any of us can reach our true potential without having our heart and mind completely devoted to what we're doing," says Bronco. "There's a great analogy in war: one free man is better than ten pressed men. If you have an entire army or an entire team that has chosen to come to a place for a purpose and represent that purpose and fight or play for a cause that's bigger than the group, you have a very formidable organization. Capturing hearts and minds—I don't believe that can happen unless it's tied to a vision or a purpose or a cause beyond oneself."

At BYU, Bronco's players love to play football. Some are motivated because their football scholarships provide a means for them to get an education. Others are seeking NFL careers. For some it's the most exciting way to stay fit. For many, the thrill of competition motivates them. What really brings them together, though, is that they see themselves as flag bearers of BYU and The Church of Jesus Christ of Latter-day Saints. They have the audacity to believe that they can be "beacons to the world," that their playing and winning can point others to the good news about things beyond this earth. They sign up by the dozens and then play their hearts out in service of this vision.

"I ask the players to play from the deepest place possible, and that's through their faith," says Bronco. "That is one of the key ingredients as to why we have success—capturing their hearts and minds around a significant cause. Faith is the number one reason they come to BYU. Our surveys say that over 90 percent came primarily because of their faith."

"Never before has any program in America put the word 'Spirit' in the middle of their stadium," says Brandon Doman. He expounds on what he means:

> This means faith in a Creator, in a Heavenly Father. It's who we are and it's our most central core value, and we're going to present it to the world. I would not have taken this job if Bronco had not wanted to do it that way. I had never aspired to be a football coach. I had no intention of quitting the NFL. My wife had informed me several times that I was never to become a football coach. But after my first conversation with Bronco, my heartbeat started speeding up. I spent a lot of time praying about it, thinking about it. If this is for the youth of the Church, then it was very clear to me, spiritually, that that was what I was supposed to do. I have learned in my life that when you receive promptings, you are to follow the promptings. Whether there were going to be fewer zeroes on my paycheck or not, that wasn't significant to me. What was significant was that Heavenly Father had made it clear to me that I was supposed to come take this job. It had nothing to do with football. Being an alum of BYU, it had everything to do with BYU, what it stood for, and what it represents. It had nothing else to do with anything because, quite frankly, I wasn't interested in coming back and just being a football coach.

Joe DuPaix feels the same. "I always aspired to be here. It's like Christmas morning to be able to wake up and know that you're going to come to Brigham Young University. Being LDS, it ties right into my core, to my soul, to my values."

In chapter 4, we talked about some techniques for impressing a vision on a group: metaphor, music, and significant emotional experience. Bronco used them when he was a new coach helping his players transition from the difficult past and join with him in envisioning a victorious future. He ran them up Y Mountain and had them ponder how much better the view is from above. He had them lie out on the grass of LaVell Edwards Stadium to relive great moments from Cougar Football's storied past. The players literally became flag bearers when he put a big blue-and-white "Y" banner in their hands to hold while they ran around the field pregame, the signature of each player affirming his commitment to the program's mission and shared principles.

One year he had a large granite boulder placed front and center in the team room. Bronco showed the team a film clip about John Rowe Moyle, a nineteenth-century immigrant stonecutter who was "called" (invited) by Church president Brigham Young to apply his talent as a mason in the construction of the Salt Lake Temple. He was so dedicated to his assignment that for years he walked over twenty miles weekly to the temple site, tending to his 160-acre farm on Saturdays. When he was kicked by a cow and subsequently lost his leg below the knee, he carved a wooden leg for himself. Walking was painful, but he taught himself to endure it and resumed his weekly trek to the Salt Lake Valley. He persisted for nearly twenty years, dying four years before the temple was finished and put into service.[4]

Bronco taught the team that Moyle was an example of the dedication it takes to build a glorious edifice. He gave each football player a chisel with which they were to engrave their own "calling." A capital "Y" was stenciled on the stone, and when they reached

Chiseling a Y

team goals or were recognized for extraordinary effort, players were invited to chisel away on the stone to bring the Y into relief.

Each day that season, the boulder had its place in the team room, rock powder dusting the carpet at its base, the Y slowly emerging from its upper surface. "What happens when you drive the chisel into the stone?" says Bronco. "Sparks. Sparks fly. Even during the team meetings, you could hear all through the course of the year: 'clink, clink, clink.' Anytime you walked into the office, there's somebody 'clink, clink,' hammering away. Then I'd have players coming to me, 'Coach, my chisel isn't sharp enough. Can you sharpen this for me?' Is that not what a leader does? For those under your care, they limp in or are beaten down, saying 'Can you sharpen this for me? Please, I need help.'"

Using metaphors such as the boulder is a favorite tactic of

Scan this QR code to see "Rock and Chisel" or go to http://bit.ly/LyF2Dt

Bronco's for reinforcing the purpose and values that tie his group together.

INVOLVE

People must be intimately involved in an undertaking if they are to give their hearts and minds in the fullest sense. The best way to get them involved is to give them a choice about what to do to accomplish a goal and how to do it. When they have a choice, they feel free and autonomous. When they feel free, their interest and commitment skyrocket.

The point is not to involve people so as to trick them into thinking that a given set of ideas is their own. The idea is to invite them to participate in the process of developing a new way of doings things. They then not only understand why the shift is merited, but they actually contribute to the bedrock of the change. When they assist with the very development of the solution or its immediate implementation, they become cocreators. They pour their own personal creative energy into the effort, and there is no more fecund human resource.

A second component for increasing engagement is personal competence. In addition to giving freely, people need to feel that they give well—that they make a significant contribution. People enjoy being challenged, but they must have the expertise required by a given task. If they do, they will have a sense of accomplishment and their curiosity will propel them to take on harder tasks and either deepen or broaden their skills.

Accordingly, Cougar players are deeply involved in the program. They do not just show up and comply with what their coaches say. "Bronco has extremely high expectations of these kids, and he lets them choose," says secondary and special teams coach Nick Howell. "He makes it clear to them that it's their choice, and he gets them to make the choice to give their best effort. That's really all he cares about—if they're trying their hardest. Not just in football, but he cares if they try hard in academics and their relationships and their families. When they're having fun, he cares if they're having fun."

The hardest-working, top-performing players are the ones who play on Saturday, which has made BYU very friendly to walk-ons. As of the 2012 season, thirty-three walk-ons have earned scholarships during Bronco's era, including standout players Nate Miekle, Andrew Rich, Dennis Pitta, Bryan Kariya, Jameson Frazier, Reed Hornung, Travis Uale, and JD Falslev. Bronco believes this could be the highest number of walk-ons in the country in an equivalent time frame.

Involvement doesn't just mean playing with gusto. Cougar players run team meetings, serve on the leadership council, and organize firesides and service projects. And when the team is facing a dilemma, the coaching response through the years has been to involve the players in finding a solution.

Special teams are a good example. Remember that special teams coaching was first rearranged after the 2005 season, when the highest ranking of these BYU units was 79 out of 117 NCAA teams—with others ranked as low as 110. Bronco instituted player-coaches because he believed that increasing player participation would have a big effect on performance. Chapter 6 included what player-elected coaches Nate Miekle, Cameron Jensen, and Kelly Poppinga had to say about leading those teams—how they had schematic help from then-special teams coach Patrick Higgins but were free to choose how to select their teams, motivate them, and hold them accountable. They had meaningful autonomy and their task was challenging without being too difficult. Cougar special teams national rankings were better in 2006 by an average of nearly sixty slots.

After 2006, the autonomy given to player-coaches slowly ebbed. When Nick Howell took the special teams reins in 2011, he and Bronco talked through several approaches that "didn't feel just right." So he recommitted to the higher-involvement approach.

But "player-coaching had lost its flavor," says Nick, "and the guys didn't know how to do it anymore." He worked with coauthor Paul and previous player-coaches Nate, Cameron, Kelly, and Bryan Kehl throughout the spring to kick off a new emphasis on player coaching. Special teams rankings at that time hovered near 55 nationally, plus or minus a few ranking spots.

"We were given a lot of freedom about what return scheme to run," says Travis Uale (safety 2008–11, team captain), who was the punt-return team captain:

> Giving the captains freedom to coach, freedom to tell what they think they should be doing, really excited the other players who were on the team because they knew that if they had something to say, they could tell the captain and if it was a viable idea, it would get integrated into the game plan for that week.
>
> It was my idea to bring back the "Wall Return," which we used to score a touchdown against TCU. There are many punt-return schemes that you can use to score a touchdown, but with the Wall Return, not only can you score touchdowns, but it's also fun for the people who run it. It was at a crucial time in the game when we needed to score and it gave our whole team life. I was just happy that it paid off.

The performance of the punt- and kickoff-return teams as well as the kickoff team improved significantly from 2010 to 2011. Player commitment is greatly deepened when other players coach special teams.

Another example of enhanced involvement comes from Duane Busby, the director of Football Operations, who volunteered to step up at crunch time. In early 2011, following the season during which Bronco reclaimed his role as defensive coordinator, Duane says, "It became clear to me that the coaches needed more time to coach; our players needed their full attention." He requested that Bronco shift some of the competitive-enabling work he was doing onto Duane's shoulders.

"Duane came to me after the season and said, 'I don't feel as though I'm doing enough for my salary.' In my opinion," says Bronco, "he wasn't making nearly what he was worth. But he said, 'Here are the things I believe I can really do to help.' He had suggestions about what he wanted to do. Actually, they were the exact same things I had been thinking of asking him to do, anyway."

Duane assumed the role of liaison with key support areas such as the equipment room, strength and conditioning, sports medicine, and the academic center. He wanted to enhance the involvement of these groups. He says:

> If these entities had more autonomy, more ownership of their areas, and if they understood the culture of the organization and believed in it strongly enough, then what they could do exceeds our imagination. On the other hand, if I told them everything to do every day, we would only get whatever my level of expertise is, because all they would be doing is following my instructions. But to really become great, we needed the full investment from each person. And to get that they had to feel they had some autonomy, that they had ownership. No one is going to reach their potential by me just continually telling them what to do. When they have the creative excitement that comes with feeling a part of something, they want it to be great.

In the past, the football staff had made some mistakes by not involving these groups in their decisions. For example, the coaches decided that the best way to motivate struggling students was to display their academic record on the screen at every team meeting. "We did that for a whole season," says Duane, "and everybody in our academic center knew that was the wrong thing to do. They knew it was counterproductive, that it was damaging those kids. They knew it all along. But an organization can get that way—where everyone is just agreeing with whatever you choose to do."

Having recognized this dynamic, Duane set out to change it. He established a weekly meeting that gathered all the support area leaders together.

> We talk about what's going on in the program. They want to know where they can help. We talk about players who are struggling in one way or another. Their opportunity to mentor in the equipment room or in the training room is stronger than even that of the coaches. If you go to a lot of players and ask them who they really talk to about their problems, they'll say the trainer, or the equipment manager. Those people are their sounding boards. There's a different relationship than with a coach who has control over whether you play or don't play. With these people, there's no barrier. So players can just go and say, "I'm so homesick; I want to go home, but I don't dare tell the coach because of how it would look." So we really improved our communication and really began looking at how we could care for our players better.

Once Duane assumed this role, Bronco notes that "there was a completely different level of invigoration and commitment in him. It's changed his job, and I think it's going to change the way these support groups interact as well."

Employees who become engrossed in their work are the most productive and satisfied. "Flow" is when you are so totally absorbed that you lose a sense of your time and self, enjoy the work for its own sake, and afterward feel gratified and accomplished. It's how a middle linebacker might feel as he lines up behind the line of scrimmage on a chilly fall day, gets a feel for the offense, reads the pre-snap formation, and then breaks toward the line of scrimmage post-snap while attending to formation changes and feeling out screen, draws, and trick plays. It's the thrill of mastery that we talked about in chapter 8, when your attention is so focused and ordered that your body or mind takes itself automatically through well-rehearsed routines and draws on extensive experience to make instinctive decisions and develop creative approaches. Total involvement happens when work flows.

UNITE

Besides feeling autonomous and effective, people also need to feel connected to others. It's basic to our well-being. We are social by nature, and we cannot be happy without caring relationships. "We are by far the most social species on earth," says Harvard psychology professor Daniel Gilbert. "Even ants have nothing on us. If I wanted to predict your happiness, and I could know only one thing about you, I wouldn't want to know your gender, religion, health, or income; I'd want to know about your social network—about your friends and family and the strength of your bonds with them."[5]

"Capturing hearts and minds cannot happen without a true and sincere love of the individual," says Bronco. Many of his coaches are motivated by their love for their young players above anything else. "You can have all the systems and the designs and all that stuff, which is great to have," says Nick Howell. "But it's the kids. It's worth facilitating the kids and helping them. Sometimes they're up here," he says, gesturing, "and we're trying to catch up with them, they're so good. It's the kids; it's the people. There are great people here. Good things happen when great people are attracted to an organization. This program just has great people attracted to it and around it."

Players such as Brian Logan have felt the energy of a student body and community closely connected by the ties of faith and shared values of kindness and respect. "I love it here," says Brian, a nondenominational Christian who came to BYU savoring the vindication that this second chance at college football afforded him. (He transferred when his scholarship was rescinded at San Diego State.) He continues:

> Everybody's been so nice. It's funny, because when I first got here, I thought it was fake. I thought this environment with everybody saying "hi" and everybody smiling was fake. I was just like, "Why is everybody being so nice to me?" Because back home, you care about yourself, you care about your family, and you go on with your life. You could care less. Everybody here is just willing to give a helping hand. Especially teammates, but just fans and people out in the community, saying, "If you ever need something, let me know, I can come over, I'll cook you dinner." I have no regrets. I told my mom, "I'm having the time of my life here."

We asked Brian how he came to believe that the caring wasn't fake. He answered:

> It kept going on! I learned more about the Church and I took all of the religion classes. The LDS Church really has a heart for God. You can really see it. You can feel it. That's when I knew that it wasn't fake. It was real. I remember my first religion class I took. People were coming up to me, saying, "If you have any questions, let me know, if I can help you on any assignment, let me know if you need to study"—I realized right then it wasn't fake.

The ties between staff members are strong and lasting. Some of Bronco's relationships go back decades. Inside linebackers coach Paul Tidwell was Bronco's head coach when he was a student at Snow

College. Offensive line coach Mark Weber knew Bronco at Oregon State. Assistant head coach and tight ends coach Lance Reynolds's BYU offense had played against Bronco's UNM defense. Lance, who was in the running for the head coaching job at the same time as Bronco and Kyle Whittingham, had been assured by Bronco before the decision was made that were Bronco to get the job, he would want Lance on his staff. "Different from what probably most people out there think," says Lance, "we remained very, very open through the whole thing. It could have been very ugly, but it wasn't that way at all."

When Whittingham was named head coach at Utah, he invited Lance to join his staff. Meanwhile, Lance's namesake son, Lance, was playing for the Cougars; his next-oldest boy, Dallas, was on a mission; and his youngest, Matt, was being recruited out of high school by colleges across the nation. The commitments of some of Matt's high school teammates such as running back Harvey Unga and wide receiver Luke Ashworth hung in the balance as well. "It was a mess," says Lance. "But Bronco was as patient and as understanding and as calm with me through that whole thing as you can imagine. He told me to take my time to figure it out. He understood. He didn't push me or anything. He didn't rattle my cage. Different from what you would think, knowing what his personality is like."

The balance of the staff members may not go back as far with Bronco, but they are closely united by shared values. "All the coaches at BYU teach and preach exactly what Coach Mendenhall teaches and preaches," says Travis Uale. "There's no other coach teaching a different thing. I think that is such a cool thing. It has brought our team together."

The BYU staff works hard to strengthen their relationships, particularly since the 2008 season, when Bronco suffered badly from burnout. As soon as that season was over, he began very consciously to try to find greater enjoyment in his work. "I was trying to loosen up," he says. Most of his attempts to find greater happiness had to do with strengthening relationships with his colleagues.

He began to focus more on his staff, not just his players. They learned about each other through assessments that described their learning style, their personalities, and their strengths.[6] "What many people think they are good at and what they are actually good at are two different things, which is an amazing concept," says Bronco.

Even as they explored how to better capitalize on each other's talents, Bronco also labored to improve communications with the staff about performance by improving his performance management process, which included developing a rating system that helped staff members clearly talk about their own aspirations and goals as well as Bronco's expectations. "I'm comfortable when I see growth," says Bronco. "When I don't see growth—when I see someone actually going backward, even if we are doing great as a team—I just can't cope with that very well. Complacency is easy when you're winning. And that's something we were fighting against. I want to see unbroken growth in our program, even when we're doing well."

"We've spent a lot of time learning how to communicate with each other, learning about who we are," says Nick. "We all know everyone else: how we think, how we learn, how we communicate, and how we act under stress. Coach Mendenhall wants us to tell him what we think we're great at, and he'll give us the chance to be put in that position. When he evaluates us, he's very honest. It's to help you improve. The feedback he gives me is to help me get better, and he's honest about it."

"I've seen Bronco show great empathy," says Brandon. "I've seen him show a great desire to allow us to grow and develop. We're

 Scan this QR code to see "Performance Management" or go to http://bit.ly/NP1CTD

certainly not perfect and probably create more headaches for him than he ever imagined. He's been very careful and private about helping each one of the coaches develop." He's also created an environment where coaches feel they can speak openly. "He's allowed me to feel as though my feedback is very valued. As long as it's something I feel very strongly about, and I voice it, even though he may not agree with it, he's created an open forum for that to happen."

"I have a way different personality than he does," says Lance. "Sometimes I can't figure out why he keeps me here because I'm so different than he is. I'm quite, quite different in the way I coach and the way I think. But he has never acted as though that was an issue. He handles our differences far more naturally, more easily than I would have thought a man of his intensity would."

But it's not all assessments and performance dialogues. "Team building isn't only for players," says Bronco. "It's for the entire organization. It's more difficult with staff than with players. Players are more idealistic and formative in their opinions. Staff bring with them experiences from other places, their wives' perceptions, their interest in their children. They have more life experiences and they're more set in what they believe and how they are. So it's much more difficult to capture and keep their hearts and minds."

To overcome these difficulties, the coaching team seeks for creative ways to connect. For example, the time when they all rode Harleys to Jackson, Wyoming (see chapter 9) was not just to meet with learning experts from BYU–Idaho, but also to talk about how they could work better together and to renew their bond in other ways.

In one staff meeting, Bronco anointed Mark Weber as their "morale coach" by presenting him with two leis: one, a blue faux fur; the other, a green jadeite necklace. "The fur is for casual days and the green one is more dressy," says Mark, clearly the right man for the job. Upon receiving the assignment, Mark immediately announced that the staff would be going to breakfast on Bronco's dime. Everyone promptly got up and left. The staff meeting was adjourned without further ado.

Paul Tidwell says that Mark is the best morale coach in the country. "It's not hard to be the best morale coach in the country when you're the only morale coach in the country," says Mark. Bronco and Mark put an event on the calendar each month, which Bronco funds. When they planned a bowling outing, Mark had some bowling shirts personalized with specially chosen nicknames, which the training staff helped Mark invent. "We had to be a little sensitive with Bronco because he is the head coach," Mark says, grinning, "so he got a decent nickname. He was the Big Kahuna." Mark won't share his nickname because the training staff called his wife and dug up an unapproved appellation from the past.

But he is willing to elaborate on some other shenanigans, such as an Easter egg hunt on Good Friday right in the football offices. "My wife and daughter and I were filling Easter eggs the night before," he says. "We found a funny little Easter egg that winds up and does a little dance. It reminded us of Bronco, because sometimes he does a little dance. So we put his name on it, and it was the golden egg." The prize was a gift certificate to a supermarket. "There's always a prize involved," says Mark. "Coaches are competitive."

They have shot clay pigeon targets at a shooting range, attended a cross-fit workout, taken motorcycle riding classes at the local Harley-Davidson dealer, and eaten barbecue together on the patio of the Student Athlete Building. The staff seizes lots of opportunities to deepen their connection. They love to be together, and having fun is an important way to enhance their team capability.

Really, their bond energizes the whole team. "I think the morale of the staff is easy for the players to see," says Paul Tidwell. "They know if we're connected or not connected. For them to see us going bowling or skeet shooting or motorcycle riding—when the players see that, they know that we're unified as a staff."

Bronco is careful to reach out to alumni players and former coaches to help them feel a continuing connection with their BYU football associates past and present. "Coach Mendenhall has always been very respectful of the past," says Mike Tanner (linebacker 2000–03; team captain). "Although he didn't play at BYU in college, he's always had a great love and respect for BYU, for the traditions that Coach Edwards built, and for former players and coaches. He really shared it with us as players. What an honor it was to be at a place like BYU with such great traditions." Mike goes on:

> The way he involves players and coaches of the past is something that's second to none. He welcomes all of us with open arms—even people who he never coached. That brotherhood, I guess you could call it, started back with Coach Edwards and definitely carries through with Coach Mendenhall and every coach who I've been involved with at BYU. They have truly created a friendship and a brotherhood that still carries on even ten years after playing. To be a part of that is pretty cool.
>
> At my first alumni reunion a few years ago, what a great experience it was to see some of the past players that I remember my grandpa and my dad talking about. Coach Mendenhall allows the ex-players and some of their family members to come down on the sidelines when the players are warming up. I look over and there's Jim McMahon. I, as an adult, am still in complete awe and shock to be able to stand next to someone such as that, who created the traditions at BYU. Seeing the Gifford Nielsons, and the storied great players of BYU in the past, and Coach Edwards, all

coming out to the alumni barbecue and still being involved in the program is phenomenal.

REVIVE

Bronco insists that his staff and players be "fully invested." This means totally committed, fully engaged. He selected this motto for his first year at the helm (and BYU's athletic marketing department used it on a mass delivery of blue T-shirts into fandom). Freely pouring all the effort they can into their purpose alongside their compadres is exhilarating and fulfilling for the BYU players and staff.

But total focus also requires high-energy output. Complete and constant dedication of your energy in one direction is exhausting. Though Bronco could not be more energized by his work with young athletes and his opportunity to represent his faith, he is by nature, as we have seen, an intensely private person and has been very open about his struggle to meet the most visible demands of his role. Media interviews, public speaking, and the very intense public scrutiny of his coaching performance drain him and wear him down. For these reasons, Bronco has warned that football coaching may not be a lifetime pursuit for him. In the meantime, he has had to cope with deep fatigue and burnout, as do most football coaches and many hard-working professionals in other domains.

High-energy output is sustainable over long periods only when we learn to take in as much energy as we give out in an alternating cycle of investment and replenishment. Just like those athletes who push their physical powers, leaders and other knowledge workers must learn to develop a rhythm of adequate rituals for rest and recovery alongside intense bursts of work.

Athletes who don't learn to add recovery to their training programs eventually begin to falter. They may find themselves unable to pass a skill plateau, or their performance may even slide backward.

On the other hand, athletes who can skillfully find opportunities to rest physically and emotionally, even in the midst of a competition, perform better over a longer span of years. The same is true for those whose efforts are dedicated to business, scholarship, or other mental disciplines.

The ways we choose to replenish our energy matter. For example, watching television is a passive, empty form of relaxation, which can actually lead to greater anxiety and mild depression.[7] Rich sources of recovery that feed us rather than dull us, such as reading, meditating, spending time with friends, or absorbing ourselves in a hobby serve to uplift us and replenish the reservoir inside of us.

We can learn to find rhythms of renewal throughout the day that resonate with the natural cycles of our bodies and our world. Frequent, short periods of rest are often enough to refresh us for the task at hand. Such disengagement is strategic—it is intentional and purposeful and just as important to the success of the mission as are periods of intense productivity.

Once a leader has brought a group or organization to its igniting purpose, involved them in striving toward common challenges, and cultivated their collaborative unity with the right network of fellow journeyers, the challenge is to keep the purpose fresh and to help people connect and reconnect to it firmly and frequently.

Bronco has sought to institute positive rituals for periodic recovery in his own life as well as in the team routine. These rituals variously foster physical, emotional, mental, and spiritual energy.

Organization rituals at BYU Football include the daily all-team meeting. "The reason we have a team meeting for coaches and players at 2:10 every day, *every day*, is to bring them all back," says Bronco. "And the next day, to bring them back. The next day, bring them back. That has to be structured and built in, otherwise the program just so easily ends up at a place you didn't want it to be. When you're a defensive or offensive coach, you're focusing only on scheme and strategy. You end up realizing you have players out there, but you have shells of the players. You don't have their full heart."

So they meet daily, beginning with a prayer, adding a spiritual thought and sometimes a short motivational presentation. The whole team participates together in calling upon God to guide their work, help them learn, keep them safe, and bless their families.

Each day the staff likewise begins their morning together with a prayer. "We ask for the Spirit to help us make right decisions on behalf of our young men," says Nick Howell. "We pray for the health of the kids and their success."

The practice of holding a fireside before each game is another spiritually restorative routine. It embodies the Cougars' belief that their highest work is not playing football but representing the message of the gospel. They share their stories and beliefs about football in the context of their faith, they sing devotional songs, they pray with fans in the audience for their collective edification.

Coach Weber sponsors a Bible study for all interested players, meeting once a week during the season. "Coach Mendenhall wants to have spiritual growth for every athlete here. We're concerned about all our players, whether they're LDS or non-LDS," says Mark, who himself is not a member of The Church of Jesus Christ of Latter-day Saints. "Maybe I just have more sensitivity to some of the needs of the kids who aren't of the LDS faith. We've got a Bible study that's open to anybody. It's actually bigger here than at other programs where I've worked." Mark has always been involved in the faith ministries at other programs and enjoys participating in Bible study at BYU. He has a passion for it. "LDS kids come, and also non-LDS, and it's very generic. It's just to give an opportunity for some more spiritual growth for kids who may not know that much about the LDS faith or who may not have any faith. They just get some general Bible learning, since they don't know of the Book of

Mormon. The Bible is universal, for the LDS kids or non-LDS kids. The study gives some life lessons and principles from the Bible."

Service projects at hospitals and children's clubs are always scheduled as part of bowl-game activities to keep the team grounded in the real reason for their play, even when competitive excitement buzzes in the air and season records hang in the balance.

The yearly run to the Y and other significant rituals remind the team of their heritage and their vision for top-notch achievement.

But amidst this panoply of invigorating practices that constantly reconnect the group as a whole to their mission, values, and highest aspirations, there is plenty of support for activities that smaller groups and individuals devise as ways to recharge.

For his physical energy, Bronco works out in the early hours of the morning. Then for a mental recharge, he takes a midday break from football concerns every day, even during the season—especially during the season. "Twelve to 1:30 is sacred time," he says. "I'm fly fishing, I'm paddle boarding, I'm riding my mountain bike. I disappear for an hour and a half in the middle of the day. I told two coaches from other institutions about that, and they said, 'What world do you live in?' But I know I need to stay fresh. Paul taught me that scheduled events happen more than unscheduled events, so I have things scheduled every day that I do for myself so that I can return and teach in the manner that I need to."

His staff is less likely to take off for fly fishing than for a spin on a stationary bike, a dip in the pool, or a pickup basketball game, offensive staff against defensive. "We try to get out and be active," says Joe DuPaix. "You've got to take care of your mind. You've got to take care of your body. You've got to take care of every part of yourself, so you can help these kids out."

We wrote earlier about the staff's scheduled monthly morale outings where they eat together, play together, or work out together. "It helps keep the tension and pressure down a bit," says Paul

Tidwell. "This is a high-pressure job and to be able to take an afternoon—go have a little bowling tournament with the head coach and the other coaches—is great."

Sometimes they share their fun outright with the players. Take the Village People incident.

You'll remember that during the 2009 season—which ended up as an 11–2 year—Bronco was trying to have more fun because he had nearly burned himself out the year before. As part of the effort, he had taken to playing "YMCA" by the Village People when Mark Weber came into staff meeting. "I don't know why," says Bronco. "It just made people laugh." One day, at a stressful time during the season, the staff hatched a plan to lip sync the song during the team meeting. Those participating took off right then to assemble their costumes. "We were getting ready for practice," says Bronco, "just in a different way."

As the time for the meeting approached, Lance Reynolds went down to the locker room to put the team on edge. He told them that their head coach had seen someone use a cell phone at an inopportune time the day before, and he was really angry, so they better not bring their phones to the team meeting. Then he told them to hurry upstairs, and he started the meeting. The team was terrified. Duane Busby had the music video cued up, and as it rolled, players quietly looked at each other, trying to figure out what was going on.

"When it got to the chorus, we opened the door and danced in," says Bronco. "Coach Weber was the construction worker, dressed exactly like the character from the Village People. Jaime [Hill] was the traffic cop. Kaufusi was the Indian chief in full head dress and chaps. I was the cowboy. Barry Lamb was the biker guy. His was the best costume by far.

"The team absolutely just went crazy. I've never seen a team—I mean, they were just rolling. They were in the aisles. They were falling on top of each other. It was just madness. We were all up front, dancing."

Sadly, there are no photos of that day. Bronco had had the foresight to make sure of it by forbidding cell phones.

This is a raucous example of an event that rejuvenated emotional energy during a time of the year when energy output is extreme for everyone.

We—Paul and Alyson—vouch for the fact that the relationships at BYU Football are based on genuine caring. All of the coaches warmly welcome us when we visit for consulting or for interviews. They invite us to join their patio barbecues. We see them joke and banter with each other.

But one interaction impressed us even more than most. Alyson was waiting for an interview with Lance Reynolds one afternoon when a starter who had recently withdrawn from the program due to an Honor Code violation came to the football offices. He stopped in the hall to chat with another coach, and then Lance arrived and saw this player before he saw Alyson. She overheard their conversation. Lance greeted the young man and joined in the chatting. After a bit, Lance said, urgently, "Don't think that we don't love you around here. Don't think that we think any less of you, because we don't."

"I would never think that, Coach," said the young man.

It was clear to Alyson that Coach Reynolds's relationship with the player was still loving and comfortable despite the setback to the young man and to the program. He had been welcomed warmly by all the coaches in the building that day, and he spent some time in the halls and their offices.

Alyson mentioned the conversation to Lance at the end of the interview, and he was a bit embarrassed that she had overheard. "You want the kid to go have success and you want him to be able to deal with his problem," says Lance. "You want anybody who has issues to be able to come out of it, doing the right thing and taking the right course and having a good life. They ought to be able to look back in ten years and believe that football was a great experience and people cared about them. You honestly hope they have success and get things worked out and get their lives rolling, whatever they end up doing."

CAPTURING HEARTS AND MINDS: 2010

Now that we've discussed the principles for capturing hearts and minds, let's go back to 2010 and remember that sinking feeling that plagued the teams and fans as BYU began the season with its slowest five-game start (1–4) in thirty-seven years.

They were a young team, with a disproportionate number of freshmen, red-shirt freshmen, and sophomores. They were reeling from having lost an "embarrassment of offensive riches practically unparalleled in the Cougars' long football history," as BYU radio broadcaster Greg Wrubell described it, referring to standouts John Beck, Curtis Brown, Max Hall, Austin Collie, Dennis Pitta, Harvey Unga, and Andrew George. "These weren't just great players," he says. "They were all among BYU's top two or three at their respective positions, all-time."[8]

In Bronco's estimation, the four key positions on the field are quarterback, offensive center, middle linebacker, and strong safety. Those four position players make the majority of decisions on game day. They call the plays in real time at the line of scrimmage and influence what everyone else does. "They each have to be a coach on the field," says Bronco.

In 2010—following the graduation of Max Hall (quarterback), R. J. Willing (center), and Matt Bauman (middle linebacker)—three of those key starters were new. Freshman Jake Heaps and junior Riley Nelson had teamed up at quarterback, though the more experienced Riley was lost for the year with a shoulder injury in the season's third game. Terence Brown was at center, and Shane Hunter was at middle linebacker. Andrew Rich at strong safety was the only returning starter in the group.

The new squad had little experience with true adversity. "My first year [2005] we went 6–5, then lost a bowl game," said Vic So'oto (tight end/defensive line 2005–10) at the time. "I don't think the guys know how much work was put in to have this string of four [winning] seasons go like they did." He was willing to assume some of the blame. "It's my fault, and our fault as seniors, for not bringing these young guys along and letting them know how it is to play BYU Football the way we should play."[9]

But the person who accepted the most blame was Bronco himself. "I was the head coach, but I wasn't leading," he says. "I was being very passive, and I had delegated a lot of the competitive work to my coaches." He felt he should have been more hands-on with this young team. After a fourth consecutive loss early in the season, Bronco released the defensive coordinator and utterly changed tactics.

For weeks the idea of making the staff change had been presenting itself to him, but it conflicted with his concern for the coach and the negative impact on his family, and he repeatedly quelled it. Firing someone mid-season is almost unheard of in college football, let alone at BYU, where replacing staff anytime happens far less frequently than in other football programs. "Those kinds of wrestles are something that any leader can associate with," says Bronco. "They're rarely spur-of-the-moment decisions. Many times people say in retrospect that they should have acted faster, not slower. But you try to see the best in others and you work as hard as you can to make it work. You try to give every opportunity, and usually it's at the expense of your organization for a while. I think any leader would understand that. But that's an individual decision that has to be handled uniquely and privately." Finally Bronco made the change, assuming the defensive coordinator's role and hiring former player and then-graduate assistant Kelly Poppinga to round out the defensive staff.

It was a shocking mid-season overhaul and the most poignant imperative for renewal Bronco had ever faced. "It was very traumatic and hard," says Bronco. It required quick action to consolidate hearts and minds.

He did it through methods that were familiar to the Cougars and that we described earlier in this chapter—a refocus on the ultimate purpose of the program, a return to an exceptionally challenging practice style, and drills and symbolic activities crafted to restore team unity by emphasizing a commitment to mutual support.

The turnaround began on the Monday morning after the Utah State loss. Bronco tossed the defensive staff's usual game planning agenda and instead reworked the vision of the defense with the involvement of the whole defensive staff. He wrote on an enormous white board as they talked, which the defensive staff has never erased and which remains a fixture in the room to remind them of their turnaround that season. It was a full-out effort to recapture hearts and minds, and it amounted to nothing short of a complete return to the established basics of Cougar Football. In Bronco's own words:

> The first thing the coaches said is that we have to become unified. The defensive staff felt that the true core values of what BYU represents, and our faith, were not being used as a real strength or point of reference for why any of us were here.
>
> The coaches believed that once that was in place, then our players would find this very exciting because they would see the change, they would notice the tangibility of it, they would embrace the connectivity that they would feel to each other and the staff. That would inspire and invigorate them

to recover from a one and four start, which hadn't happened at BYU for a long time.

If they did that, it would then start putting smiles on their faces, and they'd actually enjoy what they were doing.

Players were going to have to be challenged, but challenged in a way that would build them up and have them reaching for their divine potential. Challenged in relation to what they believed in and what they were representing. That would help them overcome the adversity because their effort was going to be tied to a purpose. Being motivated toward a purpose is one of the greatest motivators there is, which they had lost. They were just playing the game—not even *playing* the game, just being participants in the game.

Then we discussed how that was going to happen. I said that in my opinion, coaching is nothing other than teaching, and teaching is about service. The goal of service according to the scriptures is because you love somebody. "When ye are in the service of your fellow beings ye are only in the service of your God."[10]

I think that coaching is not players serving coaches, but coaches serving players. That certainly had not been the case. What I didn't think was happening is that the coaches weren't loving the players. They didn't care about them in a manner that was tangible nor noticeable nor sincere, which means that they really weren't coaching or teaching them.

So I started naming players. I asked, "Do you love so-and-so?" I paused. "It doesn't look like it. How would he know?" I tried to give tangible examples. The best examples come from the gospel, and the term that I like to use is disciple leadership. I asked, "Disciples learn from whom?"

They all said, "Christ."

I then asked, "Is it possible to coach while emulating the

Savior? That's what I would like you to do from now going forward, which is disciple leadership. Where better to do it than BYU, which is owned by The Church of Jesus Christ of Latter-day Saints, which has Christ as its cornerstone. Why shouldn't the way you lead reflect that?"

I said, "The great benefit we have now is I think all of you have been humbled to the point where you're now teachable. Without humility, you won't be teachable."

They were anxious to be taught, and they wanted to be taught. So this actually worked in our favor because they were truly seeking answers, as were our players. They were ready for something to be different.

Then after this philosophical part of our discussion, we got into the functional part or the execution part. We talked a lot about our existing strategy. We said we intend to make this as simple as we can, as easy as we can, so we can gain speed and the players' confidence and build simple successes. That would start to inspire the players. They would love us, and we would love them. We then could change their lives so they could change others' lives, which is the big picture. All of that means that the culture would change.

The defense didn't have an identity, and they needed one. We decided it was going to be based on how hard they tried. They didn't know what they were doing, especially in the run game. We had to be better in the run. We had to address that. You can't control the game if the offense of the other team can run effectively because then they control the clock, and they control the football. You can't ever make good defensive calls strategically if you are always facing 3rd and 2. So we knew we had to fix that.

The secondary was giving up big plays because the system was so elaborate that it was just too much. They were

playing slow, which made it look as though they weren't trying hard, which then deterred their confidence. They had
to know what they were going to do by practicing the right
calls, and they had to know exactly what their assignments
were so they could regain their confidence.

Then we went to the call board and erased the entire
thing. We never looked at it again. We never watched any
film from the previous four or five weeks. We started again
from ground zero. Every call had a purpose. If we couldn't
define why we needed it and how we complemented it, it
didn't go on the board. The idea was to have very few calls
so we could work on the rest of it.

"We talked about how we could help this particular group of
kids reach their potential because they weren't reaching their potential, and it wasn't their fault, really," adds Nick Howell. "We didn't
do anything to prepare for [the next game against] San Diego State,
so we were a day behind. But there's something to be said for getting
the mission just exactly right."

They had it right by the time the defensive players came for practice that afternoon. Now it was Bronco's moment to capture their
hearts and minds, even as he had done with his staff that morning.

"He brought the defense into the defensive team room and
asked us if we trusted him," says Travis Uale. "A few guys nodded
their heads, a few guys said yes. Then he asked us again. He said,
'Do you guys trust me?'" Every hand went up.

"'If that's the case,' Bronco said, 'then what I'm going to ask you
to do is commit to a completely new way of practice and mindset.'

"We were kind of looking around at each other like, 'We don't
know what that means,'" says Travis. "We found out shortly that
that means a lot of running until we were conditioned."

"I believe that physical conditioning is the habit of total effort," says Bronco. "I had someone read a sign in the defense room that says that. I had them read it every day the rest of the year out loud. They weren't in the habit of giving total effort. They didn't want to, they didn't know how, and they didn't know really why. That had to be rebuilt. What I found is that they were craving it."

"We were just hungry for a win, because we had been losing for so long," says Travis. "We were just desperate to do whatever it took to get a win."

"The pace of practice changed," confirms Steve Kaufusi. "There was a sense of urgency in all the drills. We went back to being more physical. Intense effort through every drill to the finish. Normally, during the season you kind of tone it down a little bit because injuries pile up. We felt as though we were going back to boot camp. For him to come back in the driver's seat and take over—some of those younger kids didn't quite know his style. For a lot of the older kids, they welcomed him back, because they knew what he had done in the past."

"I'll never forget that week of practice," says Travis. "I would come home and I couldn't even stand because we would be running—just running, running, running. I didn't realize the importance of just conditioning itself. He made practices so hard that games became easy. He worked on conditioning first, and then we started working on our fundamentals." Travis continues:

> It helped us come together as a defense. It helped us to lean on each other because there were times where one guy was tired and we needed to help him out. Coach focused our drills to being able to do it as a whole defense. If one guy didn't do it right, then that rep didn't count. So we realized that we had to stick together and we had to trust in each other to be able to play good defense.
>
> All that translates into life. Sometimes I think things

are hard in life, but they're really not. Coach Mendenhall took my mind to places that I hadn't ever thought it was possible that I could run that much or last that long in a game. I never thought that a game could be easy, but he trained our minds to be able to go past our limits and exceed expectations.

To emphasize the importance of precision effort, Bronco instituted a point system for the defense that held them accountable for every ball they allowed the scout team offense to advance past the line of scrimmage. (We mention this system in chapter 8.) To pay off any deficit in their accounts, Bronco put them through a new line drill that developed a little notoriety of its own. It has since come to be called "Perfect 10s." Again, in Bronco's own words:

> At the end of practice, I had them line up as a defense, five yards away from a line of scrimmage that was clearly delineated. There were three commands.
>
> Number one was, "Walk up." They had to walk up together to the line of scrimmage. If they walked up in a wave, some outpacing the others, it wasn't going to count.
>
> Then I would say, "Down." They all had to put their hands down at the same time, in precision, not one after the other. Not a hand could touch the white line.
>
> Then when I moved the football, they had to sprint off the line of scrimmage together as hard as they could go through ten yards.
>
> That would count as one point in terms of erasing the debt that they'd incurred for practice. So the precision in execution would erase the mistake that they'd made earlier. I had two coaches stationed at the line of scrimmage and two at the plus-ten line, some even lying down. After the drill I

would look to the coaches. There had to be four thumbs up for that rep to count.

The first day the team had twelve or sixteen points to account for. We did maybe seventy reps of the drill to erase those points. Again, when you're talking now about forty players who had to walk up together, put their hands down together, come off the ball at the same time and finish running as hard as they could run—if any one player didn't, it didn't count for the entire group. They had to rely on each other.

What happened is the people who were walking out of the building stopped, equipment managers stopped. Practice was over, but everyone stopped to see what was going on. It went on for a long time. It went on until they did at least twelve or sixteen right. The clear message was that they would be accountable for every practice and every play in practice because they said they trusted me. If they can't run ten yards hard together, they can't play the game.

About halfway through that drill that first day with the defensive players, they were getting exhausted. They realized this wasn't going to go away. They started to reach out to one another and hold hands so they would approach the line of scrimmage together. If someone was slightly behind, they would pull him up. I'd never anticipated that would happen but within a half hour, they were holding hands and the barriers were gone. They weren't told to. It wasn't even suggested they do that. That just happened.

From that point, the defense never lost another practice with the scout team the rest of the year. Not one. The reason the change happened so quickly is that they were just simply held accountable to something they wanted to do anyway.

I show film of the drill at the coaches' clinics that I go to. It becomes dead silent. No one can believe what it looks like.

From that point on, every single thing on the white board that recorded the new vision happened. With the right design elements and with the right accountability, our vision transferred to the entire team.

The solution that season was a defensive solution, but the solution really was a leadership solution. I had been playing an advisory or support role, but the players needed someone on the ground to link arms with and to see a tangible example every day and up close of what real effort is supposed to look like.

It was not easy. It was tough love. It wasn't coddling. It was just the opposite of that. But the motive was love. It was very hard, and we were all tired. But it was for the right reason. The coaches hadn't been seeing what coaching and love needs to look like, so they didn't know how to do it, nor were the players responding. But once they saw it, they recognized it.

This is when the old Band of Brothers T-shirt made its appearance on game day. Bronco wore it at the next game, which was against San Diego State in Provo. So did the players.

"We are all wearing that shirt now because that's who we want to be," said Travis Uale at the time. "That's who we tell the world we are. It's not just to show people, but to actually be that person, to be a brother."

At the start of every series, Bronco lined the defense up on the sidelines in a three-point stance, sending them onto the field in a sprint. "That man is crazy," said Kyle Van Noy (linebacker 2010–). "When you have us in a three-point stance to start, it's crazy; but to us, it means the world. He's our leader. He's the man. He tells us what to do and we do it, because we trust him."[11]

Their trust in Bronco rippled throughout the team. "As a defensive unit, we feel more united than ever," said Travis. "We feel more comfortable out there. The emphasis was on us being a unit and not being separate entities, like the defensive backs or the linebackers or the D-line, but playing together as a defensive unit and trusting the guy in front of you, knowing he's going to get his job done."[12]

Trusting relations are required for learning and change. "Nothing is as fast as the speed of trust," says Stephen M. R. Covey.[13]

The Cougars certainly needed a fast turnaround. Their 24–21 win over San Diego State was "just half a notch beneath essential," according to Bronco, "because there were some pretty drastic changes made, and you like to have something substantial to show as soon as possible."[14]

"When trust is high, the dividend you receive is like a performance multiplier, elevating and improving every dimension of your organization and your life," says Covey.[15]

Brandon Bradley was inspired to give his trust because he felt so much love from Bronco. "You could feel the emotion, the desire and the love he has for us as well as the program and this school," Brandon said at the time. "Anytime you have a coach such as that, it makes it so much easier to go out and give everything you have. The intensity was taken to another level."[16]

Other defensive players echoed the sentiment—and this is a group of young men who had been worked to the bone all week. "You can really see how much he cares about us," said J. J. Di Luigi (running back 2007–11). "He's more involved with us now than he ever has been. It showed all week through practice, and I think that's why we came out and played so hard, because of what he was showing us, the emotion that he sent to us."[17]

"You saw Coach Mendenhall wearing his 'Band of Brothers'

shirt," said Shane Hunter (linebacker 2007–10). "I mean, that's what we're all about, being together as a team. The offense was cheering for the defense and the defense was cheering on the offense. Everyone was lifting each other up, and it was contagious."[18]

"Noticeable immediately was the change and the attitude of the players, their work ethic, how they bought into what he wanted," says Paul Tidwell. "It wasn't just defense. It was the offense as well. It started that Monday and it went all the way through spring ball. At the end of the season when we finished our bowl game, I think the players were still hungry for more. They weren't ready for the season to end, because we were just really hitting our stride. When we ended spring, the last day was just as energetic as the first day, which is difficult to do in spring ball, because usually spring is a grind."

After a 1–4 start, BYU would win six of its final eight games, with the only losses coming at 7-ranked TCU and 22-ranked Utah. The 7–6 season culminated with a blowout victory over UTEP in the New Mexico Bowl.

Before moving on, we want to tell of a small mid-season incident that had buoyed Bronco through this turbulent autumn. On the Monday after the loss to Utah State and the ensuing staffing shuffle, even before Bronco had met with players to win their trust as their new defensive coordinator, he left campus for his usual midday break.

I took off on a drive, going nowhere in particular, just to get out of the office. I've always given Carey, my secretary, strict instructions that no one can find me between noon and 1:30. I was rounding the Point of the Mountain, heading toward Salt Lake, when my phone rang. I saw that it was Carey. I said, "What?" in an annoyed tone.

Her voice was kind of cracking, and she said, "I have a phone call for you from President Packer. He's on the line." Once I heard it was President Packer [a high-ranking Church leader], I realized this could be a turning point. I wondered if he was calling to release me from my position or for something church related. I just wasn't quite sure.

In about a ten-second span, before he picked up the phone, I did a life evaluation. That's really all it took, even though I was forty-five at the time, to review everything that I've done in my life. It only took about ten seconds to see if I was living in a way that I should be.

I said, "Hello," in kind of shaky voice. I knew that President Packer, by reputation, speaks very bluntly. He asked if the head cheerleader position was open. I wasn't sure if he was making a joke or if he was inquiring maybe for a granddaughter. There was an awkward silence, and then I realized he was making a joke, but I had missed the window. I kind of laughed after the fact. He went on to say, in effect, "We want you to know how much we support what you're doing and not only what you're doing, but how you're doing it." He said if the head cheerleader job wasn't taken, he would like the job. Then he hung up.

I pondered what he had said. Number one, the fact that he had called really touched my heart. Number two, with all the things that he had going, it mattered that he was showing support, that he was sensitive enough to look after a leader who might be struggling. That phone call mattered a great deal to me, and it was a turning point for the season.

CAPTURING HEARTS AND MINDS: 2011

We know what happened as 2011 began: even bigger changes. A new offensive coordinator (Brandon Doman) and two new offensive position coaches (Joe DuPaix for the running backs and Ben

Cahoon for the wide receivers). A new offensive strategy. Football independence. And a quarterback shakeup that nobody could have predicted.

As we mentioned in chapter 8, Jake won the starting job coming out of the 2010 season. While Riley adjusted to his backup role, even volunteering for the scout kickoff and punt-cover teams, Jake was deepening his relationship with Brandon and working with him on the new pro-style/West Coast offense.

"I've been around a lot of great quarterback coaches, and [Coach Doman] is one of the best there is," Heaps says. "To be able to be around him and pick his brain and to be able to have the opportunity to not only have him as my coach but now as the offensive coordinator, being able to be on the same page and work[ing] together, it's just phenomenal. We're very close. It gets as close as you can get between a coach and a player."[19]

But five weeks into the 2011 season Jake was faltering, and BYU was on the verge of a second consecutive loss to Utah State, which would have dropped the Cougars to 2–3 on the season. Brandon inserted Riley into the game against the Aggies late in the third quarter, with BYU trailing 21–13, and it was Riley who captured the hearts and minds of his teammates, his coaches, and the fans. He rallied BYU to a pair of fourth-quarter touchdowns, the last of which came in the closing seconds, as Riley capped a ninety-six-yard drive with a touchdown pass that gave the Cougars a dramatic 27–24 comeback victory.

How did he have their hearts so instantaneously? Long before the game, he had won the devotion of his teammates with his hard work, persistence, and good humor. Journalist Jay Drew gathered together many of their comments:

> Two of his teammates have called him "a gritty dude"
> the past few days. Another referred to him as a "California

surfer-type of guy" while a senior defensive back called him a "survivor" and a "mister positive" type of person who never, ever gets down on himself or his teammates.

BYU backup quarterback Riley Nelson has been called a lot of things since he came off the bench. . . .

Quitter, slacker, malingerer or malcontent is definitely not one of them. Leader, hard worker and fierce competitor definitely are.

"I believe in him," said linebacker Brandon Ogletree. " . . . Riley is one of the hardest workers I know. He is gritty, and he is tough. Man, props to him, because he has had a tough road, and he has stayed with it. And it is inspiring. You saw the way the team rallied around him [at the Utah State game].

"Riley is just a gritty dude, you know? He is kind of ugly," BYU center Terence Brown said with a laugh. "He is just a guy that plays hard. He is not 6-2, he doesn't have an arm, he can't throw the ball 80 yards. But the dude plays hard, and he plays with his heart."[20]

In the final analysis, Jake's struggles may have been largely because the playful and persevering Riley had won the hearts of his teammates long before Jake arrived fresh from high school to begin spring ball with the Cougars. "He had been with them longer and the team had a deeper relationship and a deeper tie to Riley," says Bronco. "Riley was just a different personality and a different maturity level." He had served a mission as had so many of the other players, and he had Division I experience from his year as a backup to Max Hall and his freshman season at Utah State.

Jake gamely battled for the starting spot and won it at last, but Riley's moxie served him well when it came to making plays and inspiring players. In the end, that became the deciding factor.

CHAPTER 11

Impossible

BYU is such a unique place that what would work in another place really wouldn't work here. I'm not sure that what Bronco does here could be replicated because as he has often said, football is not only not the *only* thing, it's not the *first* thing on the list.

Bronco has been not only a consistent leader, but he's been a clear leader. He's always been focused on mission. One of the great things about Bronco is that what you see is what you get. For example, when he has a challenge, and you hear him talk about it, he says the same thing in private as he does in public. So the young men that are in his program understand what his expectations are and what the University's expectations are.

—CECIL O. SAMUELSON JR.
PRESIDENT OF BRIGHAM YOUNG UNIVERSITY 2003–PRESENT

BRONCO MENDENHALL wanted to build a sustainable competitive advantage for the BYU football team, and he wanted to do it while firmly adhering to—even promoting—the values of his faith and holding his players to the same standard. Thus, he discouraged his players from making football their top priority. He asked them to put their faith, their families, their schooling, and even their friendships ahead of the game. Is this possible while still fielding an elite college football team? "If it sounds like fantasy, it probably is," wrote Chad Nielson for *ESPN: The Magazine* in 2005.[1]

It was not a fantasy.

THE RESULTS

• The Cougars' record during Bronco's first seven years was 66–24. Only fourteen other teams won more during that time.[2]

• BYU achieved ten or more wins in five of Bronco's first seven seasons. Only seven other college teams equaled the feat,[3] and only four other teams put up more double-digit winning seasons.[4]

• In the six seasons from 2006–2011, BYU was ranked five times at season's end in the *USA Today* Coaches Poll. Only eight other teams achieved this kind of consistent success,[5] with only one of those eight being ranked nationally all six seasons.[6] BYU was also one of only eleven programs nationally to achieve that consistent level of final national ranking when considering both major national polls.

• BYU won five bowl games from 2006–2011, one of only seven schools to do so. The Cougars' 2011 win over Tulsa in the Armed Forces Bowl was BYU's third consecutive bowl victory, a program first.

Now, what of those higher priorities that outrank football?

• Seven Academic All-American citations were received by six BYU football players between 2005 and 2011. This was the third highest in NCAA Division 1 programs.[7]

• Between 2007 and 2011, twenty-five players were recognized by the National Football Foundation & College Hall of Fame (NFF) as members of the Hampshire Honor Society. This honor, first bestowed in 2007, is given to collegiate players who maintain a cumulative 3.2 GPA or better throughout their college career. BYU had the most honorees among NCAA Division I schools in 2010 and tied for the most in 2011. In 2012 it was tied for the second-most honorees.

• Between 2005 and 2011, 258 players served two-year missions for The Church of Jesus Christ of Latter-day Saints across the globe. Regularly, one fourth of the players on the Cougar roster are on missions. In each recruiting class, at least half of the signed players leave for a mission before enrolling at BYU; a dozen or so players return from missions each year to rejoin the team.[8]

• One hundred thirty-three team members played as married men—far more than any other program in the country.

Leaving the Mountain West Conference and entering football independence in 2011, BYU's steady performance helped the program secure an eight-year contract with ESPN, with many of BYU's games broadcast on "The Worldwide Leader" and its family of networks. The agreement allowed BYUtv to rebroadcast all ESPN games and also to broadcast live any games not claimed by ESPN. At the same time BYU's new TV deal was announced, the football program also entered into a six-year series with Notre Dame.

"True to their mission as flag bearers, they had achieved broad, nationwide access to [their] games for [their] large, national following," BYU President Cecil O. Samuelson Jr. said of the Cougars at the time of the announcements.[9]

In BYU's first year of independence, ESPN broadcasts of Cougar football far exceeded the minimum quota of games required by the contract. Including the bowl game, five BYU contests were broadcast on ESPN, four aired on ESPN2, and two more were seen on ESPNU—that's eleven games with an average total audience per game of 1.2 million households or 1.6 million viewers. Another game was offered on KBYU/Fox College Sports Pacific, and one game was broadcast exclusively on BYUtv. Before the start of the season's third game, 2011 viewership had already surpassed

BYU Football's combined TV audience during Bronco's previous six years. BYU Football's distribution in 2011 had a cumulative total of 1.2 billion homes.[10] When ranking teams that had games available during the season to a national audience of 100 million homes or more, only five programs ranked ahead of BYU's nine such telecasts in 2011: Notre Dame, Louisiana State, Ohio State, Oklahoma, and Wisconsin.[11]

Not only did national exposure increase BYU's audience considerably, but it greatly enhanced the interest of potential recruits. Brandon Doman explains:

> In past years, we'd go out and recruit and the only game anybody had seen was our bowl game because it was the only game that people had access to on television. Now in 2011 we were on two or three Friday night games where the entire country watched. Every college football team in America is in a hotel on Friday night watching one game, and it was us. Now if you're winning those games, your credibility increases significantly, and that's what's happened. The Utah State game when Riley came into the game and we came from behind and won—that was a Friday night game. It was seen by a massive audience. The exposure is phenomenal. Our ability to share the message that we have to share has increased tenfold.

Recruiting coordinator Joe DuPaix adds that "the increased exposure has definitely attracted more recruits and more coaches, and it has educated the coaches and recruits throughout the country on what BYU is and what BYU stands for and the success of our program." The number of calls and e-mails and unsolicited highlight films received from high school athletes shot up considerably compared to previous years.[12]

President Samuelson gives Bronco high marks not only for

266

leading the team to merit such massive exposure, but for the values he has championed along the way. "We're proud of Bronco," he says. "We're grateful for what he's done."

> We think that BYU is a great place. He understands that it's bigger than the football coach, or the team, or University president, or anybody else. He's made a tremendous effort with real success to ensure that everyone, both in and out of the University, understands what a special place we think this is.
>
> I agree with what the coach says. A winning record makes it much easier for people to pay attention to the real reason that we play football. It would not be nearly the success that it is if we were winning only one or two games a year rather than losing only one or two games a year. I have great admiration for him, great respect for what he's done.
>
> It is a remarkable thing to recognize that here's a man of high character who expects his people to be of high character. He's very, very clear that BYU Football is part of something much bigger and much more important than just athletics, and therefore those that are here need to understand that and be willing not only to tolerate it, but to buy into the mission. I think he's had great success in doing that. I've observed with both appreciation and admiration that the young men who come here, even those that are not Latter-day Saints, do understand that the place does have a unique mission and do understand that it is not only a responsibility but a privilege to represent these things.

"Bronco's success on the field has been noteworthy and important because the principles that have guided the football program, which are certainly in alignment with the principles that guide the university, have resulted in a winning football team," says Kevin

Worthen, BYU's Advancement Vice President. "I was not in my current position when he was hired. At the time, as a fan looking on, I admit that there was part of me that wasn't 100 percent sure it would work. But I believed the experiment was worth trying, because I know those principles are effective in other contexts. Now we know they can help create a successful football team as well."

LEARN AND APPLY

Bronco believes that what has been accomplished at BYU Football could not have come to pass without organization design principles and practices honed in the world of business and then adapted to the world of collegiate football. These are summarized as the five smooth stones. Bronco learned them from coauthor Paul and from his extensive readings and then creatively applied them in the unique milieu of BYU Football. He recommends them to you. You can turn to section 2 for more about them and for suggestions about how you can put these tools to work as well.

There are many other factors that have also contributed to the success of the Cougars—the dedication of outstanding teacher-coaches, the strong support of university and Church leaders, the extraordinary effort of student athletes, the steadfastness and encouragement of family members, and the quiet, consistent promptings from the Spirit that helped Paul find the right advice at the right time and that assured Bronco of what to do in the face of his challenges.

THE RESPONSIBILITY

BYU Football's success has been a joy and pleasure to Cougar fans, to players who've found a spot on the BYU roster, to coaches who've worked at this family-friendly place with top notch youth, and to Bronco.

But there are some costs.

"I don't think people realize how mentally and emotionally hard football is, and how hard it is here, especially when you're young and you're trying to establish yourself," says Jan Jorgensen. "When you first come in, you're trying to perform and you're trying to earn a spot, and it seems you can't do anything right. Everything is extremely tough. At times it sends you into depression because it's so hard."

Matt Bauman felt the pressure academically. "There's a lot demanded of you, and I think for every player there's a different answer." Matt received numerous awards for his accomplishments as a student-athlete including two *ESPN: the Magazine* Academic All-American citations and a prestigious NCAA Postgraduate Scholarship. But it wasn't easy.

I had an academic scholarship and that required at least fourteen credits. I usually took at least two more. I had fifteen or sixteen credits every semester. I had to maintain a 3.9 grade point average to keep that academic scholarship as well, so the rigors of being a scholar-athlete were really demanding, especially at BYU. It's challenging at school academically. Then in the position I was—mike [middle] linebacker—there was a ton of weight and pressure put on me to really understand the defense, to know our opponents better than anyone else on our defense. It was a lot of pressure put on me just to watch extra film, to spend extra time with the coaches, and so, for me, the toughest thing was really just the demand on my time.

I learned to use every moment I had. I would literally have papers in my backpack—notes from a class—and I would be reviewing them for a test while I was walking between classes. Any spare second I had where I didn't have something I was doing, I planned for it. I figured out something I could do in that little half-hour window. So I just really utilized all my time well. I learned time management, learned how to handle a lot on your plate, which is a valuable life skill as well.

Matt Reynolds felt that no matter where he went, he had to always be on his best behavior:

BYU Football has been so popular over the years. Because it's a Church-owned school and because it's recognized throughout the country, there are followers everywhere. You really are recognized as a football player for BYU everywhere you go. That's obviously going to put stress on you, and you do have to remember that. But there are pluses to that as well. It's a huge blessing to be able to be a part of the program and people see you in a positive light because you are a BYU football player. But at the same time you also have the pressure to keep that light positive.

For example, my wife and I went shopping, and a lady got mad at me because it was raining and my wife ran to the car. The lady thought I had sent her to come pick me up. In reality, I just had a hot dog and I wanted to finish my hot dog before I left. My wife was freezing so I gave her the keys to go warm up in the car. I told the lady what happened. She said, "Oh, that's good. I didn't want a BYU football player to not be chivalrous." I wasn't wearing anything with BYU on it; she just recognized me.

At the same time I do think it's a good thing, because that's something that I think we need to learn especially if you're a member of the LDS faith or any faith or any other type of community. You should always be aware of what type of impression, what type of person you're being in any situation.

Bronco himself has felt the pressure as keenly as anyone. "The first two seasons, I threw up every day before work," he says. The self-doubt he had felt since a child combined with his keen desire to please culminated in anxiety that plagued him until only recently. "How I got like that, I'm not sure," says Bronco. "My parents were my biggest allies and advocates of confidence and peace and joy. I might have come out of the pre-mortal existence like that."

But Bronco has changed.

"Finally, after all these years, my purpose in life is not tied in my mind to performance on the field. It's taken me a long time. That's why I'm so passionate about saying that football is just a game. I've lived the other life and ultimately, when we leave this world, it's not going to matter how many games we won. What's going to matter is what kind of husband and father we were and what kind of faith we had. Did we help other people? That's what's going to matter."

His players and colleagues have watched him morph right before their eyes.

"Coach Mendenhall has changed tremendously from when I first saw him as a defensive coordinator," says Cameron Jensen. "He wasn't social at all with his players. I think I probably must have said ten words to him my whole redshirt year, even into my sophomore year. He was very closed, very closed. Now he's more open. He's more sharing of the knowledge that he's learning. I would have never thought at the start that he'd give me control of special teams. Never. He did everything his way, and he loved having control of the defense. When he decided to give more ownership to the players, that was not natural."

By all means, Bronco remains strict. "He clearly defines the goals and objectives that he's after," says Nate Miekle. "Nobody runs a tighter ship than he does. At meals, you don't talk on your cell phone. You respect your teachers. You go to class. You practice full bore. You know in any situation what he would want you to be doing, whether it is in the classroom, or at church, or anywhere." Nate adds:

> The paradox comes that in this framework, no coach has given us so much ownership and freedom. In some sense, you have no freedom. But by living by his standards, it actually enables you and gives you more freedom than you've ever been entrusted with on a sports team. To be able to walk that line—nobody does it better than he does.

"He is basically a Marine drill sergeant by nature," says Lance Reynolds, but in the next breath says, "He's way engaging, way involving. He's not at all worried about adapting, changing, taking new directions. Pretty amazing, really."

Lance, who worked for both LaVell Edwards and Bronco Mendenhall, says that he sometimes hears people say that their personalities are similar. "Not even close," he says firmly. "They are different guys. One is very warm; the other, way standoffish." But on reflection, he says there are some similarities. "They are both unshaken," he says "not easily rattled. They both provide a consistent model of what they think you should be to be here—your conduct as an athlete, on and off the field."

"Leadership is discipline," says LaVell Edwards. "Bronco brought consistency, discipline, and he's also brought a sense of accountability. Any leader, if you're going to have any success at all, I think you have to have those two elements. You show players what they need to do, and then when their discipline starts coming from them, that is the best form of discipline. Because in that case the kids are making their own decisions on what's going to be good for them and the team and the school and whatever else."

Everyone can see Bronco's soft side if they're with him long enough. They have seen him dance on the practice field. They have seen him lip sync to the Village People dressed up as a cowboy. They have seen him ride out on his beloved motorcycle. "You know when he's the coach and you know when he's himself," says Scott Johnson. "He's usually himself when he's around his family. He kind of softens up and you see his real personality."

"I think I've become a lot more confident and more capable of handling the wide variety of tasks and challenges that come every day," says Bronco.

> I've described the experience when I was a brand new coach as being in a constant state of readiness because so many different types of things were coming at you with such diversity from all angles so frequently that you had very little time to think and make appropriate decisions. Over time, I learned some core principles and perspectives. There really aren't that many true emergencies. People actually can wait for an answer.

About being standoffish, Bronco says:

> I was hesitant early on to show any signs of weakness or to let my guard down. Because it was so intense, I didn't want to relax or indicate that there was anything other than just a ton of work to do. With the success and consistency we've built, being more assured and clear as to what the program was going to produce, I've learned it is completely okay to show a more human side and that it can actually work to your benefit. I think that allows you to capture hearts maybe a little bit more than the other way.
>
> When you surround yourself with great people who are capable and who are eager, then you can confidently give them more responsibility to help them grow personally, to try to tutor and mentor them through mistakes that they make. You realize that the program will actually move faster

and be more effective when there are more people involved and feeling ownership. I don't ever claim to have all the answers. It's kind of the Church principle: "Teach people correct principles and let them govern themselves."[13]

As part of his effort to keep focus on the right things, Bronco wrote his ultimate mission in his journal recently. He shares it:

I will live my life with faith, hope, optimism, confidence, gratitude, and peace. I will inspire my family and those I have stewardship over to seek and understand their ultimate mission in life and the plan of salvation. I will inspire others to reach for their divine potential, by teaching and developing human decency, kindness, and compassion as sons and daughters of God. I will be at peace as I become an instrument in my Father in Heaven's hands as I serve my fellow man through my personal commitment to discipleship.

"That's what I think I'm here to do," he says, granting that football may not always be the playing field on which he carries out his mission. "I'd be okay if I'm not supposed to do this anymore, because I am a teacher. That's what I'm supposed to do. I'm supposed to develop people, to help them become better. The more clear that is, the easier it is for me to deal with everything else."

Bronco has neared the end of the journey he began in Ruston, Louisiana, to find his life's purpose. He's just not yet finished carrying it out.

THE FUTURE

Bronco has five goals for the BYU football program's immediate future:

1. Inspire others to seek excellence in living through championship football.

"It's not about the game, it's *through* the game," says Bronco. "I want other people to say, 'Man, I want to be better. Man, because I saw a BYU football player, or watched the game or had contact with the team, I'm now going to be this or reach that.'"

2. Create the greatest home-field advantage in college football.

"I care a lot about how we play at home because of whose name the stadium bears. That's LaVell Edwards's name. I use this story a lot: If I came in to visit your home, my guess is I would leave with an impression of how your family is, by the spirit in the home, by just how the interaction is. You'd want me to leave saying, 'That's a special place.' I would like people who play here—usually, they leave in defeat, but with respect to the experience they have while they're here—I would like them to say, 'That was amazing. There's something special there. Who are those guys and why would they play like that?' It's to honor the past, but also to pique an interest in the Church. That only happens if you play well. For a while, we had the longest winning streak in the nation at home and the longest ever here at BYU. That was good."

3. Build the most complete college football program in the world.

"Our program encompasses faith, family, finding knowledge, friends, then football," says Bronco.

LaVell Edwards's philosophy was similar. "I've always felt that if an athlete has his grades, his activities, and his personal life in order, then football is going to take care of itself," LaVell says. "Bronco has shown that these are his priorities for his players. He understands what players need to do to be successful, not only on the playing field, but I think more importantly in the classroom and in their personal lives. He is consistent that way on things that are important to him."

"It's not just football," Steve Kaufusi agrees. "We're trying to build good men who have good character and be good in the community and be leaders at church and teach other kids. Football's last in all this. That's what's unique about this place."

"Every player is different," he adds. "Some are more spiritual than others. Some need more work than others." He goes on:

> To see the growth that takes place, that's what's gratifying to me. There are a couple of guys who went on missions who I never thought would go. They were sitting on the fence. To see those two young men have a change of heart and leave just before their senior year—most folks would be mad, probably. "Why are two starters leaving? We can't have them leave!" My first reaction is "Yes!" I'm so excited for them. I love to see the maturity and the growth that takes place in the young people. To see them get married and have a family. You hope that during the four or five years they are here that you had something to do with guiding them along in the right direction, to do with teaching them that there are more important things than football.

Bronco wants fans who cheer for his players' nonfootball accomplishments as well for their victories on the field. Most BYU Football supporters appreciate the team's broader mission and purpose. Bronco has been known to chide some for losing sight of the larger picture. He once called out boosters for pressing him about 2011's 17–16 loss to the University of Texas. "It felt as though I was in front of the Pharisees and Sadducees," he said, appealing to his audience's scriptural familiarity with those who have missed the point in a big way. "Sometimes what play we run on 3rd-and-20 is more important [to them] than what we're trying to do here."[14]

Bronco's appeal to all fans: "My hope is that you support us with your heart as you try to find what's most important in life and see the bigger picture, and join us in that purpose."[15]

4. Compete for a national championship.

Bronco has defined a series of landmarks that are likely to precede winning a national championship. First, BYU must be ranked consistently each season as one of the top twenty-five Division 1 teams. They have achieved that, but the rest of the landmarks have so far been elusive. They must regularly achieve in-state dominance against Utah and Utah State. Then the Cougars will need to go undefeated in order to break into the realm of the top ten. If they do that, then they'll secure an opportunity to play in an elite bowl game. They'll need to repeat the performance to qualify for a national championship opportunity.

To achieve that level of consistency, the Cougars are even now working to build their competitive-enabling processes. They'll need NFL-ready strength, nutrition, and conditioning preparation. Medical and training care must be top notch. Academic support, technology, and scheduling, all must be outstanding. And of course, masterful teaching and coaching will continue to be a requirement.

"I'm not afraid to mention winning a national championship as the ultimate goal from the football perspective," says Bronco. It's just that it's not the only perspective.

5. Develop leaders to impact and serve families, communities, and the world.

"These kids, these players here today, are all going to take the seats you and I currently occupy, and they're going to be better than we are," he says. "That's the intent—that the next generation is the better generation."

"Coach Mendenhall cares about the kids," says Nick Howell. "Everything he does is for the kids. I've never seen a person search as much as he does. He's always seeking new knowledge and trying to implement new things that will help them. He really wants them to learn and grow. All the decisions that he makes are to help them learn something. A lot of times coaches will give kids the easy way out or just discipline them to hold them accountable. But he really puts a lot of thought into just helping them learn and making this experience at BYU a learning process."

INDEPENDENCE AND
THE NATIONAL CHAMPIONSHIP

Is winning a national championship realistic for BYU? The football environment was a whole different world when the 1984 Cougar team pulled it off—the same year Bronco graduated from high school. There was no BCS with rules that all but prevent schools outside BCS automatic-qualifier conferences from obtaining a berth in one of the elite BCS bowl games. With or without the BCS, Bronco believes BYU must go undefeated repeatedly to have a shot at the national championship. On the other hand, "Now that we're independent," says Bronco, "we're going to be playing better competition, more of which will be on the road than at home." Their wins will be tougher, but every win more meaningful.

"The other top-twenty-five teams in the country may have more depth than we have, but our first and second string guys are pretty darn good," says Brandon. "I think we can play with anybody in the country. And somebody's got to win. It may as well be us. Somebody's got to carry that trophy home at the end of the year. Why not us? Is it really that impossible? No, because somebody's got to walk away with it."

"What if we could win a national championship here?" says Bronco. "With all these missionaries, with this shortened workday, with these principles? The exposure for the Church would—I bet there would never have been an event that would have been more significant to piquing people's interest. That would be a great thing."

After the team became independent, Bronco had the visual display on one of the long walls in the football department changed. He had the word *Impossible* affixed in the center in enormous letters and surrounded by photos of inspirational men and their words on the subject—Muhammad Ali, Gandhi, Abraham Lincoln, Neil Armstrong, Christopher Reeve, Albert Einstein, Martin Luther King Jr., and others. There's a poster on Bronco's door crafted especially for Cougar football. In a pigskin-filled font on a gray background it says, "Impossible is nothing."

Impossible is just a big word thrown about by small men who find it easier to live in the world they have been given than to explore the power they have to change it. Impossible is not a fact. It's an opinion. Impossible is not a declaration. It's a dare. Impossible is potential. Impossible is temporary. Impossible is nothing.[16]

"This idea that we can't win a national championship under the current circumstances and that it's impossible—I don't buy it," says Bronco. "The goal is a national championship. To say that it's not possible, I refuse to believe that. It's possible sooner rather than later. That's the reason I keep going. Not for the trophy, but for the exposure that that would give to the Church. For people to see you can do both—you can be excellent at what you do but more importantly you can be exceptional about how you do it and who you are. You don't have to have thirty players who are in jail to do it; you don't have to have a coach who is breaking rules to do it. You can do it the other way. And that would be a good thing for the world."

Since BYU became independent, the scope of Bronco's vision has changed. "My thoughts about our strategy have simply shifted from a large scale to a world-wide scale," he says. It's because BYU football games are now available in hundreds of millions of homes.

That is why the reticent Bronco agreed to this book.

"The only motive for me to tell this story is to show that you can do it all," he says. "Hopefully, we can continue to be successful on the field so people are drawn to this idea. If we're not successful on the field, they won't care. That's the truth. But if we are able to sustain our success, it will motivate people to look and see what we've done here. They will get a real surprise. They'll be blown away with how it's happened.

"What we do here shows that you can do a lot more than what you think you're capable of if you're just willing to reach a little deeper."

SECTION 2

IN THE FOOTBALL OFFICES

CHAPTER 12

Everyone Has a Goliath

Framing the Coaching Experience

W E INTRODUCED you to Bronco Mendenhall in section 1. We took you on his journey from a youngster watching his gifted brothers play football to a safety and linebacker in college to a young defensive coordinator wondering if the sacrifices required by his job were worth it. When he became head coach of the Brigham Young University Cougars, we told you how lost he felt but how the business principles coauthor Paul shared with him helped him know how to press forward in forming a unique strategy and designing a program that could carry it out. We showed you what we believe is his enormous creativity and courage in applying the things he learned.

· Section 2 is *your* coaching session. Here we reveal a bit more about the ideas and research behind each smooth stone. We'll refer you to some of the readings that were most influential to Bronco. We'll offer some examples about how others have applied these principles, and we'll ask questions to help you think of ways you can make them work for you. It's *you* sitting with Paul in the football staff meeting room of the Student Athlete Building and finding new ways to tackle the challenges you face. As you read, imagine yourself in your workplace, or with a community group you have joined, or in your home. What is your strategy to accomplish your goals? If you were to have a chance to start fresh, what would you do first to set things on a path toward greater success? What would you do better? What would you do differently?

The five smooth stones are a metaphor for five sets of principles and practices that are handy for anyone hoping to improve an organization to which they belong—their family, their work group, an athletic club, a band, a volunteer community group, or any other organization you can imagine. The hero David used five small stones to conquer a well-clad warrior in a battle that was to determine the fate of his people. In some ways, we fight similar battles every day as we seek to improve our own lives and the lives of those for whom we care.

The armies of the Israelites' archenemy, the Philistines, challenged their biblical rivals by sponsoring a formidable warrior named Goliath to stage a championship fight-to-the-death, the survivor of which would win for his nation the enslavement of his opponent's entire people.

Goliath stood a towering figure before the amateurish Israelite soldiers, terrifyingly dressed to the nines in brass mail, armor, and helmet, carrying an enormous spear, and shouting bluster. The Israelites were paralyzed with fear, and it wasn't until the jaunty lad David came in on an errand to deliver some cheese that the standoff was broken.

David thought that he could take on this monster and convinced the king to let him do it with talk of his past exploits as a shepherd against fearsome predators and also with an earnest reminder about the power of the Lord.

David tried on some armor and tested out a sword but found that they cramped his sling style. So he threw them off and instead "chose five smooth stones out of the brook." Tossing these in a shepherd's bag along with his sling, David handily confronted the very contemptuous Goliath, who soon lay dead, beheaded by his own sword at David's hands.[1]

So goes the story of David and Goliath. Dark-horse David found an unpredictable way to best his formidable enemy. It derived from his own unique capabilities developed in long hours spent defending sheep from predators in the hill country, not by engaging in the same warrior rites and rigors by which Goliath was likely trained. Similarly, the BYU Football staff has drawn on each of the five smooth stones in the seasons and years with Bronco as head coach. Applied steadily and thoughtfully with the inventive insight of Bronco, his coaches, and his players, they have contributed to the Cougars' sustained competitive advantage in the world of college football.

You can add the five smooth stones to your shepherd's bag even as Bronco added them to his. We invite you to ponder, as the Cougars did, how these ideas can augment your talents and help the groups to which you belong, or which you lead, achieve the success that you and your companions long for. Put your ideas into practice, see how they work, and continue to renew your approach to make a greater and greater difference in your work, your family, and your life.

First, a quick review.

Smooth Stone #1: Organizations can craft a sustainable competitive advantage through differentiation.

When Bronco became head coach at BYU Football, he was acutely aware that it was his duty and privilege to set the direction for the program. What he needed to know is that winning is all about establishing the team's uniqueness, about finding the inimitable things it can do, not *better* than rival teams but *differently*, to give them a competitive advantage.

Any group to which you belong has a purpose, and it's worth taking a close look at your strategies for moving toward that purpose. How is your family or group different from similar families or groups, and how can that difference be used to the advantage of the participants? We don't mean to imply that all groups should be competitive—far from it. But each group is unique and must find its own singular strengths in order to thrive.

Smooth Stone #2: Organizations are perfectly designed to get the results that they get.

If a group or organization's results are disappointing, the explanation lies in an understanding of its infrastructure: its strategies and systems and the derivative culture. And the good news is that's where the remedy lies as well, because the way an organization works can be changed. People can overhaul the rules they have put in place about how to do things. They can change procedures, remodel, rework, restore, revamp, and reconnect. By making thoughtful choices about organizational design—by adjusting design elements such as the goals and principles that provide guidance, work activities and facilities, decision-making processes, approaches to recruiting and training and rewarding and learning—a team can remake itself systematically.

We suggest that you take a close look at the design choices that characterize any group whose outcomes you'd like to change. This applies not only to business or community organizations, but to families as well—*especially* families.

Smooth Stone #3: Organizations are made up of business processes, and not all processes are created equal.

Fundamental to the workings of a company or team are the activities carried out every day to create value. The devil is in the details, as the saying goes, although here we'd want to say that it is in the activities. Decisions about which activities a group chooses to do should be strategy-driven, and those that are more relevant to competitive advantage should be cherished over those that provide little marketplace upside. When organizations become set in their ways and take the daily work they do as a given, the work most critical to marketplace positioning can be swamped by the vastness of everyday concerns. It's a good idea to look under the hood occasionally, to do some reevaluation and revitalization. To ask, what are the crucial activities we do here that are really impactful? Which of them are most to our advantage? On what work should we focus our finances and our time? What work is most helpful to us when it is performed as efficiently as possible, or outsourced?

BYU Football made its own choices about what its distinctive work would be, and you can too.

Smooth Stone #4: Knowledge is the purest form of competitive advantage.

What we mean here by knowledge is really an organization's *dexterity* with knowledge. And when we say that it is the purest asset of a group, we mean that acuity with knowledge itself can see the group through all kinds of changes in technology, management, markets, and the environment. The ability to discover, create, codify, diffuse, apply, and renew knowledge protects it from being missed, dismissed, lost, hoarded, or squandered. There is tremendous power in the minds of the people in an organization, but the organization itself must develop or encourage the systems and agreements and networks that spark this knowledge, that draw it out and capture it, that apply it to create an advantage.

As Bronco and the staff studied the critical knowledge that relates to football, they made some discoveries and formulated some secret sauce. In section 1, we focused on quarterback knowledge. What knowledge should you be managing in your family? In your Little League team? Your religious study group? Your hobby enthusiast club?

Smooth Stone #5: Effective leaders capture hearts and minds.

As Bronco began to envision the future of the football program, the task ahead of him was to communicate this vision and engage coaches, players, and fans. He needed to ignite their energies, involve them, and unite them, as any leader must do in any type of enterprise, large or small, profit or not-for-profit, if enduring success is the goal. Then he would need to revive the team periodically and ensure they found regular ways to reconnect with their aspirations for faith, family, finding knowledge, friends, and, of course, football.

How do you direct your group's or family's attention to fundamental priorities? How do you help them feel energized and passionate about their work? Bringing people together and helping them channel their energy toward a greater good is the most important role of a leader—and the most rewarding.

CHAPTER 13

Smooth Stone #1

Organizations Can Craft a Sustainable Competitive Advantage through Differentiation

T HE SEMINAL THINKING about the importance of differentiation is explained in the 1996 *Harvard Business Review* article by Michael Porter, "What Is Strategy?", that Bronco read before his first meeting with Paul.[1] Porter wrote that sustained success in the marketplace comes from being *different* from competitors, not from being *better* than they are.

The classic case that Porter used to illustrate his insight is Southwest Airlines. Southwest has turned a profit for decades longer than any other major airline. By the end of 2011, fifteen years after Porter wrote the *HBR* article, the airline had a market capitalization of $7.5 billion, second only to Delta, among U.S. carriers. Southwest had been in the black for thirty-nine years, had paid dividends for 136 straight quarters, and had amassed billions of cash and hundreds of millions in available credit. It had closed on its purchase of AirTran and was poised therefore for major growth in its domestic offerings and an expansion into the Mexican/Caribbean getaway market. The carrier had regularly received top honors in customer service, corporate social responsibility, environmentally friendly performance, web experience, and more.[2]

Southwest's *modus operandi* was and remains totally different from that of its competitors. Nailing low-cost airfares as its chosen strategy, it has hung from this choice a web of practices and systems that are mutually reinforcing. For example, Southwest has used only one type of aircraft—the Boeing 737—saving millions of dollars in maintenance costs (though the purchase of AirTran means that its 717s are being integrated into the Southwest fleet). Southwest flies directly—point-to-point—and thereby avoids crowded hubs that would otherwise slow its schedule and ruin its industry-busting on-time average. They have fun over there at Southwest Airlines, the cultural power of which cannot be underestimated. Though they are highly unionized, they employ 30 percent fewer workers per aircraft, resulting in the lowest non-fuel cost per available seat. Streamlined in-flight amenities—replaced perhaps in entertainment value by a witty rampage over the speaker throughout the obligatory airline safety talk or a song upon arrival at the destination—reduce aircraft turn-around time to less than twenty minutes.

Committing to a marketplace position—in Southwest's case, as a provider of low-cost airfare—is only the first step of defining a strategy. The fabric of that strategy is knit when a system of activities and structures is sewn together, aligning with and reinforcing each other. Only then does a solid strategic idea provide a competitive advantage, and one that will last. "It is harder for a rival to match an array of interlocked activities" than it is to imitate any one program, as Porter said.[3] A harmonized system is nearly impossible to reproduce. The fact that Southwest's practices still stand out as so completely different from the rest of the industry, even after all these years of success, is a testament to their inimitability.

So BYU Football chose to be different by designating players as "flag bearers" for BYU, a mission in sync with the university's purpose of helping students "learn, then demonstrate, that their allegiance is to higher values, principles, and human commitments rather than to mere self-interest." Program leaders chose to recognize the strengths of their religiously faithful, well-rounded players and design an organization to capitalize on those strengths—a service mentality, a strong work ethic, and mature leadership capabilities. They choose not to make the athletic abilities of their recruits the end-all of their recruiting goals. In this way, they got the right players on the bus and offered them unique opportunities to become coaches and leaders themselves.

To apply Smooth Stone #1 in your life, identify your distinctiveness. Be brave. You are in business to do something different from what is done elsewhere, or even if you do something similar, to do it in an entirely different way. This is true even if the business we are talking about is the business of building a family. How can you help each other at home in a way that no one else can? What can you teach there that cannot be taught in any other setting?

Once you've answered these questions, prepare to develop a set of mutually reinforcing and even idiosyncratic practices to embody your chosen point(s) of differentiation.

For example, Discover Books is a Tacoma-area recycler of books. Phil McMullin started the company to rescue some of the millions of books donated to thrift shops each month from landfills. Like all organizations that receive book donations, the company must sort the titles that they receive, elsewhere a labor-intensive process. This is where Discover Books differentiates itself. Scanning technology reads the books' barcodes and a proprietary algorithm takes into account sales history, edition, weight, and recent consumer demand to determine each book's best use: to be donated to nonprofit organizations, resold through Amazon or another online outlet, or "pulped" and recycled. The company processes thirty million pounds of books a year this way, which is equivalent to nearly 1 percent of the total volume of books published annually. Its unique use of technology has contributed to fast growth and the recent infusion of 8.5 million dollars in venture capital.[4] Other methods of differentiating itself include establishing strategic partnerships with local literary councils and Friends of Libraries groups for both giving and receiving books. In this way, Discover Books succeeds as a for-profit organization with an explicit social purpose as well, giving out donations of books worth $5 million in 2011.

In a family, we have found it helpful to talk about the idea of differentiation as a strength just as Porter does. For example, co-author Paul has a daughter who once was in the habit of pointing out to her parents that all of her friends got to stay out late, so why couldn't she? Smooth Stone #1 to the rescue! "We are different from other families," said Paul and Kris Anne, "and that difference is a strength that will help you stay safe, make wise choices, and enjoy the weekend well-rested."

SMOOTH STONE #1 SUMMARY

Principle: To gain competitive advantage, do something different from your competitors, or else do something similar but in an entirely different way.

Cougar application: The Cougars developed a unique mission to be flag bearers of BYU, a mission in sync with the university's purpose of helping students "learn, then demonstrate, that their allegiance is to higher values, principles, and human commitments rather than to mere self-interest." They recruit players who embrace the mission and who evidence balanced athletic, academic, and spiritual values. They capitalize on the work and service ethic of these young men and on their leadership experience.

Your application: What can you identify that you do differently from anyone else, or what you would *like* to do differently? Your organization's mission may guide you. You may be inspired by a cause that unites your workforce, or an igniting vision that provides energy and draws people together. Be brave. Just be sure that you are in business to do something different from what is done elsewhere, or even if you do something similar, do it in an entirely different way. Then prepare to develop a set of mutually reinforcing and even idiosyncratic practices to embody your chosen point(s) of differentiation.

CHAPTER 14

Smooth Stone #2

Organizations Are Perfectly Designed to Get the Results That They Get

S MOOTH STONE #2 teaches that if you want different results, you'll need to change your current practices.

Bronco and his staff did not go about changing the organization's embedded practices haphazardly. As we described in section 1, he followed a map for moving the Cougars back into winning territory. We showed a simplified version of this map in chapter 5. In this section, we'll build on this simple model toward the more complete map that provided detailed guidance to Bronco.

ORGANIZATION DESIGN FRAMEWORK

This is the simplified map we introduced in section 1:

It shows, moving from left to right, that if you want different *outcomes*, then you need to influence the *culture* of the organization, including what people feel they can achieve, the way they behave in striving toward those achievements, and the personal attributes that define their abilities. But since you cannot control all of the forces outside the team and within its individual members that impact the culture, you instead influence that culture by choosing to modify elements of the organization that you can directly change, such as goals, routines, and policies. Because these can be intentionally designed, we call them *design choices*. Thus, design choices affect culture, which in turn drives outcomes.

Say, for example, that a football team wishes to be a flag bearer, an icon of its sponsoring institution. The team believes that it is going to need to catch people's attention to be an effective representative, and that it can best do this by winning games and playing in bowl contests. These are the desired *outcomes*.

The belief may be that this can only be achieved if players are accountable for high personal standards, execute schemes with discipline, and give their best effort to every practice and every game. This is a short description of the desired *culture*.

Working backward, then, leaders are going to have to make some choices that will drive this culture of accountability, discipline, and effort. Choices, for example, about how they recruit, run practices and camps, structure the team, communicate goals, and manage football and academic performance. These are *design choices*.[1]

Now the external environment is the context within which all

strategic and tactical action takes place. It is like the gridiron itself, the size and bounds of which profoundly shape what happens between teams and among players. So we represent the influence of the external environment like this, and the diagram begins to expand from what we described in chapter 5.

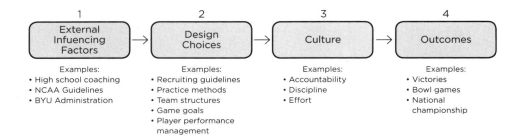

Notice the second box, *design choices.* This is the box over which leaders have the most direct control. If organizations are perfectly designed to get the results that they get, which is Smooth Stone #2, then to get different results, leaders must create a different organization design. They must choose different ways of performing everyday activities, or they must choose to perform different activities altogether.

But as we saw in section 1, we're not just talking about Xs and Os. For the Cougars to concentrate only on strategies and schemes is akin to Procter & Gamble concentrating solely on making toothpaste. There's a lot more to do in any organization than produce and deliver its product or services. There's research and development to think about, as well as marketing, hiring, training, information systems, and much more. All these activities are interdependent. Depending on how well they are orchestrated, their aggregate effects can either fulfill or kill the strategy. Remember what Bronco came to know: it is the effects of a signature set of broad, interlacing practices that bring sustainable competitive advantage to an enterprise.

To help an organization think about all the different types of design choices it makes that drive culture and outcomes, consider another diagram that expands on the second box of the path. Start with one category of design choices—choices that give *direction* to all the activities and decisions made in an organization. Then add another category of design choices—the *systems* assembled to execute the direction:

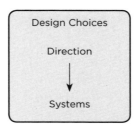

Design choices that give *direction* answer questions such as, what is our mission or purpose? What principles guide our actions? What strategies do we choose to influence groups and forces outside our organization? What are our specific goals for achieving our outcomes?

People in organizations design different kinds of *systems* to implement the answers to these questions. We can name six general types of systems: technical, structural, decision-making and information, people, reward, and renewal.[2]

This model shows the way to new, improved results, and it expands on all the many variables that can be tweaked or overhauled in an organization to influence culture and change results. It is called the Organizational Systems Design model, or OSD model.[3]

Bronco used the expanded OSD model to picture all of the different systems in his organization. It is a framework which you, too, can use in any organization you lead to evaluate and reconstruct the organization's mix of practices, practices that you should align

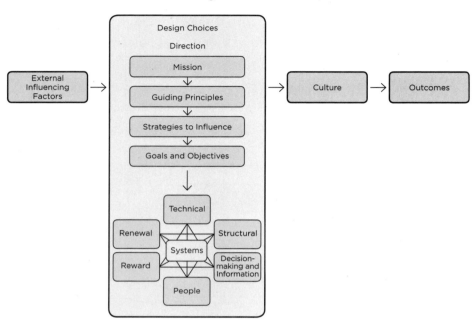

with the aim of setting yourself apart. You can use this model to develop strategic coherence, to think through which systems will be most important to achieving your objectives. What key activities will result in marketplace differentiation? Are they unique? What systems will support those activities—what organizational structures, information systems, training, and reward plans will underpin these critical tasks? If you hope to provide web design services, produce eco-friendly construction materials, or raise funds for the opera, what work routines, short-term goals, and employee incentives do you think will bring you customers?

ALIGNMENT

Since each design element is dependent on the others, leaders must pay careful attention to their interaction. Even one design element, if it is out of sync with the whole, can cause a sub-optimization of the entire system. Synchronizing design elements so they are mutually reinforcing is called *alignment.*

If you remember nothing else about Smooth Stone #2, remember the concept of alignment. *This is the most important idea associated with Smooth Stone #2.* Bronco mentions it often. He became an advocate for aligning organization choices by looking at them systemically to ensure they are in harmony and that they work in concert to drive the strategy of the program and support its values. For example, if a team really values faith and family over football, then late nights watching film at the office and Sunday staff meetings might be off the table. They are at BYU.

The Cougars innovated design choices like crazy throughout the first few years of the Bronco Mendenhall era. In section 1, we shared BYU's design choices for all of the boxes in the model: outcomes, culture, mission, guiding principles, strategies to influence, goals and objectives, and all the systems—technical, structural, decision-making, people, rewards, and renewal. These choices continue to develop as Bronco's team discovers what works well and what doesn't, as they experience staff and conference changes, and as inspiration comes from man and heaven.

The following table shows the full set of aligned choices that have come to define the Cougar system. Of course, these choices weren't all put in place in sequence. In fact, the system is still changing as the environment changes (BYU becoming independent, for example) and as players and staff learn, gain experience, and change. But this snapshot represents a robust example of an intentionally designed and aligned organization.

Cougar Football Design Elements

Design Choices	Summary/Illustration
OUTCOMES: The high level accomplishments that an organization desires such as market share, return on investment, customer satisfaction ratings, and more.	Our end results will be a football program aligned to BYU's aim of educating students who are renowned for who they are as well as for what they know and can do.
CULTURE: The set of shared basic assumptions, emotionally charged beliefs, and behavioral patterns that develop over time among organization members. It is manifested in symbols, stories, rituals, routines, and behavioral norms.	We will aim for a culture characterized by accountability, discipline, and effort.
MISSION: A statement describing an organization's primary reason for being and its distinctive competency.	Our mission is to be the flag bearer of Brigham Young University through football excellence, embracing truth, tradition, virtue, and honor as a beacon to the world.
GUIDING PRINCIPLES: Statements that express underlying beliefs about the best way to do business.	We value *tradition* because of the program's rich history of football excellence; *spirit* because we are committed to

Design Choices	Summary/Illustration
(GUIDING PRINCIPLES continued) They guide an organization's actions as they carry out the mission and seek to achieve the desired outcomes.	(continued) seeking the Spirit, living by the Spirit, and turning to the Spirit to guide our priorities and our actions; and *honor* because we wish to cultivate an atmosphere consistent with the ideals and principles of the gospel of Jesus Christ, which means we will maintain the highest standards of honor, integrity, morality, and consideration of others in personal behavior. The order of our priorities is faith, family, finding knowledge and learning, friends, and finally football.
STRATEGIES TO INFLUENCE: Plans identifying the offerings and activities that will differentiate the organization from its competitors. They also encompass methods of influencing the environment to both meet the requirements of outside groups and achieve the organization's desired outcomes.	We achieve sustained success on the football field by differentiating ourselves according to our unique mission and strengths. We will influence on- and off-campus entities by monitoring and meeting with them periodically to assess and influence their expectations.

Design Choices	Summary/Illustration
GOALS AND OBJECTIVES: Measures that indicate progress toward achieving the desired outcomes.	Each year we wish to be champions on and off the field, to be conference champions (applicable prior to 2011), and to win a bowl game.
TECHNICAL SYSTEM: The organization's business processes (sometimes called value streams)—the activities it routinely carries out to create and deliver value for customers. Also its physical facilities and technology for interacting and exchanging knowledge.	We identify our work processes, name a process owner for each one, and strive to align our processes to deliver results. Specifically, for example, we practice and play with reckless abandon, we practice efficiently so we can go home in the evenings and on Sunday to be with our families, we build team unity, and we regularly perform service in our own community and the communities in which we play.
STRUCTURAL SYSTEM: The way the enterprise is organized—what groups are formed to do the work.	We augment the traditional football program structure with a leadership council, a Band of Brothers program, and rotating conditioning and locker assignments, all to strengthen the interaction of players and their communication with leaders.

Design Choices	Summary/Illustration
DECISION-MAKING AND INFORMATION SYSTEM: Decision-making responsibilities as well as the identification, capture, distribution, and display of information.	We identify and drill the "three pillars." We encourage leadership council members and other players to take ownership. We establish a rigorous academic goal of a 3.0 cumulative GPA for each player.
PEOPLE SYSTEM: Attraction, selection, orientation, training, and performance management systems.	We have unique recruiting requirements. We gather 360-degree feedback for coaches. We intervene early to prevent Honor Code or academic violations.
REWARD SYSTEM: Formal pay and incentives as well as informal rewards and recognition.	We grant scholarships year by year. We reinforce our goals with helmet stickers and an academic banquet.
RENEWAL SYSTEM: The way the organization ensures continuous improvement.	We schedule renewal events and efforts—both for process improvement and recommitment to our team mission.

As for you, you can use the OSD model to test the alignment of your own organization. Are the systems and structures that embody your organization harmonized toward fulfilling your strategy? Could you make a change in one or more of the categories that would make a difference in your outcomes? For example, does your structure—your reporting relationships—bring the right people together to optimize how you deliver your chosen product/service mix to your chosen market segments? Have you been systematically thoughtful about how you select, train, and reward your people? And are they clear about your organization's goals and objectives?

We have a challenge for you. Grab your laptop or some notebook paper and list all of the boxes in the OSD model. Choose a group to which you belong and that you'd like to see improve, and summarize your aspirations for the group—the results you'd like to see it achieve and the culture changes you believe will be important to get it there. Now describe the current design. What is the mission? What are the goals? What is the everyday work? How are people grouped to do work? What information are they given? How are they selected, trained, and rewarded, and how does the group periodically find ways to improve itself?

Once you have fleshed out the current design, look closely to see if there are any misalignments. This group is perfectly designed to get the results that it gets. How might the design be changed to get different results?

For example, we know of a business school alumni group in the Silicon Valley area that once attracted a dozen or so members each month for a cold-sandwich lunch meeting in a college classroom. Their leaders wanted the society to flourish as a place where like-minded professionals could build their associations with each other to develop careers and leadership skills, to serve the community, and to support their alma mater. To get different results, they knew they had to do something differently. They started out with a facilities change—they moved the time of the meeting to breakfast and the location of the meeting to a series of restaurants, landing finally at the Silicon Valley Capital Club on the penthouse level of the Knight-Ridder building for "not only a 360-degree view of the downtown and the valley but also a real step up in [the] professional surroundings."[4] They sought to enhance the content of their meetings by inviting speakers of the highest caliber—the mayor of San Jose, for example, or the president of the metropolitan Silicon Valley Chamber of Commerce, or the head of a successful and exciting nonprofit. Soon attendance had increased by eight-fold. They formed a group called Silicon Valley Women that met quarterly and tailored their meetings to the specific interests of professional women. They held brown-bag lunches at Google, Apple, Adobe, and Novell, where alumni who were employed at these notable companies described what it was like to work there. They added other forums like movie nights and workshops on topics such as work-life balance and estate planning. They partnered with an employment services organization to hold career events, and with mentoring organizations (such as Score) to help entrepreneurs and small business owners connect with experienced veterans. Soon they were holding 150 activities a year. They raised funds to offer tens of thousands of dollars in scholarships to students attending local colleges who demonstrated moral and ethical leadership. They partnered with other alumni groups from the same institution to expand their membership. They developed a huge master list of potential members, and they distributed a monthly newsletter that promoted their offerings and welcomed all of their school's alumni and other interested friends. Membership soared to over 900 and the society won the Dean's Gold Chapter of Excellence Award.

The alumni group made changes to their management structure in order to support the planning required to carry out these activities. They created a solid executive board of fifteen members that met in person quarterly and more often by teleconference. They formed an advisory board well equipped with contacts to potential speakers. They systematized every type of event so that minimal time was required from board volunteers. They tenaciously adhered to a limited set of goals and studiously reviewed the metrics they set out each year in a one-page annual business plan. They became intentional about developing future leaders so that a new president was ready to take over the reins at the end of each president's two-year term, sending them to an annual worldwide leadership meeting at their sponsoring university to learn best practices for leading a chapter. Coincident with the chapter's growth, the mission of the organization was more clearly articulated by the society's leaders: growing moral and ethical leadership around the world. In short, the chapter's success was the result of reworking every organizational system—from mission to processes and facilities to goal-setting and training.

This group is the Silicon Valley chapter of the BYU Management Society, and marketing professional Joel Deceuster was its volunteer president during the early years of its blossoming. He is now the chairman of the Management Society's Global Steering Committee, and his vision is to welcome business professionals from around the world with the same beliefs about right behavior. "We really want to reach out to people," he says, "not just to people who went to BYU, not just people who went to college, not just people that are of the LDS faith, but we want to reach out to all people, be all-inclusive."

> If you believe in ethical standards, if you believe in a code of morality, if you believe in being a leader and leading by example, then we want you to come and stand with us. We want to give people a place to stand and to say, "This is where I belong." This society is where like-minded people— like-valued people—come together. By being together we

will be strong as we move forward, and we can do things that can make a huge difference in the world. Sometimes the reason why people give up is because they think, "Who am I? I'm just one person." But when you can bring a group of people together that believe in the same things like moral and ethical leadership, then they can really start to have a presence in the world, a presence in the community.*

A second example of Smooth Stone #2 in action is a church congregation that wanted to ensure a culture where each person felt loved and blessed by other members of the congregation. They wanted people to feel more closely connected than they would by seeing each other only in the context of worship services and formally organized activities. So they selected an existing program to bring this outcome to pass—a program where every member was visited personally each month in their home by a pair of other members. When they began their renewed effort, the rate of this "home teaching" or "visiting teaching" had stood at roughly 24 percent per month for nine years. Representatives from the congregation met together to discuss what could be done to increase the regularity of visits.

First, they revamped the assignments regarding who would visit whom with an eye toward making logistics as effortless as possible. They connected people who were available at similar times during each day and who lived in close proximity to each other. Second, they encouraged participants to meet anywhere that was convenient—in homes, at lunch, before or after dances at the church, or wherever. Third, the leaders themselves committed to serve as better role models and held each other accountable for being regular participants in the program. Fourth, knowing that what leaders talk about

---

* To learn more, visit https://marriottschool.byu.edu/mgtsoc/about.cfm.

impacts the feelings and behaviors in an organization, they made a conscious effort to simply tell stories about the benefits and successes of visiting whenever they could. The agenda of every meeting was modified and someone would recount a story about the love felt during a visit. When leaders met personally with members of the congregation for whatever reason, they brought up the benefits of home teaching. In hallway conversations, they found ways to talk about how lives could be touched through these visits. In short, they tried to bring the topic into focus in every interaction. Fifth, they produced a film about the blessings of monthly visits and showed it to every new member of the congregation.

Did results change? Visits increased to 90 percent monthly, peaking once at 96 percent. More important, members of the congregation believed they were blessed for their efforts as their feelings of love and goodwill for each other seemed to swell. Other numerical indicators of group well-being rose also.

These examples show how bringing many organization design choices into alignment helps an organization achieve its goals. Modifying structures, facilities, meetings times and agendas, and communication methods helped these groups head in a new direction.

SMOOTH STONE #2 SUMMARY

Principle: Organizations are perfectly designed to get the results that they get, so design an organization comprised of systems and structures that are all aligned toward the development of sustained competitive advantage and the realization of a shared set of objectives and aspirations.

Cougar application: The "Cougar Football Design Elements" table (pages 300–03) summarizes and illustrates design choices that characterize the BYU Football program.

Your application: Use the OSD model to evaluate alignment in your company or group. Do the choices you've made with regard to your mission, principles, objectives, processes, structures, and people practices drive cohesively toward a clearly defined result? Or are they at odds with each other? As a whole, are they distinctive in a way that prevents imitation so as to preserve your competitive advantage?

CHAPTER 15

Smooth Stone #3

Organizations Are Made Up of Business Processes, and Not All Processes Are Created Equal

I N CHAPTER 7, we saw that the work done in organizations can be understood as a collection of processes that deliver value to customers. But we emphasized that these work processes differ in their relative strategic impact. Some directly contribute to the organization's competitiveness in the marketplace (*competitive* processes), while some provide critical support to these processes (*competitive-enabling* processes). Some are necessary to stay in business and may be important for one reason or another but have no strategic upside (*essential* processes). Some are simply required for legal reasons (*compliance* processes).

STRATEGIC IMPACT OF WORK

This powerful method of categorizing work was first laid out by our colleagues Lee Perry, Randy Stott, and Norm Smallwood in their book *Real Time Strategy*[1] and further elaborated in practice by our friend and associate Kreig Smith. It is the most effective way we know to help businesses make wise strategic decisions about how to allocate resources.

Focusing resources on enhancing competitive and competitive-enabling processes will provide maximum upside in the marketplace. For most organizations, turning the accounting department into a world-class operation has no competitive upside, unless a company has designated some aspect of accounting as providing specific distinctiveness in the marketplace. Indeed, essential and compliance work, as we have defined them here, only need to be done at par. It is not the case that being excellent in everything will ensure your excellence in the marketplace. *Au contraire.* The most successful enterprises know exactly what signature processes must be outstanding, and they are perfectly content for their performance in every other area to be at industry standard. Categorizing your work by its strategic impact provides a rationale for designating one area of excellence over another.

For example, Perry and his colleagues offer the example of a company whose strategy is to be a world-class provider of technology. Though such subprocesses as "developing the technology," "identifying customer requirements," and "designing the product" all fall under the category of competitive work, "manufacturing the product" does not. This company made the strategic choice not to attempt to develop world-class manufacturing practices because doing so would not create competitive advantage *for them.* Their focus was design, and that's where they chose to lavish the most resources. That's where they chose to excel.

To be sure, performing essential and compliance work poorly can lead to competitive disadvantage and legal risk. Even though this work does not have a strategic upside, it most certainly has a strategic downside if done poorly. To say that it does not contribute to strategic advantage is not to say it is not important. It *is* important. For example, payroll is a process that is most often categorized as "essential" work. Yet employees greatly appreciate being paid accurately and on time. Havoc can break loose if the process goes awry. When essential and compliance work are being performed under par, it may be a short-term necessity to direct resources temporarily away from competitive work in order to bring them up to speed. Organizations sometimes need to overcome any competitive disadvantages that are causing them to lose market share. Such initiatives may take priority in the short term alongside enhancing competitive work.

Making the effort to discuss and agree on the strategic relevance of work activities helps a leadership team then make wise trade-offs. Leaders will want to ensure that competitive and competitive-enabling work is protected from being swamped by the largely transactional, repetitive nature of essential and compliance work, but instead supported with strong funding and top talent to encourage effectiveness, innovation, and the development of distinctiveness. Attention and resources devoted to essential and compliance work will ensure its efficiency, but this work need not be performed at world-class levels since doing so has no advantage in the marketplace.

The BYU Cougars capitalized on these principles by categorizing their work according to the four classes of impact: competitive, competitive-enabling, essential, and compliance. They named recruiting as one of the most important processes for competitive advantage; others include effective practicing and game preparation.

PROCESS IMPROVEMENT

We wrote in chapter 5 that the essence of managing the organization is to manage its processes (also called value streams), and we introduced the process owner, who is the leader who has responsibility for a given process. It is his or her job to lose sleep over process performance. It is his or her imperative to ensure that the process will be outstanding (or outstandingly efficient, if it is a business essential or compliance process), both now and in the future. To do so effectively, he or she must have a passion for the process.

Part of the operating rhythm of the Cougar staff is to regularly revisit their processes and change them to make them better. "We have a very calendarized, very sequential approach," says Brandon Doman. "We know exactly week for week what we're going to do throughout the year. We take two or three weeks to actually evaluate and analyze and change our game and recruiting processes. Once a year we'll reevaluate each one of our core processes and then refocus our energies," he says.

Their yearly cycle includes process improvement efforts; coaches generally seek to reduce essential and compliance work so that they can devote their creative juices to competitive and competitive-enabling work.

YOU AND YOUR PROCESSES

To apply Smooth Stone #3 yourself, get your leadership team together, map your processes, and then categorize all your work by its strategic impact. Discuss ways to ensure that the people who perform competitive and competitive-enabling work have the time and space and money to "go for it." At the same time, help the folks who do essential and compliance work to achieve or maintain industry standard levels of quality in the most efficient way possible. Set goals and resource initiatives so as to enhance the *effectiveness* of competitive and competitive-enabling work and drive toward the *efficiency* of essential and compliance work.

NuSkin, a skin care and nutrition products company, is one company that identified its business processes and named global process owners. The company positioned itself from the beginning to obtain and maintain product distinctiveness through scientific innovation. To this end, the company's competitive work included forming partnerships with research institutions focused on the biological processes of aging, and a new $85 million Innovation Center will soon be completed to supplement NuSkin's three existing research centers.

Another strategic differentiator for NuSkin, one of the largest direct-selling companies in the world, is the success of its individual distributors. The company identified a single point of ownership for its sales process, and this process owner's responsibility is to ensure that all distributors worldwide are supported with the tools, training, and commission structures they need to launch them effectively and help them grow their businesses. Because access to Internet connectivity varies in NuSkin's fifty-two markets around the globe, the Big Planet division of NuSkin offers reliable Internet and telecom services to its distributors.

It takes leadership to proclaim outright that your aspiration is to be average . . . in certain areas. But on the other hand, such insight will allow you to be so much better when it comes to delivering the value that is distinctive to you and your group alone.

The idea that all work is not created equal certainly applies in the home. If you think carefully about what is the "competitive" work in your family—that is, the distinctive work that only a family can do—you may be surprised at your insights. Kathleen Slaugh Bahr and Cheri A. Loveless have made a counterintuitive but compelling case that mundane family work—the daily life-sustaining tasks of feeding and clothing each other, tidying our surroundings inside and out, maintaining our vehicles, and caring for the young and the elderly—is some of the most significant work done by a family. They explain that menial family work, because of its simple and repetitive nature, can provide the perfect relaxed and easy environment for intimate conversations between parents and children, for spontaneous play, for discussing values, for singing together and quarreling together and crying together.[2] When carried out in this way—when families routinely accomplish these simple tasks by coming together rather than delegating them to a lonely individual—family work is competitive-enabling work because it facilitates the work that is of highest value. It facilitates interactions that strengthen bonds, build character, and teach about love. It has a unique and powerful role in linking family members. A wise family may choose to develop family work routines that they regularly do together, such as preparing meals, washing the dishes, changing the beds, pulling the weeds, and folding the laundry—and then protect these routines from too much disruption in our overly busy society.

SMOOTH STONE #3 SUMMARY

Principle: Organizations are made up of business processes, and not all processes are created equal, so identify your business processes and categorize activities as either competitive, competitive-enabling, essential, or compliance. Assign resources and tailor improvement efforts to develop distinctive and excellent competitive processes; drive toward efficient essential and compliance processes.

Cougar application: The BYU coaches identified and categorized their football processes, identifying recruiting practices as some of the most important work for delivering competitive advantage. Their yearly cycle includes process improvement efforts; coaches generally seek to reduce essential and compliance work so that they can devote themselves to competitive and competitive-enabling work.

Your application: Map your processes and decide how to categorize all your work activities by their strategic impact. Then use these discussions as a leadership team to set goals and resource initiatives so as to enhance the effectiveness of competitive and competitive-enabling work and drive toward the efficiency of essential and compliance work.

CHAPTER 16

Smooth Stone #4

Knowledge Is the Purest Form of Competitive Advantage

I N DISCUSSING SMOOTH STONE #3, we wrote about the collection of business processes that delivers value to fans (or customers). We noted how important it is to recognize their potential for creating differentiation and to resource them accordingly. We talked about improving them, aiming for excellence when they are strategically crucial, and striving for efficiency when their impact on the marketplace has only a downside. However, although a careful examination of the *work* in the organization is crucial, it is not sufficient to build an organization that can deliver.

Smooth Stone #4 is a shift to thinking about the *knowledge* required to develop and execute these processes. It's about managing the knowledge required to create value for customers.

When we say that knowledge is the purest form of competitive advantage, what we mean is that although technologies, processes, and customer requirements all change incessantly in our twenty-first-century world, what remains constant is the tremendous power of the minds of the people in an organization—the capacity to generate new ideas, share them, and convert them into value for customers.

Having made strategic decisions about what is competitive work, leaders of an organization can seek to understand what knowledge is required for marketplace success and determine how well they are converting that knowledge into customer value. In other words, they can scrutinize their *learning capability.*

Identifying crucial knowledge, developing methods for teaching or sharing it, and finding ways to make it broadly accessible are all part of good *knowledge management.* Chapters 8 and 9 shared the Cougar Football approach to knowledge management. We talked in chapter 8 about the types of organization knowledge and the different ways of learning different kinds of things (knowledge *discovery*), and we discussed these topics in the context of the BYU quarterback factory. Then in chapter 9 we discussed knowledge sharing across organizational boundaries, or *diffusion.*

KNOWLEDGE AND PERFORMANCE

Smooth Stone #4 is important because organization performance is linked to organization knowledge. Organizations that foster the right conditions and processes for learning to take place will perform better in the marketplace. Performance is related to organization knowledge as depicted in the OP–OK cycle shown on the next page.

Similar to the organization design model we discussed in chapters 5 and 14, **organization performance (OP)** outcomes are depicted at the end of the cycle because they are the ultimate purpose for all knowledge management activities in an enterprise. **Organization knowledge (OK)** comes before because it is required to achieve those aims. The cycle shows that **organization learning processes (OL)** must be in place earlier to facilitate the acquisition of all types of knowledge. **Organization conditions (OC)** begin the

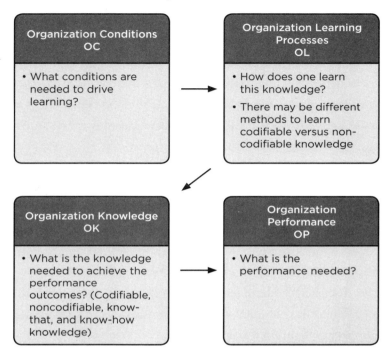

cycle because they drive learning in the first place. These activities are the essence of knowledge management.[1]

The OP–OK cycle and many of the ideas pertaining to Smooth Stone #4 come from the work of our long-time friend and colleague Bill Snyder, coauthor of *Cultivating Communities of Practice.* It is the cycle Brandon Doman had in mind as he took on the challenge of reestablishing BYU's quarterback powerhouse. He set about identifying the knowledge critical for the team's offense leader, and then putting in place an array of conditions and methods to help quarterbacks learn.

Let's take a closer look at the OP–OK cycle and review some ideas about organization knowledge, organization learning methods, and finally the organization conditions that support learning.

ORGANIZATION KNOWLEDGE

The knowledge needed to deliver outstanding performance in any organization is not just technical expertise—how to design a computer operating system, engineer production machinery, or throw a football. It also includes tacit values and attitudes. Nowhere is that truer than at BYU, with fans' unrelenting expectation that all the players be stellar examples of Mormon values as well as expert athletes who perform in the top echelon of college football.

The grid below shows the four types of organization knowledge we discussed in chapter 8:

Four Types of Organization Knowledge

	Codifiable	Tacit
Know That	Facts	Beliefs
Know How	Routines	Expertise

The horizontal dimension makes a distinction between explicit and tacit knowledge. **Codifiable knowledge** is knowledge that can be described and codified. **Tacit knowledge**, on the other hand, refers to knowledge that is hard to explain. It is difficult or impossible to put into words, or to systematize in any way.

The vertical dimension differentiates between cognitive knowledge and experiential knowledge, or skill. **Know-that** involves knowledge of facts but also includes intuitions and beliefs. **Know-how** refers to the ability to perform tasks either in your head or in action.[2]

These dimensions together describe the four kinds of knowledge that Brandon Doman vetted at the Alumni Day in 2006.

• **Codifiable know-that** includes facts, data, information, and ideas. In organizations, codifiable know-that is often embodied in memos, reports, and symbols. At BYU, it's inscribed on the walls of the Student Athlete Building in displays of past championships, current goals, and missionary whereabouts. It is also represented by team and player stats on the NCAA website and the results of national ranking polls.

• **Codifiable know-how** includes procedures and routine skills that are archived in work flow diagrams, organization charts, policies, manuals, equipment, and the design of facilities. At BYU, they reside, for example, in the Cougar playbook, in Bronco's continuously updated policy manual, and in the quarterback protocols on Brandon's bookshelf.

• **Tacit know-that** includes values, outlook, intuitions, beliefs, and assumptions that are so complex, dynamic, or implicit that they resist explanation. The LDS returned-missionary dynamic on the Cougar roster involves this type of shared beliefs about God and service to others. Another example is the commitment to living the BYU Honor Code.

• **Tacit know-how** refers to complex skills that are highly developed yet little understood by the people who use them. It resists codification. It includes expertise and artistry. This is a quarterback moving through play without conscious thought, his body instinctively reading and responding to visual cues on the field.[3]

In organizations that compete on knowledge, more than half of their knowledge is tacit, and an even greater proportion of *the most valuable knowledge* is tacit.[4] That might be obvious in football, where physical prowess is revered (or blunders are reviled) and reviewed in cycling loops of playback tape. Yet in many organization settings the tendency is to attend mostly to knowledge that is explicit. Only when both kinds of knowledge—both explicit and tacit—are recognized, developed, and aligned can performance results begin to approach their potential. Tacit know-how is absolutely crucial for managing processes and providing products and services.[5]

All four types of organization knowledge must be **aligned** and **balanced**. In other words, they must not contradict each other, and they must all be of the same relative strength. For example, if work routines (codifiable know-how) are changed without a corresponding development of the expertise (tacit know-how) required to carry out those routines, performance outcomes will be compromised. Likewise, if new beliefs (tacit know-that) about the importance of customer service are developed, customer satisfaction outcomes still will lag if new systems such as performance management systems relating to customer service (codifiable know-how) are not put into place or are only weakly communicated.[6]

ORGANIZATION LEARNING METHODS

Explicit knowledge is easier to coach than tacit, so part of the knowledge management challenge is to find ways to share tacit knowledge even when it's difficult to describe the nuances of the skills that need to be learned. But without a doubt it is possible to accelerate tacit learning. Tacit knowledge is more likely to be developed with unstructured methods, while codifiable, explicit knowledge is learned best in conventional, structured settings. Know-that is learned just fine through cerebral methods such as study, conversations, and reflection, while know-how is best learned in action-oriented ways.[7]

In chapter 8, John Beck was a case study for how to develop each type of knowledge.

He gained codifiable know-that by studying the facts and figures of football—football rules, team formations and plays, game situations, and defensive fronts.

He absorbed a lot of codifiable know-how about the mechanics of throwing, drop sequences, and coverage reads by watching film. Plus, Brandon codified BYU's quarterback protocol in the binders on his shelves, which were always available for John's reference. Then he ran his quarterbacks through those routines over and over again until the checklist was part of each player's muscle memory.

This is exactly the learning process that mathematician Keith Devlin describes in *Goodbye, Descartes*. He says that developing expertise begins with the halting execution of explicit routines. An example he uses is learning to drive a car. At first, new drivers must consciously think about the rules and routines of driving that they have learned in driver's education or read in a handbook: how to shift, when to signal a turn, how to parallel park, and so on. With more experience, the actions of driving become increasingly natural, and the driver begins to execute driving procedures with little or no conscious thought. Eventually, the driver can encounter even unexpected situations and react instinctively and immediately.[8]

Running through the protocol and similar exercises were among the first steps of Brandon's QB training camp. As he explained, "The quarterbacks couldn't start on the noncodified knowledge, because they wouldn't be able to learn the offense, and they wouldn't be able to understand and then transfer the knowledge." So Brandon first focused on basic, explicit routines.

A big challenge for John Beck after two losing seasons was to rebuild his confidence; tacit know-that can't simply be picked up from film or position room discussions. Bronco and Brandon's "simple successes" practice philosophy refashioned John's belief in himself and eventually led to the poise and patience that he displayed in the last drive of the 2006 Utah game when he shuffled from pressure for over ten seconds while waiting for a receiver to get open.

The most important type of knowledge, which is also the most difficult to coach, is tacit know-how. It is what a golfer relies on when he finds his ball in the rough just off the green or buried in a bunker and must create the perfect combination of grip strength, feet position, swing plane, and force to get the ball close to the hole. It is knowing just what to say to finally close the deal with your outsourcing contractor, or expertly performing the right technique for removing a lesion from the prefrontal cortex of an eight-year-old girl. This is knowledge that at its best allows a person to make the right choice in a situation he has never experienced before or to conceptualize an idea so new, so different, or so true that it revolutionizes physics or medicine or the marketplace.

The tacit know-how that John needed was how to execute even in the "fog of war." This term was introduced to the Cougars by Mark Rhodes, our colleague whose expertise in strategic decision-making has been tapped by BYU athletics. The phrase comes from the pen of Carl von Clausewitz, a Napoleonic-era military theorist who wrote the venerated tome *On War*. Clausewitz famously described the uncertainty of battle by saying that "all action takes place, so to speak, in a kind of twilight, which, like fog or moonlight, often tends to make things seem grotesque and larger than they really are."[9]

A young football player is most likely to run into trouble when he encounters something complex and new. It's the same as learning to drive a car. The day will come when you first face traffic on the interstate and cannot seem to make your way into the exit lane, or you hit black ice on an overpass in the dark. You have to think very explicitly about what to do: change lanes at the speed of traffic! Turn in the direction of the skid! But as our exposure to such complex scenarios is repeated and our brains become attuned to the various patterns and responses involved in driving, we eventually come to perform them automatically and even calmly. We become experts.[10]

We owe the ability to develop automatic responses to complex stimuli to our cerebral cortex. This is the largest part of the brain; it surrounds more primitive brain structures and is responsible for higher thought and learning. It is the region of the brain where stimulus-response patterns are developed and lodged. Our brain's ability to learn to deal with the sophisticated response requirements of intricate scenarios is an extension of the primitive brain's instinctive response to danger that comes hardwired within each of us.[11] Just as we jump when we hear a sudden clap of thunder, so also can a quarterback instinctively shoot off a pass that sails over coverage and anticipates where the receiver will be by the time the ball arcs toward the earth. The startle response is innate; passing prowess is learned. But both are executed without deliberation.

How does a quarterback's body acquire nondeliberative wisdom about when and where to send the ball? The surprising answer that comes from neuroscience is that it's all in his *emotions.*

The process, simplified, goes like this: in daily, weekly practice, a quarterback repeats the protocol for every play hundreds of times. His reads and gestures become automatic. His body learns to take him fluidly through a cascading gamut of possible handoffs and passes. In gamelike practice in particular, he encounters a range of scenarios. Some of these are unexpected and require improvisation. Alone and with his coaches, he reflects on his performance and studies how his responses could have been more effective.

Over time, his brain begins to recognize patterns on the field.[12] Certain formations and actions betray the defense's intentions to him. The movement of cornerbacks and safeties signals either danger or opportunity. His brain learns to expect certain outcomes from these configurations based on experience. If the brain foresees a positive outcome—a receiver wide open in the red zone, as an obvious example—special neurons release a tiny squirt of dopamine, a feel-good neurochemical elixir responsible for pleasure. A part of the brain called the anterior cingulated cortex immediately saturates the brain with the corresponding emotions—anticipation and excitement—directing the quarterback's attention to the good news and preparing his body for action.[13] Simply reacting, the quarterback chooses that alternative among all those on the field.

If the brain foresees a negative outcome—a cornerback converging on the tight end—the brain withholds dopamine. The player senses danger and experiences fear or alarm. He is motivated to choose another alternative, and fast. All of this happens almost instantaneously, and the quarterback is quite unaware of what moves him. But his actions feel natural, and he makes his decisions effortlessly.[14] He is guided by his emotions, not by a complicated thought process. In fact, the critical role that emotion plays in decision-making is one of the big stories of modern neuroscience.[15]

To develop these easy instincts, the coaching staff relies on repetition, gamelike practice, and mentoring. We discussed each of these in chapter 8.

ORGANIZATION CONDITIONS
FOR LEARNING

Bronco says BYU Football is a "learning organization." He tries to ensure that everything about the place is conducive to learning. Likewise, organizations should cultivate environments propitious to gaining and sharing knowledge. **Organization conditions** are the design elements of the OSD model—work and work processes, structure, decision-making and information systems, people systems, reward systems, and continuous improvement practices. All of these can be designed to encourage learning. For example, when process improvement projects are made part of the yearly goals of leaders, teams are more likely to take the time to review their outputs to see how they can make them better.

Organizations should recognize that the most important

learning is unlikely to take place in formal, classroom-type situations. It's more likely to happen when folks discover something unexpected and have a chance to bat it about with peers and mentors, to test it and wrangle with it. Organizations must be able to tolerate—no, encourage—informal discussions where people are most likely to swap war stories about how to answer tricky customer service questions or which new materials are working well in product design and construction.

When Xerox researchers studied the use of service documentation, which had been helpfully designed to guide technicians through correct repair procedures, they found that the technicians not only didn't use it, they didn't need it! They already knew the procedures for routine repairs. What tripped them up were unexpected and non-routine tasks for which no documentation was available. The researchers—ethnographers who study *behavior* to discover what people believe, not just what they *say* they believe—found that technicians turn to their peers and to technical experts for help, not to documents. Then they share stories with each other and pass on their wisdom in water-cooler-type discussions.[16]

This is true at BYU as well. As we explained in chapter 8, water breaks provided just the kind of informal setting where backup quarterback Riley Nelson was likely to ask starter Max Hall about footwork or other actions that puzzled him.

Time for knowledge explorations can be built into the work routine. At Google, engineers are famously given 20 percent of their time to devote to projects not necessarily within their job descriptions. This time has resulted in new features and offerings, not to mention bug fixes and other improvements to existing systems.[17] People are motivated to learn and innovate when they can delve into interests beyond their everyday responsibilities. Formal classroom training will never be enough to spawn the most complex types of exploration and skill development.

Opportunities to attend professional conferences and to benchmark processes in other organizations give employees exposure to ideas outside their usual purview. Both the BYU offensive and defensive staffs visit yearly with teams or coaching staffs from other conferences or even from the NFL that are doing something of interest. This is standard practice in the football world—"there's a kind of fellowship between coaches," says Brandon.

To deepen such enrichment opportunities, learners can be asked to reteach the most important "takeaways" of their outings. After Nick Howell attended an NFL camp with the Pittsburgh Steelers, Bronco asked him to present to the whole staff. "That was awesome," says Nick, "because I got to get in front of everyone, tell them exactly what I saw, what I learned, what concepts I thought would be good for our program, and what I thought we should implement."

The BYU staff even explores knowledge that is perhaps outside the boundaries normally trolled by football coaches for information about football strategy and technique. After two new coaches joined the staff in early 2011, the BYU coaching team reread and discussed Jim Collins's *Good to Great*, chapter by chapter. New and unaccustomed to such wide-ranging learning practices, wide receivers coach Ben Cahoon expressed the tension naturally created when learning time is devoted to topics not directly encompassed in job descriptions. "We spent two and a half hours talking about Level 5 leaders," he says. "I like learning about new things, but at the same time, I have forty videos I've got to evaluate!"

Organizations can ease this kind of tension when expectations and systems are in place to reinforce extra- or ultra-curricular studies. They can cultivate voluntary structures (such as communities of practice) or systems (such as internal wikis) that accelerate the trading of knowledge. They can establish mentoring systems that assign novices to experts as a way of fostering conditions for the transfer of know-how, such as the Band of Brothers program at BYU. These are just a few of the many possible examples of design elements that can foster a learning environment.

YOU AND ORGANIZATION LEARNING

What have you done to identify knowledge in your organization—your work, or perhaps the soccer team you coach? Can the people around you identify what is the most important thing to learn?

What learning processes have you developed? Repetition, game-like practice, and mentoring are three learning processes that BYU Football relies on to train young athletes. What about the learning processes at your work? Have you developed strategies for passing on crucial competitive knowledge? Jobs that require top-notch physical performance are not the only ones where well-developed learning practices can improve on-the-spot success. Do you have a mentoring program, and have you been involved in both sharing your expertise as well as learning from someone else whom you respect? Do you benchmark practices that would improve your marketplace situation? Does your group simulate tense customer moments in order to practice your skills at calming customers and solving their problems? Do you ensure that those new to your area are oriented to the basic rules and routines that govern your work? Do they have a chance to rub shoulders with experts and hear their war stories? Have leaders developed the innate ability to improvise strategically in the fog of war when employee or customer situations don't go quite as planned?

What about organization learning conditions? Are you a learning organization? Have you developed structures and routines to foster learning, both formal and spontaneous? Have you built a cost structure into projects that allows for some "innovation time off" as at Google? Do you take time in staff meetings to discuss a relevant new book, technology, or news event? Have you assigned decision rights so that new ideas get a fair hearing? Have you crafted reward policies to encourage learning explorations and continuous improvement?

Superior knowledge is the purest form of competitive advantage. If you or your group has discovered or developed new knowledge, have you shared it abroad? That's the topic of chapter 9, a continuation of Smooth Stone #4—why and how to spread new intellectual wealth to those who could use it beyond the boundaries of your immediate group.

KNOWLEDGE DIFFUSION

With its emphasis on acquiring new knowledge, chapter 8 focused on knowledge discovery. **Discovery** means *inventing* programs, products, processes, procedures, and so on, and learning how best to *implement* them. For example, a left-handed quarterback might discover a solution to a problem he's having securing snaps. Or a department in a company, responding to employee interest in job rotation, might work with its HR partner to invent a useful Employee Development Planning process and teach the managers how to use it to discuss their employee's hopes and dreams and make arrangements accordingly.

Chapter 9 extended the discussion of knowledge management by considering the importance of diffusion. **Diffusion** (or *dissemination*) means broadly *sharing* the concepts of new products, programs, and processes as well as the know-how to relevant groups across the organization. The ability to implement must be transferred as well. A pro quarterback sharing his knowledge with a young southpaw about how left-handed offense leaders can take snaps from right-handed centers is a good example of diffusion, especially if he gives him some personal coaching. Transferring the Employee Development Planning process would mean telling other departments about the program and even providing mentoring to those interested in adopting the practice.

Organizations must provide for effective knowledge transmission across boundaries. Because of far-flung corporate, supplier, and customer locations, there has never been a greater need. Too often, knowledge has been locked and forgotten on individual laptops, shared network drives, and old e-mails. People duplicate efforts because they don't know which groups have already dealt with similar problems. Collaboration has been plodding and cumbersome because of time and geographic distances.

Application is as important as dissemination, because it's not very helpful if a lot of very good ideas have been developed and shared but used by only a very few people. The gist: focus knowledge management efforts not only on helping people learn something new but also on passing their new insights to others in a way that spreads the ability to *implement* the knowledge as well as just *comprehend* it. This may mean applying it directly, but often it means collaborating to develop it further, to reinvent it into something of greater relevance and efficacy.[18]

Many organizations, when rating their ability to learn, score their ability to *discover* new information much higher than their ability to *diffuse* new discoveries throughout the company. But improving their diffusion capabilities could have a multiplicative effect on knowledge transfer.

One famous example of knowledge insularity within an organization is the technological innovations made at Xerox's Palo Alto Research Center (PARC) in the early 1970s. Within a few years of its inception, this research group rapidly invented or developed some of the most important technologies of the century: the personal computer; user interface devices such as the mouse, icons, and pull-down menus; laser printing; and local area networks. But only one of these technologies was commercialized by Xerox itself: laser printing.

Part of the problem was that Xerox Corporation understood itself to be in the business of copiers, not personal computers. Despite funding PARC, they had developed no effective mechanisms for transferring knowledge out of research and development and into manufacturing and marketing. And not only were its Connecticut headquarters geographically a continent away from PARC, its con-servative East-Coast business culture clashed with the youthful, hippie-like culture at PARC. As it happened, Apple was a significant beneficiary of PARC's innovations. Steve Jobs paid a visit to PARC in 1979 and subsequently hired some of the PARC employees for the skunkworks that developed the Macintosh desktop computer.[19]

SOCIAL NETWORKING TOOLS AND DIFFUSION

The good news is that with the advent of social networking tech-nologies, there have never been more tools and ideas to help with knowledge diffusion. In fact, some observers believe that perhaps the most important potential business use of resources such as Facebook, Twitter, and other social media is not for *marketing* but for *learning.*[20] Tweets, RSS feeds, blogs, and podcasts can push questions and ideas to the mobile devices of followers interested in a topic. Knowledge can be searched and accessed by those for whom it is relevant on internal social networks, internal wikis, and hubs of aggregated blogs and videos. Leaders or technicians can come together in virtual worlds that simulate critical work situations and help them deepen their competencies in a context that imitates their daily work.

Consider this example of diffusion and application from *The 2020 Workplace* by Jeanne C. Meister and Karie Willyerd: a sales professional downloads product overview videos to his iPad one evening then reviews them the next morning as he rides the train to a client. The presentations have been created and uploaded by people who have sold the product before. Because they are tagged and rated, selecting a highly regarded, relevant presentation is easy. The sales pro learns what he needs to know to make a good presen-tation to his client, and he does it on his commute to work.[21]

BT, the British telecommunications firm, found that 78 per-cent of employees prefer peer learning.[22] As we saw in chapter 9, peer-to-peer instruction is when people learn from each other rather than relying on a designated expert or course instructor. They question each other, discuss, collaborate, and develop new knowledge together. BT launched its corporate social network Dare2Share to promote peer learning, and along the way reduced corporate training costs. Peter Butler, head of learning at BT, said that the network tapped "an enormous amount of enthusiasm among BT employees to be involved in their own learning. They have contributed content in areas ranging from product overviews and leadership thoughts to general best practices in doing their jobs," all delivered in a variety of formats. "The excitement we unleashed is priceless," he says.[23]

Social media, of course, is not the only organization design element that promotes knowledge sharing. Think through the OSD model that we introduced in chapter 5: knowledge transfer is also impacted by work processes, facility layout and equipment, work structures including and apart from traditional hierarchies, performance management systems, recognition practices, and continuous improvement methods.

For example, research pursued by Steelcase, a supplier of innovative office furniture, revealed that learning and collaboration are enhanced when learners are physically oriented toward each other rather than toward the instructor, as they are in the traditional classroom layout. The company designed a classroom where learners face the center and look over one another to view content replicated on monitors in all the corners. The facilitator can stand anywhere in the room and operate a switcher to toggle the projection between instructor and student laptops.[24]

The BYU Football defense, as we explained in chapter 9, found that a change in its use of facilities resulted in an exciting improvement in collaboration—so effective, in fact, that they remodeled the defensive meeting room to further enhance the defensive team's ability to meet in position pods all together in the same space.

Standardizing process improvements across departments and facilities is another way to ensure enhancements are diffused throughout the organization. Additionally, communities of practice can bring technical experts together (in-person and virtually) to share developments in their business units and to craft, certify, and maintain professional standards.

Regardless of the size of an organization or the sophistication of the technology they currently employ, leaders can still recognize the span and depth of the approaches that help people improve their skills and solve problems. BYU Football, for example, is not a large organization, nor has social media (yet) proved to be a tool it relies on to help football players enhance their expertise. But as we saw in chapter 9, BYU coaches have pursued experiences outside their ordinary work environment that help them develop specific competencies, and they also have developed procedures that promote learning within the context of their daily meetings and practices. They have recognized and experimented with the power of peer-to-peer learning. They have identified ways that their physical space can be enhanced to facilitate collaboration and knowledge transmission. These are learning principles that any organization can apply, large or small, well-resourced or cash-strapped.

We include a few additional notes below about some of the Cougars' methods of diffusion discussed in section 1.

ORGANIZATION-TO-ORGANIZATION DIFFUSION

We described how BYU Football turned to BYU–Idaho's Clark Gilbert and Henry J. Eyring for their findings about how students learn best. Gilbert and Eyring provided principles and tactics for peer-to-peer instruction. We share here the background about how innovative instructional methods became so important to administrators and scholars at BYU–Idaho.

For many decades the LDS-owned institution in Idaho was a large, two-year junior college known as Ricks College. In 2001, Church leaders announced the decision to expand it to a four-year institution because they desperately wanted to meet the soaring demand of LDS young people for an education at a Church-owned school. Since they planned to do so while keeping cost-per-student down, however, they made the choice not to offer graduate degrees nor to aspire to recognition as a research institution. They were crystal clear on their strategy and they knew what the trade-offs had to be. They implemented a year-round calendar to maximize the use of facilities through even the summer months, and they eliminated the school's successful but expensive intercollegiate athletic program.

Most fundamentally, leaders of BYU–Idaho decided that the new, four-year university should become best-in-class at *teaching undergraduates.* They envisioned that the school would, as expressed by then-university president David A. Bednar (a former quarterback, as it happens), "play a pioneering role in understanding learning and teaching processes."[25] Faculty would have dual competency in their respective fields—"mastery of both the subject matter and the art of conveying it for maximum student learning."[26]

Gilbert was an innovation specialist who had been invited to join the administration after his former dean at Harvard Business School, Kim Clark, succeeded Bednar as president. He had taken note of recent scholarly evidence that one of the most effective forms of learning is peer instruction. (Not just a favorite method, as we saw in the BT example above.) He and his colleagues, including Eyring, had been developing the concept and had created courses at BYU–Idaho founded on the principles of student-to-student interaction.

One of those principles, as we discussed in chapter 9, is strong *student preparation*, which allows class (or team) time to be used for deepening understanding rather than dispensing information. But finding ways to foster preclass preparation, they warned, is easier to say than to do. It involves developing a culture of accountability. Teachers must check preparation because students will revert to poor habits in the absence of oversight. Teachers can do this through preclass online quizzes or discussions, for example, or "cold-calling" on students during class. They must be sure that the preparation they require is relevant; busy-work jades students and hampers their engagement. And, of course, they must be sure they themselves are well prepared in order to set the example.

Gilbert and Eyring also described some of the *tools* used by teachers in Idaho. As we showed, the football coaches took those ideas, augmented them with some of their own, and each developed a repertoire of methods for involving students in teaching each other. This kind of application is exactly what good knowledge managers do: when they learn something new, they adapt it and elaborate on it to mold something uniquely suited to their own situation.

Gilbert and Eyring also told the coaches that when BYU–Idaho implemented a new learning model across the campus that encourages student-centered teaching methods, some faculty worried that peer instruction might "simply become a case of students swapping ignorance."[27] But if students prepare ahead of time, if classroom activities are carefully planned with a definite learning outcome in mind, and if *peer interactions are monitored and redirected by teachers* as needed, then the result is a depth of understanding and an ability to apply learning far beyond what would be possible through the traditional lecture format.

TEAM-TO-TEAM DIFFUSION: LINKING MECHANISMS

When it comes to encouraging people within an organization to share knowledge about customers, equipment, technical expertise, and more, organizations must figure out how to help people span the organization chart boundaries between different departments and groups. They can make all kinds of choices to get this to happen—they can put in place councils, projects, policies, wikis, internal social networks, and even matrixed reporting relationships. This type of design element is called a "linking mechanism" because it links people together across verticals. Some of these designs are more complex than others; some work better than others at ensuring knowledge held in one area is made available throughout the company to those who can also use it.

DIFFUSION IN YOUR WORLD

Now pause for a minute to consider the learning environment at your own paid or volunteer work. Can you articulate your most significant weaknesses and opportunities? Are you constantly looking for novel ideas about how to make things better? Have you set up the expectations and made the accommodations to give people with a good idea a little extra time and space to explore it?

If you participate in a high-performing team at work, do you sometimes volunteer to help other teams? Have you tried to codify—film, record, or write about—what's working well and to make it available to those who are interested? Have you joined a community of practice? Do you participate in online discussions? Have you found a mentor to challenge you and answer questions, or have you become a mentor to share your knowledge with younger employees? If you are more mature, have you yourself been reverse-mentored by a younger employee to learn more about social media? Have you participated in a Six Sigma or Lean project to tackle a persistent problem and shared your outcomes?

Are the learning practices in your organization replete with peer instruction? If you teach a community college class or lead training events at work, do you see yourself as "a sage on the stage," or do you understand your job to be the chief engineer of the learning experience? If you perhaps teach at church, when is the last time you found a gentle way to hold people accountable for preclass preparation? Split folks into "huddles" to discuss an assigned topic? Let young or reserved class members prepare and teach part of the lesson?

What about your role as a mother or father? When you give advice, is it a lecture? Or do you devote some effort to crafting experiences where your teen can safely and honestly discuss her thoughts with you? Do you think it is possible for children to teach each other as the Cougar players coach each other? Maybe you could bring up a scenario at dinner that the family can work through together; for example, you could ask children what to do when they hear an unkind story about someone on the bus. A parent, too, can be a sort of learning craftsman who creatively finds ways to help kids talk through current events, personal challenges, and values and virtues.

You don't have to be a leader or teacher to concern yourself with knowledge diffusion. Ideas that spread are *gifts*, says Seth Godin, author of *Linchpin*.[28] Giving gifts satisfies us and "magnetically" signals to others that we have "plenty more to share."[29] To give effusively, without thought of recompense, is to feel joy. It is to please others, maybe to touch them or change them in a way that gladdens them. Giving shows that you trust someone, that they are worthy of your efforts, investment, and attention. When you give, you strengthen your community, whether it is at work, at home, in the neighborhood, in your congregation, or online. Giving creates a bond, a partnership with the receiver. In an organization, giving ideas that spread helps you become valuable, maybe even indispensable—a linchpin.[30] And when you are well appreciated, you will be rewarded with gifts worth getting, such as "massive amounts of responsibility and freedom," the opportunity "to expend emotional labor," assignments that are intriguing and challenging, and the pleasure of collaborating with colleagues who also love to give.[31] Indeed, Godin suggests thinking of your job as "a platform for generosity."[32] Sharing your ideas earnestly and openly may be the best way to work.

SMOOTH STONE #4 SUMMARY

Principle: Knowledge is the purest form of competitive advantage, so learn to actively manage the knowledge in your organization. Identify what knowledge is crucial and then develop learning processes to help people acquire or enhance their expertise. Make sure mechanisms are in place for knowledge to move easily across organization boundaries.

Cougar application: BYU Football is a learning organization. The players and coaches study best-practice learning methods. To overcome the weaknesses in their team as well as to move toward their highest football aspirations, they search out new knowledge about the game and about coaching. They have made a thorough study of quarterback knowledge in particular and rely on repetition, gamelike play, and mentoring as just a few of the ways to efficiently deepen the capabilities of all players. Coaches strive to teach using the most effective pedagogical methods; specifically, they see themselves not just as men who dispense their technical game wisdom but as the designers of top-notch learning and practice experiences.

Your application: Discover what knowledge is most important to your organization, group, or family. Understand how those you guide learn. Get to know their learning preferences. Then seek out the most effective ways of learning and teaching this knowledge, which are unlikely to include formal classroom training and much more likely to involve hands-on processes such as peer-to-peer instruction and mentoring. Find ways to share what you have learned.

CHAPTER 17

Smooth Stone #5

Effective Leaders
Capture Hearts and Minds

M OST OF SECTION 1 up until chapter 10 was about how the
Cougars approach strategy, organization design, and knowledge management. These disciplines are exquisitely helpful in creating successful organizations that can claim an advantage in the
marketplace or otherwise achieve their goals.

But the truth is that an estimated 70 percent of change efforts
falter.[1] Most strategies never achieve the results that were expected;
the majority of organization transformation or reengineering efforts
peter out before reaching their potential. A large part of the reason
is that leaders are unsuccessful at energizing people about the new
vision and helping them to sustain that energy.[2] As strategy expert
Gary Hamel has written, "The goals of management are usually described in words like 'efficiency,' 'advantage,' 'value,' 'superiority,'
'focus,' and 'differentiation.' Important as these objectives are, they
lack the power to rouse human hearts."[3]

So in chapter 10, we talked about what leaders can do to rouse
human hearts: ignite them with a higher purpose, involve them in

the cause, unite them in rich, caring networks, and revive them when energies flag.

IGNITE

We said in chapter 10 that a noble purpose energizes people more than anything else.

We had in mind the work of psychologists Edward L. Deci, Richard Ryan, and their colleagues when we claimed that pursuing intrinsic rewards results in greater happiness. They have shown that holding out extrinsic goals (i.e., external rewards) such as money and power tend to result in poor mental health, manifested in such conditions as anxiety and depression, while placing a higher premium on intrinsic goals, such as personal development and community contribution, results in a greater feeling of well-being and self-esteem.[4]

Gallup has found that a good job is the most dominant and prevalent desire of the world's seven billion inhabitants.[5] But once they have a good job, now more than ever, workers—and share-owners—crave a meaningful answer to the question, "Why?" They long for an answer that feels more personal than merely "for profit." People feel most satisfied and engaged when they find or orchestrate a satisfactory response based on intrinsic aspirations. David and Wendy Ulrich explore this topic in *The Why of Work: How Great*

Leaders Build Abundant Organizations That Win. They show that the effort of seeking meaning has inherent value for mankind *and* that it also has market value. It is noble *and* profitable.[6] When employees find meaning in their work, they are more committed and energetic. The Ulriches cite a slew of statistics that show that the full engagement of employees results in stock appreciation, increased market returns, better customer outcomes, higher sales, and reduced turnover.[7] Purpose is a matter of revenue as well as right living.

It's interesting that the question of meaning is now important to workers on both ends of the demographic spectrum. Baby boomers, which as a group have made up the largest segment of the workforce for many years, are fueling a new emphasis on meaning as they retire healthy and fit and seek noble pursuits to cap their productive lives.[8] On the flip side of the workforce are the Millennials—those born between 1977 and 1997—who will shortly replace baby boomers as the largest generational work population, a group to which the Cougar football team soundly belongs. A 2008 survey of this group revealed that they are meaning-driven. Among other expectations, they want to work for an organization whose purpose aligns with their beliefs.[9]

National leaders and economists throughout the world have conceded that a nation's well-being includes much more than its economic output, as reported recently in the *Harvard Business Review*.[10] They now talk about "well-being" or "happiness" measures and are diligently engaged in finding new ways to track more than just economic output. One such measure is "GNH"—gross national happiness.

What is a leader's responsibility in helping people find meaning at work? The Ulriches say that the heart of a leader's job is "creating a direction for their organizations that is charged with meaning— that resonates with not only the minds and hands but the hearts of those they lead." Such leaders guide their groups or companies in *"meaning-making,"* not just moneymaking.[11]

Inspired people and organizations all over the world are choosing to put moneymaking in the service of meaning-making. They create organizations of varying forms to get at this purpose. A for-profit organization that is both clear and sincere about how it brings greater well-being to customers can be very inspiring to its employees—as long as leaders are devoted to vigorously sharing this mission internally.[12] We are all very familiar with charities and nongovernmental organizations, such as the Red Cross, that have made social missions their priority from the beginning. More recently, traditional money-making enterprises have sought to act with "social responsibility" by improving quality of work life for employees and taking steps to reduce their environmental impact. Some companies such as IBM and Pfizer have created programs to develop rising leaders as well as contribute philanthropically to underdeveloped regions of the world. In these programs, young managers spend a term working at a local business in a market where the organization plans to grow.[13]

"Social enterprises" go much further by incorporating both profits and social improvement into their fundamental mission. The micro-lending Grameen Bank was a pioneer in finding a profitable way to bring banking services to the poor in Bangladesh, one of the world's most impoverished countries. Founder Muhammad Yunus, an economics professor, won a Nobel Peace Prize for his work. In 1983, he designed a bank to serve people so utterly destitute that they had no hope of providing a credit history or any form of collateral—traditional requirements of credit-worthiness. The bank relied on lending circles made up of the poor—women, mostly, who may have never before touched any money—to mentor and monitor each other in borrowing to start or grow tiny businesses called "micro-enterprises." It worked fabulously. As of 2012, the repayment rate is 96.57 percent,[14] and the bank routinely makes a profit. The Grameen Bank has lifted millions above the poverty level, and as its mission has expanded, it has built hundreds of thousands of homes and awarded tens of thousands of scholarships and student loans.[15] By 2012, microfinance had become a $65 billion industry serving more than ninety million of the world's poorest customers.[16]

Most of us have heard of or even benefited from social businesses with a variety of aims. Take TOMS Shoes. Last year, co-author Alyson's twelve-year-old daughter could not live without a pair. Grandma took her to buy some, so according to the company's mission, another pair was donated to a child in need somewhere in the world. Then Grandma bought a pair, too. Boom: another disadvantaged youngster was shod. On a smaller scale, Malawi Pizza in Cougar territory is "pizza with a purpose." Each pie purchased in Provo means a meal served to a child in the impoverished country of Malawi, Africa, hit hard in recent years by drought and the HIV/AIDS epidemic. More than one million free pairs of shoes for children from TOMS; nearly two hundred thousand meals for Malawis. Many American teenagers satisfied in both style and stomach.

Cougar football found its transcendent purpose in the cause of generating additional interest in The Church of Jesus Christ of Latter-day Saints, whose tenets and practices have made such a difference in the coaches' and players' own lives.

What's your noble cause? Bronco said, "I ask the players to play from the deepest place possible." What the deepest place for you? It doesn't need to be explicitly religious to have the power to coalesce and impassion your investors and workforce and customers.

Once you know your noble cause, you will need to find a way to coalesce your organization around it. As described in chapter 10, our most memorable experiences are those that involve significant emotion, metaphor, and/or music. Bronco creates significant emotion when he runs his players up Y Mountain or throws helmets representing an old uniform in the bonfire. He makes memories when he lodges a granite boulder in the front of the room and asks players to chisel a "Y" into its surface as a metaphor for the total dedication required by those who have given themselves over to the effort of building faith in the community. Music in team meetings and firesides—hymns or other songs of praise, sung or played by musician-athletes—creates a worshipful undercurrent to business as usual.

How can you craft memorable methods for coalescing people around a worthy cause? Memos and webcasts generally aren't particularly arresting. But a story or symbolic gesture might just do the trick. John Kotter in *The Heart of Change* recounts the actions of one savvy leader who created a Glove Shrine to draw attention to a purchasing problem. He piled 424 different types of work gloves on the boardroom table as evidence of disjointed requisition approaches that resulted in far too much variation in the supplies ordered and prices paid by different facilities in the company.[17]

Share your message in a way that evokes surprise, hope, excitement, or even outrage. Use a metaphor or incorporate music. Make it memorable.

INVOLVE

To describe how important it is to involve people in an undertaking if you really need their hearts and minds in the fullest sense, we turn from Millennial football players to mid-century housewives. These housewives showed Kurt Lewin, a social psychologist working at the University of Iowa during World War II, how to really help people change.

At that time, meat was rationed because of war-time shortages, and if you wanted to serve your family a steak or a chop, you had to use a scarce ration stamp to get it. But there was plenty of liver, brain, tongue, and heart for purchase without any stamps. How interested do you think women were in feeding their families these secondary cuts of meat? Probably about like you: not very. Lewin's job was to find out how to get more liver on the tables of U.S. families.

He discovered that when he organized a sample group of women (then and now the primary gatekeepers of the family dinner table) and had them listen to an informative and compelling lecture on how to provide their family with optimal nutrition during the war and how to do it economically, only 3 percent of the moms served up any of the nonrationed meat. The researchers even talked about patriotic duty and distributed recipes, but to little avail.

But when Lewin organized another sample of women into discussion groups, gave them the same topics to discuss, and asked them how they could help the war effort, 32 percent of the moms purchased the previously undesirable cuts. Lewin concluded that among other factors, being involved in the discussion and decision-making was instrumental to the higher rate of behavior change.

It was Deci who decades later conducted research that showed that people have a basic need for autonomy. In other words, they need to feel free in their actions; they need to feel that they are their own masters. The opposite is to feel controlled or pressured. When people feel autonomous, they act with interest and commitment. When people feel controlled, they may comply, but they will not be fully engaged, nor will their performance rise to the heights possible when they freely act in accordance with their own desires.[18]

The question for leaders is not, "How do I motivate people?" accordingly to Deci, but rather, "How can I create the conditions within which others will motivate themselves?"[19] This is just the question Deci and his colleagues studied in a series of experiments at the University of Rochester, studies that led to the knowledge that giving people choice increases their sense of autonomy.

When people were given a set of puzzles to solve and offered a choice of which ones to work on and how much time to spend on each, the subjects showed more indications of intrinsic motivation than subjects who were not offered a choice. The former group spent more time playing with the puzzles and enjoyed the experience more.[20] People who have choice regarding an activity commit themselves to it and feel greater volition. They work with greater concentration, spend more time at a task, and have more fun. Their creative energies so given may contribute to a better solution than one imposed on them without their input. This is why Lewin's housewives were so much more willing to cook with less favorable meat cuts when they were involved in deciding how they could help the war effort.

We also had in mind Deci's research when we claimed in chapter 10 that feeling challenged is another condition that fosters high engagement. The challenge must be commensurate with people's skills so that they are neither overwhelmed nor bored, but rather stretched. They will then feel proud of their accomplishments and eager for more.[21]

The condition of becoming totally engrossed in your work has been studied by Mihaly Csikszentmihalyi, and he is the one who used the word *flow* for this kind of utter absorption. This is work at its best, and leaders can ensure that jobs are designed to have the best chance of creating flow opportunities for employees. Says Csikszentmihalyi, "The more a job inherently resembles a game—with variety, appropriate and flexible challenges, clear goals, and immediate feedback—the more enjoyable it will be regardless of the worker's level of development."[22] Think of the Cougars' Supergames—conditioning assignments so enthralling that players achieved more while hardly being aware of their increased exertion. Jobs provide workers with a sense of discovery when the task matches their abilities and beckons them to see if they can get better. When people strive for higher levels of performance, they enjoy their work, and their output is enhanced. As we said in chapter 10, total involvement happens when work flows.

Flow is not a matter of lofty slogans or off-site rallies. It involves job design and thoughtful leadership. If managers can put the principles of optimal experience into practice in jobs, making sure there is a strong element of choice, and if the goals of those jobs align with the group or enterprise mission, they will have employees who give their all.

The Cougars get their players involved in a myriad of ways off the field—they participate in the leadership council, organize firesides and service projects, give service in the community, coach special teams, mentor newer players, and speak or play an instrument or sing at a fireside, just to name a few.

UNITE

A feeling of connection to others is the third condition for total engagement. Our relationships in the workplace, where we rely on others and give to others in reciprocal relationships of friendship and collaboration, are an important part of our total social network—the quality of which, according to Harvard psychology professor Daniel Gilbert, is predictive of one's happiness.[23]

Let's explore how caring and connection are related to learning and performance. We cannot learn without the help and collaboration of others, and close relationships with people we admire intellectually make it possible for us to learn more from them. If we trust them, we can ask them questions, reveal our concerns, and feel comfortable opening up about the deficits we want their help to diminish. Think of Riley Nelson and James Lark and the new quarterbacks they mentored in their last year.

Hearts and minds are engaged when there is an exciting discharge of energy along the vertices and nodes of a rich social system—when people reach out with enthusiasm to share the mission and solicit help and when others are attracted to this buzz of energy and commit their ideas and efforts as well.

The main idea is simply that organizations thrive when people work well together. Cooperation flourishes when the basic qualities of our interactions include trust and reciprocity. You are willing to help me with my problem if you believe that I or someone else in your network will help you sometime in the future. In a strong network, good-will giving happens frequently and predictably.

Consider the neighborly interactions that characterize coauthor Alyson's street in a Midwestern college town: when her family was out of town for a few days last summer, one neighbor made his way into their garage to turn off the automatic sprinklers when they failed in the "on" position. The Von Feldts often include neighborhood children in their family dinner if they happen to be playing at their house at dinnertime. The mom across the street drives the schoolchildren of three families to school when the temperature falls below 25 degrees F so they don't have to walk on those cold (for Kansas) days. Yet another neighbor rounded up garden chairs from the neighborhood to assist a family close by in finding seating for mourners coming to greet them when their son died in an accident. The residents in the neighborhood feel neither obligated nor pressured to help; they are all glad to offer what they have and don't find it to be an inconvenience.

This is the same kind of vibe that emerges when people are engaged at work. There's a mix of reaching out and offering up that happens ad hoc. If people are withholding information, if they're reluctant to volunteer for a committee, if they don't get their work done on time, then you can be sure that their hearts and minds are elsewhere.

The ideas from chapters 8 and 9—uniting all sorts of other people in aspects of your knowledge journey, along with igniting your compatriots with a noble purpose and involving them in the work—align with the research of Deci and his colleagues on relatedness, purpose, autonomy, and mastery. This research and Csikszentmihalyi's ideas about flow, along with much more, are beautifully discussed in the popular book *Drive* by Daniel Pink.[24] Bronco and all of the Cougar staff read this book and were greatly influenced by its ideas. We'd like to include one more essential ingredient for capturing hearts and minds: energy management.

REVIVE

Everyone who knows BYU Football knows about being "fully invested." Full engagement in an effort generates vast outputs of energy in a person or a group, doing amazing good in the world and releasing the unbounded joys of creativity, productivity, and friendship. But it can also be taxing to the body and the mind.

We emphasized the importance of an alternating cycle of energy investment and replenishment in chapter 10. This idea comes from Jim Loehr's and Tony Schwartz's work, which they share in *The Power of Full Engagement* and which has been very influential to Bronco.

They describe their work as beginning with Loehr's study of world-class tennis players. He noticed that performance differences were best understood not by studying the athlete's competitive habits during active play, but rather between points. "While most of them were not aware of it, the best players had each built almost exactly the same set of routines between points," they write. "These included the way they walked back to the baseline after a point; how they held their heads and shoulders; where they focused their eyes; the pattern of their breathing; and even the way they talked to themselves."[25] They were "instinctively using their time between points to maximize their recovery," while "lower-ranked competitors . . . had no recovery routines at all." What Loehr learned is that "the performance consequences of instituting these precise between-point rituals were dramatic"[26] and that led to his and Schwartz's advocacy of restorative routines for high performers of all types.

Loehr and Schwartz encourage us to work intensely but also to develop positive *rituals* for disengagement and renewal. Such rituals are "precise, consciously acquired behaviors that become automatic in our lives, fueled by a deep sense of purpose."[27] Because they are inviolable, they ensure that we periodically restore our energy even when deeply engrossed in a task or idea. For example, habits such as brushing your teeth or saying your prayers are so strong that we do them even when we're rushed or exhausted. When rituals are automatic, it takes very little conscious effort to rouse ourselves to do them. For many runners, their routine is so firm that they do not have to daily conquer the urge to skip their exercise. Rituals that embody our dearest values ensure that we are constantly acting on our beliefs. Attending church routinely on Sunday ensures that we are reminded of the path that we mean to take in this life. A regularly scheduled weekly visit to a parent in a nursing home establishes an ongoing opportunity to express our appreciation for their lifetime of love for us and to show our affection.

Staying fully invested involves monitoring and protecting four sources of energy: physical, emotional, mental, and spiritual. We preserve *physical energy* when eat regularly and healthily, sleep well, and exercise. Taking a short break every 90–120 minutes to stretch your legs or have a small, healthy snack can serve to enhance your productivity levels all day long and leave you with enough energy to give your family your full attention in the evening. Bronco's midday respites in the canyon help restore his physical energy.

Emotional energy comes from positive, happy feelings. These are tapped when we have fun with friends and invest time in the loving, supportive relationships of family life. These are the folks that we meet with to laugh, tell stories, relax, and share a meal. If they include our children, we help them with their homework and drive them to their piano lessons, and they love us and inspire us as they learn new things and find their own way in the world. Likewise, our spouse and friends know us well and care for us no matter how our day has gone. We can smile with them when we accomplish something big and laugh with them at our knuckleheaded mistakes. And they rely on us to help them rejuvenate from their energy expenditures as well. Protecting family life even during the football season provides for sound replenishment of Cougar emotional energy.

Mental energy is restored when we alternate periods of intensely focused analytical or sequential activity—which describes the jobs of many people across the globe—with looser periods when our mute right brains are liberated to incubate our challenges offline. Many of our best insights come to us when we are drowsy just before falling asleep, quietly awake just after arousing, or when we zone out in the shower or on a long drive. The brain rhythm correlated with such moments is known as "theta." Building theta time into your day and cherishing opportunities to go into the zone will enhance your opportunity to find that creative illumination that redirects your work when it is stalled or unsatisfactory.[28] Bronco's daily motorcycle ride does so much for his mental energy that he's come to rely on it.

Spiritual energy comes from living by your values and working for a purpose greater than yourself. Reflecting on your life periodically to honestly ask yourself if your actions are aligned with your priorities and values is an important step in rejuvenating your spiritual reserves. Serving others, reading scriptures, and praying are self-renewing behaviors that take energy at the very same time that they regenerate it. These types of activities are embedded in the personal routines of Cougar coaches and players.

Regeneration is important for organizations as well. Loehr and Schwartz provide the insight that capturing hearts and minds means nurturing your own energy at the same time that you are mindful of the energy of the organization. "Leaders are the stewards of organizational energy—in companies, organizations, and even in families," they say. "They inspire or demoralize others first by how effectively they manage their own energy and next by how well they mobilize, focus, invest, and renew the collective energy of those they lead."[29]

Just as Bronco did, leaders can institute regenerative organization rituals as well as support personal renewal whether it's performed by individuals at work or away. In chapter 10, we gave BYU Football examples of efforts to protect and renew physical, mental, emotional, and spiritual energy.

Though the Cougars choose prayer and group scripture study as some of their spiritually restorative routines, other organizations may choose spiritual rituals that are not necessarily religious. For example, an organization could publically read letters from customers whose lives have been enriched by a product or service. They could review the outcomes of community initiatives. When one of the Payless ShoeSource stores in Joplin, Missouri, was destroyed by the 2010 tornado, the leadership team of Collective Brands, their parent company, made audio contact with one of the employees in her hospital room to hear her story and wish her well. She tearfully recounted sheltering under a desk in the back storeroom and then emerging to a debris-strewn wasteland where the store had once stood. Collective Brands donated all the shoes that survived the tornado to the local community, and the retail group purchased and assembled 200 bicycles for school children who had lost possessions in the disaster. Activities such as these connect people to priorities of fundamental importance and restore their spiritual energy.

What about you? Do you find ways to regenerate throughout the day? Do you sprint all day and then flop at home, with nothing left for your family? Is there a way you can better pace renewal periods so that you have something left for others—and for yourself—after work? Are you selecting activities that rejuvenate you richly (such as reading or hanging out with your family without the television on), rather than dull your senses and make you listless (such as watching TV or surfing the Web)? Are you helping your children learn about the ebbs and flows of energy and how to manage their own sources of animation wisely? How would you rate yourself as a steward of your work group's energy? Your family's energy?

SMOOTH STONE #5 SUMMARY

Principle: Effective leaders who want to capture hearts and minds cultivate four conditions: a noble *purpose, involvement* in deciding what and how to work for that purpose, *unity* with others, and personal and organizational cycles of both energy expenditure and *renewal.*

Cougar application: BYU Football frequently engages in activities that reconnect coaches and players with their transcendent purpose and unite them together. For example, they meet together and pray together, serve the community, hold firesides, and study the scriptures together. Players are heavily involved in off-field activities such as serving on the leadership council, organizing firesides, planning service projects, coaching special teams, and mentoring each other. Cougar staff members are encouraged to seek out activities daily that revive their energy; head coach Bronco takes ninety minutes at lunchtime for a solitary activity. They hold regular social outings organized by "morale coach" Mark Weber.

Your application: Find your group's noble purpose and develop traditions for reconnecting to it often. Involve others in defining the best way to work and make sure their tasks are challenging. Develop relationships at work to facilitate social and emotional connections that are strong and satisfying. Stick to routines that help you and your group manage energy: sprint hard and push yourselves often, but be sure to recover wisely and regularly.

CHAPTER 18

Hearts Knit Together

I T WAS OUR VARIOUS life purposes that brought Bronco and authors Paul and Alyson together for this book.

Bronco had long before embarked on a journey to help young men see for themselves their own power and potential by putting them through athletic experiences requiring such discipline and devotion that they mimic the most daunting coming-of-age rituals of the world's warrior cultures. At BYU, he turned full force into the stiff wind of opportunity by requiring high moral standards of his players as well as extreme mental and physical effort.

Paul had once been a young man like those Bronco coaches now. He had been mentored at BYU by LaVell Edwards, the legendary football coach, and by Bill Dyer, the pioneering organization change scholar and practitioner. These teachers had fostered in him such a fondness for his alma mater that he was thrilled to proffer professional expertise gratis when BYU Football's new head coach requested that he join him on his path.

Alyson was the mother of a young man who loved football, too. When her adolescent son began to flex his powers and explore his potential, Alyson was thrilled to find at BYU an admirable set of athletes—and leaders—who were proclaiming their values frankly, living by high standards fearlessly, and achieving competitive success as they did so.

What purpose brings *you* to this book? Whatever it is, we hope that you have learned something that will help you feel a little more strongly of *your* own power and potential as a source of good in the world. Perhaps you have found stories that are inspirational to you. Perhaps you have gleaned some ideas that will help you in your organization as you make strategic decisions and craft a system that can carry out your aspirations. Maybe there is a young man in your life—or a young woman—who will enjoy knowing about many other young people who strive to work hard and do right. Perhaps you yourself will have a little more determination to unabashedly set your standards high and live as an example of wise and ethical leadership.

If the story we've told in these pages has ignited a good idea in you, if you are clearer about how you can involve yourself or others in changing things for the better, if you feel closer to like-valued folks, or even if you've simply been revived to move forward with greater energy on your life's path, then we hope to hear from you. Tell us what you connected with in these pages. Share with us how you are adapting the smooth stones for your shepherd's bag. Describe how you have defined your strategic distinctiveness, and what you've done to create a coherent organization around that uniqueness. Tell us about the young men and women in your life and how they are finding friends and role models with high standards.

We are eager to hear from you. Reach us at authors@running intothewind.com.

Acknowledgments

We could not have written this book, of course, without the generosity of Bronco Mendenhall. Not only did he spend hours with us reflecting on his first seven years as head football coach at Brigham Young University, but he also gave us open access to the football offices and endorsed our efforts to his staff and players. He is courageous and determined in doing the right thing. When he came to believe this book was the right thing, he gave his heart and mind over to it, even though we all knew it would mean greater public exposure for him, which he deplores. We are blessed that he has been willing to make the sacrifice.

Our heartiest thanks go to Kris Anne Gustavson, Paul's wife. She has encouraged us to collaborate on a book for years, and when we finally found the right topic, she put her money where her mouth was by scheduling appointments, assisting with interviews, transcribing hundreds of hours of tape, and reading multiple versions of the manuscript. Kris Anne, thank you.

We are grateful to the players and staff at Brigham Young University who were so willing and candid in their interviews. Cameron Jensen and Nate Miekle were particularly instrumental in helping us navigate the BYU Football fraternity. They provided background material, helped with chronology, sat in on interviews, and commented on versions of every chapter. Many thanks also go to players Matt Bauman, Brandon Bradley, Curtis Brown, Jonny Harline, Scott Johnson, Jan Jorgensen, Brian Logan, David Nixon, Jordan Pendleton, Brady Poppinga, Matt Reynolds, Andrew Rich, Mike Tanner, Travis Uale, and Harvey Unga. Every BYU Football staff member generously gave as well: Robert Anae, Duane Busby, Ben Cahoon, Brandon Doman, Joe DuPaix, Patrick Hickman, Patrick Higgins, Jaime Hill, Carey Hoki, Nick Howell, Steve Kaufusi, Barry Lamb, Shaun Nua, Jay Omer, Kelly Poppinga, Lance Reynolds, Paul Tidwell, and Mark Weber. Special thanks to Tom Holmoe for his insights and support. We greatly appreciate the contributions of UNM players Charles Moss, Nick Speegle, and Josh Bazinet. Our thanks also to Holly Mendenhall, Paul Mendenhall, President Cecil O. Samuelson Jr., Joel Deceuster, Kevin Worthen, LaVell Edwards, Paul Gilbert, and Shane Cragun.

We also are indebted to Greg Wrubell, Brett Pyne, and Mark Rhodes, who were meticulous in providing suggestions and corrections. Their help was indispensable. A host of other readers each helped us make improvements: Dave Ulrich, Norm Smallwood, Richard Feller, Kreig Smith, Reed Deshler, Stephen M. R. Covey, Rhett Evans, Kerry Patterson, Bonner Ritchie, Bill Snyder, Michael Colemere, David Nielson, Mark Richards, Marc Swartz, Stew Liff, Keith Nelleson, Ric Mitchell, Tim O'Hara, Chad Jensen, and Mindy Bash. Thanks to Adam Sanft for heroics in clarifying the NCAA rules that impacted the contents of this book.

Big thanks to those who guided us at Shadow Mountain: Sheri Dew, Chris Schoebinger, Laurel Christensen, Suzanne Brady, and Gail Halladay, and to Rachael Ward for the typography. Props, in particular, to Leslie Stitt, our editor, who is truly an angel.

We appreciate all those who have helped us chase away errors and confusion. Paul and Alyson claim full responsibility for any flaws that still remain.

On a more personal note, Paul wishes to thank Keith "Mad Dog" Rivera, whom he met in 1971 as a returned missionary living in Helaman Halls and attending BYU. They talked football; they talked religion. Mad Dog was a star defensive end who invited Paul to lift weights with him and then encouraged him to walk on to the football team. Paul's work with Bronco has been a way to give back to the team where he so loved playing under LaVell Edwards. Paul went on to graduate school at BYU; his thinking about organizations was profoundly influenced by the late Bill Dyer and by Bonner Ritchie. Thanks also to Paul's colleagues at the Woodland's Group—especially the late Forrest Belcher—for many years of intellectual stimulation and friendship. Paul is grateful for all those in his learning community who inspired him—Herb Stokes, John Cotter, Jim Taylor, the late Cal Pava, Bill Beltrop, Paul Thompson, David Cherrington, Stephen R. Covey, and many others. Thanks to all Paul's clients and to the associates with whom he served in church assignments through the years—these partnerships provided for the development and refinement of the five smooth stones. Special thanks to Truman Hunt and Claire Averett, CEO and VP of Human Resources, respectively, at NuSkin, who hired Paul to help the company through a major business transformation effort. This project in Provo made possible Paul's many early morning meetings with Bronco in his first few years as head coach.

Finally, a big "hurrah" for Paul and Kris Anne's four children: Jule, Amber, April, and Jason, plus his son-in-law, Tad, and daughter-in-law, Tauna. They each take great interest in his work. They also admire Bronco's coaching and are particularly pleased with his love of surfing, which they share.

From Alyson, a shout-out to Steve and Heidi Pugmire and their girls, Lindsay, Cassidy, Joelle, and Hannah. The Pugmires' basement accommodations and a hot breakfast were always ready when Alyson was in town for interviews. Deepest appreciation for Colleen Evans, a dear friend and a ready backup when Alyson is juggling mothering with other pursuits. Kudos for Alyson's family as well: first, for her husband, Doug, who was an ardent supporter of the project from the start and never complained once about taking on Alyson's share of the shopping, cleaning, cooking, laundry, and chauffeuring for months at a time; also for her children—Jacob, Sophia, Meredith, and Aidan—all of them the very lights of her life. Jacob especially gave to this book; he graciously granted permission for his story to be included in the preface (even though his perspective of events is quite different).

Notes

CHAPTER 1: WARRIOR COACH

1. Jeff Call, "Being Bronco: Mendenhall Developed Work Ethic at Young Age," *Deseret News*, March 30, 2005, http://www.deseretnews.com/article/600122374/Being -Bronco-Mendenhall-developed-work-ethic-at-young-age.html.

2. Call, "Being Bronco."

3. Davis Knight, as quoted in Call, "Being Bronco."

4. Ibid.

5. Ibid.

6. Ibid.

7. Paul Mendenhall, telephone conversation with Alyson Von Feldt, May 1, 2012.

CHAPTER 2: HEAD COACH

1. See LaVell Edwards with Lee Benson, *Airing It Out* (Salt Lake City: Shadow Mountain, 1995).

CHAPTER 3: DIFFERENT

1. Michael E. Porter, "What Is Strategy?" *Harvard Business Review* (November– December 1996): 61–78.

2. "Princeton Review College Ranking, Most Religious Students," Princeton Review.com, accessed April 23, 2012, http://www.princetonreview.com/schoollist .aspx?type=r&id=753.

3. "The Most Popular National Universities," USNews.com, January 24, 2012, http://www.usnews.com/education/best-colleges/articles/2012/01/24 /the-most-popular-national-universities.

4. "Princeton Review College Ranking, Stone-Cold Sober Schools," Princeton

Review.com, accessed April 23, 2012, http://www.princetonreview.com/schoollist .aspx?type=r&id=753.

5. "The Mission of Brigham Young University," Aims.BYU.edu, accessed April 23, 2012, http://aims.byu.edu/.

6. "Aims of a BYU Education," Aims.BYU.edu, accessed April 23, 2012, http://aims.byu.edu/p/aims.

7. Both quotations are from "Aims."

8. Ibid.

9. Spencer W. Kimball, as quoted in "Aims."

10. "Aims."

11. Spencer W. Kimball as quoted in "Aims."

12. "Church Educational System Honor Code," BYU.edu, accessed April 23, 2012, http://saas.byu.edu/catalog/2011–2012ucat/GeneralInfo/HonorCode php#HCOfficeInvovement.

13. Chad Nielsen, "A Question of Faith: Can Bronco Mendenhall return BYU Football to glory and still honor the school's mission?" *ESPN The Magazine*, October 10, 2005, 102–8.

14. Bronco Mendenhall with members of the BYU 2006 Football Team, *Tradition, Spirit, Honor* (Salt Lake City: Deseret Book, 2007), DVD.

15. Mendenhall, *Tradition, Spirit, Honor.*

16. As quoted in Mark Beck, "BYU Football Promotes, Truth, Virtue, Bronco Says," *Deseret News*, June 5, 2008.

CHAPTER 4: ON THE BUS

1. Jim Collins, *Good to Great* (New York: HarperCollins, 2001), 44; italics in original.

2. Bronco Mendenhall, at a presentation at Utah Valley State College, winter 2005. DVD copy in possession of the author.

3. Gordon B. Hinckley, "My Dear Young Friends," *BYU Magazine* 60 (Spring 2006): 24.

4. Thomas S. Monson, "Guidepost for Life's Journey," *BYU Magazine* 62 (Spring 2008): 33.

5. See Kurt Lewin, "Frontiers of Group Dynamics," *Human Relations* 1 (1947): 5–41.

6. See Ned Herrmann, *The Creative Brain* (Lake Lure, NC: The Ned Herrmann Group, 1993), 222–26; see also Bob Samples, *The Metaphoric Mind: A Celebration of Creative Consciousness*, 2d ed. (Rolling Hills Estates, CA: Jalmar Press, 1993).

7. Stephen R. Covey was one of Paul's professors when Paul was an organization design student at BYU. He spoke in class about "beginning with the end in mind." See also Stephen R. Covey, *The Seven Habits of Highly Effective People* (New York: Free Press, 2004) and Charles A. Garfield with Hal Zina Bennett, *Peak Performance: Mental Training Techniques of the World's Greatest Athletes* (Los Angeles: Warner Books, 1984).

8. Bronco Mendenhall, *Tradition, Spirit, Honor.*

9. Peter A. Gardner, "The Bronco Way," *BYU Magazine* 61 (Winter 2007): 24.

10. Vale Hale, "Another Victory for LaVell," *Provo Daily Herald*, April 3,

2005, http://www.heraldextra.com/sports/college/article_cdba6401-2745-53c9
-ba50–995777786640.html.

11. Quoted in Dick Harmon, "All That's Old Is New Again at Y: BYU's 'Old School' Uniforms Usher in New Era for Cougs," *Deseret News*, April 4, 2005, http://www.deseretnews.com/article/600123123/All-thats-old-is-new-again-at-Y.html?pg=1.

12. "Dick Harmon, "'Challenge' Aims to Help Cougars Finish Games," *Deseret News*, August 18, 2005, http://www.deseretnews.com/article/1,5143,600156770,00.html.

13. Mendenhall, *Tradition, Spirit, Honor*.

14. See the choices continuum in Stephen R. Covey, *The 8th Habit: From Effectiveness to Greatness* (New York: Free Press, 2004), 265.

15. Larry Wilson (founder of Wilson Learning), in discussion with Paul Gustavson and others, Pecos River, New Mexico, 1994.

CHAPTER 5: WHAT YOU DESIGN FOR

1. Jeff Call, "Mendenhall Vows Cougs Will Be More Consistent," *Deseret News*, March 14, 2005, http://www.deseretnews.com/article/600118544/Mendenhall-vows -Cougs-will-be-more-consistent.html.

2. See, for example, Lynda Gratton, *Hot Spots: How Boundaryless Cooperation Fuels Innovation* (San Francisco: BK, 2007), and Dave Ulrich and Wendy Ulrich, *The Why of Work: How Great Leaders Build Abundant Organizations that Win* (New York: McGraw Hill, 2010).

3. Bronco Mendenhall, "Faith First" (unpublished manuscript, July 15, 2010).

4. Jeff Benedict, "An Alarming Number of College Athletes Charged with Serious Crime," Sports and Society, SI.com, September 8, 2010, http://sportsillustrated.cnn.com/2010/writers/jeff_benedict/09/08/athletes.crime/index.html.

5. "NFL Hopeful FAQs," NFL Players Association online, accessed May 7, 2012, https://www.nflplayers.com/About-us/FAQs/NFL-Hopeful-FAQs/.

6. John Barr, "Painkiller Misuse Numbs NFL Pain," Outside the Lines, ESPN .com, accessed May 7, 2012, http://sports.espn.go.com/espn/eticket/story?page=110128 /PainkillersNews.

7. Mendenhall, "Faith First," emphasis added.

8. Mendenhall, "Faith First."

9. Bronco Mendenhall, interview by Greg Wrubell and Marc Lyons, "BYU Football with Head Coach Bronco Mendenhall," KSL Newsradio, October 6, 2010. Written recap: http://www.ksl.com/index.php?nid=498&sid=12727109& title=byu-football-with-head-coach-bronco-mendenhall-week-6.

10. For a photo of the BYU Broadcasting facility and Big Blue, see http://byutv. org/seethegood/post/Excited-about-our-truck-and-building.aspx.

11. Stewart Liff and Pamela A. Posey, *Seeing Is Believing: How the New Art of Visual Management Can Boost Performance throughout Your Organization* (New York: Amacom, 2004).

12. Ibid.

Notes

CHAPTER 6: CHAMPIONS ON THE FIELD AND OFF

1. See http://web1.ncaa.org/stats/StatsSrv/rankings?doWhat=archive&sport Code=MFB.

2. John Beck, "John Beck's Account of the Final 2006 Drive," *Deep Shades of Blue* website, accessed October 14, 2010, http://deepshadesofblue.com/john-becks -account-of-the-final-2006-drive/.

CHAPTER 8: KNOWLEDGE

1. Jonah Lehrer, *How We Decide* (Boston: Houghton Mifflin Harcourt, 2009), 1–8.

2. As quoted in Jeff Call, "BYU Football: Receivers Catching on to Cahoon's Vision," *Deseret News*, March 29, 2012, http://www.deseretnews.com /article/765564175/BYU-football-Receivers-catching-on-to-Cahoons-vision.html.

3. Lehrer, *How We Decide*, 8.

4. Malcolm Gladwell, *Outliers: The Story of Success* (New York: Little, Brown, and Company, 2008), 39–42, citing K. Anders Ericsson, Ralf Th. Krampe, and Clemens Tesch-Romerand, "The Role of Deliberate Practice in the Acquisition of Expert Performance," *Psychological Review* 100 (1993): 363–406.

5. John Beck, "John Beck's Account."

6. Tom Wyrich, "The Make-A-Jake Foundation," *Seattle Times*, September 2, 2008, http://seattletimes.nwsource.com/html/highschoolsports/2008152518 _heaps02.html.

7. Greg Wrubell, "Cougar Tracks: Bronco on Career, QBs, 2012 and 'Winning a Lot of Games,'" (recap of interview with Bronco Mendenhall), KSL.com, January 11, 2012, http://www.ksl.com/?nid=498&sid=18835936.

8. As quoted in Brad Rock, "BYU's Nelson Enjoying a Summer of Security," *Deseret News*, Jun 27, 2012, http://www.deseretnews.com/article/765586405 /BYUs-Nelson-enjoying-a-summer-of-security.html?pg=2.

9. Farid Rushdi, "BYU Football: QB Jake Heaps' Talent Not Enough to Replace Riley Nelson's Drive," Bleacherreport.com, October 16, 2011, http://bleacher report.com/articles/896292-for-byu-qb-jake-heaps-talent-not-enough-to-replace-riley -nelsons-drive.

10. As quoted in Jay Drew, "BYU Football: Cougars Go from Idle to Idaho," *Salt Lake Tribune*, updated Nov 7, 2011.

11. As quoted in Andrea Adelson, "Riley Nelson Makes Most of Second Chance," ESPN College Football Nation Blog, ESPN.com, October 28, 2011, http://espn.go.com /blog/ncfnation/post/_/id/51114/riley-nelson-makes-most-of-second-chance.

12. Ibid.

13. Ibid.

14. "Fans Crazy for BYU QB Riley Nelson's Hair," *BYU Universe*, October 3, 2011, http://universe.byu.edu/index.php/2011/10/03/fans-crazy-for-byu-qb-riley-nelsons -hair/.

15. Jay Drew, "Only at BYU: QB Riley Nelson Gets his Hair Cut, then Apologizes

for Letting it Get too Long," *Salt Lake Tribune*, Oct 5, 2011, http://www.sltrib.com/sltrib/blogsbyusports/52679283-65/friday-hair-whether-nelson.html.csp.

16. Amy Donaldson, "The Nelson Family Focuses on Doing their Best—Not Besting Others," *Deseret News*, October 11, 2011, http://www.deseretnews.com/article/700187168/The-Nelson-family-focuses-on-doing-their-best-2-not-besting-others.html?pg=all.

17. As quoted in Jeff Call, "BYU Football Notebook: Riley Nelson's Mobility Has Been the Key to an Improved Offense," *Deseret News*, Oct. 19, 2011, http://www.deseretnews.com/article/700189689/BYU-football-notebook-Riley-Nelsons-mobility-has-been-the-key-to-an-improved-offense.html.

18. As quoted in Jeff Call, "BYU Football: Riley Nelson Sparks Cougars to Comeback Victory in Armed Forces Bowl," *Deseret News*, December 30, 2011, http://www.deseretnews.com/article/700211397/BYU-football-Riley-Nelson-sparks-Cougars-to-comeback-victory-in-Armed-Forces-Bowl.html?pg=2.

19. As quoted in "Nelson's fake spike leads BYU to victory against Tulsa," *USA Today*, December 31, 2011, http://www.usatoday.com/USCP/PNI/SPORTS/2011-12-31-PNI1231spt-bowlrdpPNIBrd_ST_U.htm.

20. As quoted in Call, "Riley Nelson Sparks Cougars."

21. As quoted in "BYU Coaches Wanted Jake Heaps to Come Back," *Deseret News*, December 19, 2011, http://www.deseretnews.com/article/700208496/BYU-coaches-wanted-Jake-Heaps-to-come-back.html.

22. As quoted in Jeff Call, "Quarterbacks Get Chance to Perform in BYU Scrimmage," *Deseret News*, March 24, 2012, http://www.deseretnews.com/article/865552819/Quarterbacks-get-chance-to-perform-in-BYU-scrimmage.html.

23. James Lark, interview video available online at http://www.deseretnews.com/article/865552819/Quarterbacks-get-chance-to-perform-in-BYU-scrimmage.html?pg=2.

24. As quoted in Brandon Gurney, "BYU Football Notebook: Bevy of Young QBs Learning from Riley Nelson, James Lark," *Deseret News*, March 6, 2012, http://www.deseretnews.com/article/765557288/BYU-football-notebook-Bevy-of-young-QBs-learning-from-Riley-Nelson-James-Lark.html.

25. As quoted in Jeff Call, "BYU Football: Brandon Doman Confident Riley Nelson Can Run the Traditional Offense Efficiently," *Deseret News*, March 22, 2012, http://www.deseretnews.com/article/765562222/BYU-football-Brandon-Doman-confident-Riley-Nelson-can-run-the-traditional-offense-efficiently.html.

26. Ibid.

27. Ibid.

28. Ibid.

Chapter 9: Diffusion

1. David A. Bednar, "Seek Learning by Faith," *Ensign* (September 2007): 64, and quoted in Clark G. Gilbert, Steve Hunsaker, and Brian Schmidt, "Peer Instruction: Faculty as Architects of Peer Learning Environments," *Perspective* 7 (Autumn 2007): 103, http://www2.byui.edu/Perspective/contents7_2.htm.

CHAPTER 10: FULLY INVESTED

1. Scott Johnson, "Scott's Thoughts: 'Bronco's Back,'" KSL.com, October 7, 2010, http://www.ksl.com/index.php?nid=883&sid=12734701.

2. Dick Harmon, "The Message behind the Message in Bronco Mendenhall's T-shirt," *Deseret News*, September 11, 2011.

3. See Mihaly Csikszentmihalyi, *Flow* (New York: Harper Perennial, 1990).

4. Dieter F. Uchtdorf, "Lift Where You Stand," *Ensign* (November 2008): 55, and "Only A Stone Cutter LDS Movie," YouTube video, 3:42, clips from the movie *Only a Stonecutter*, uploaded by dbstores on December 5, 2008, http://www.youtube.com/watch?v=A053foVUVmI.

5. Daniel Gilbert, "The Science behind the Smile," interview with Gardiner Morse, *Harvard Business Review* 90 (January–February 2012): 88.

6. They have used the Herrmann Brain Dominance Instrument, StrengthsFinder 2.0, and the Myers Briggs Type Indicator, among others.

7. Jim Loehr and Tony Schwartz, *The Power of Full Engagement: Managing Energy, Not Time, Is the Key to High Performance and Personal Renewal* (New York: Free Press Paperbacks, 2003), 76–77.

8. Greg Wrubell, "BYU Offense Struggling to Replace All-Time Greats," *Deseret News*, September 27, 2010, http://www.deseretnews.com/article/700069207/BYU-offense-struggling-to-replace-all-time-greats.html?pg=1.

9. As quoted in Jeff Call, "BYU Football: Losing Streak Is a First for Cougars," *Deseret News*, October 2, 2010, https://secure.deseretnews.com/article/700070542/BYU-football-Losing-streak-is-a-first-for-Cougars.html?pg=1.

10. Book of Mormon, Mosiah 2:17.

11. As quoted by Greg Wrubell, "T-shirt Signifies Return of BYU Football," *Deseret News*, October 12, 2010, http://www.deseretnews.com/article/700072900/T-shirt-signifies-return-of-BYU-football.html.

12. As quoted in Jeff Call, "BYU Football: Cougars Are a 'Band' Again," *Deseret News*, October 12, 2010, http://www.deseretnews.com/article/700073168/BYU-football-Cougars-are-a-band-again.html.

13. Stephen M. R. Covey with Rebecca R. Merrill, *The Speed of Trust: The One Thing That Changes Everything* (New York: Free Press, 2006), 26.

14. As quoted in Wrubell, "T-shirt."

15. Covey, *Speed of Trust*, 19.

16. As quoted in Wrubell, "T-shirt."

17. Ibid.

18. As quoted in Call, "Cougars Are a 'Band' Again."

19. As quoted in Andrea Adleson, "BYU is now Jake Heaps' team," ESPN College Football Nation Blog, ESPN.com, August, 17, 2011, http://espn.go.com/blog/ncfnation/post/_/id/44923/byu-is-now-jake-heaps-team.

20. Jay Drew, "BYU Football: Cougs Believe in 'Gritty Dude' Riley Nelson," *Salt Lake Tribune*, October 7, 2011, http://www.sltrib.com/sltrib/sports/52681962-77/nelson-byu-heaps-riley.html.csp.

Notes

Chapter 11: Impossible

1. Nielsen, "A Question of Faith," 108.

2. Boise State, TCU, LSU, Virginia Tech, USC, Ohio State, Florida, Oklahoma, Texas, Alabama, West Virginia, Oregon, Wisconsin, and Penn State.

3. Alabama, LSU, Oklahoma, Oregon, Texas, USC, and Wisconsin.

4. Virginia Tech (7), Boise State (6), Ohio State (6), and TCU (6).

5. Virginia Tech, Boise State, Louisiana State, Ohio State, Oklahoma, Oregon, Texas Christian, and Wisconsin.

6. Virginia Tech.

7. Penn State and Nebraska.

8. Dick Harmon, "Rookies Selling Y Brand Just Fine," *Deseret News*, February 4, 2012, http://www.deseretnews.com/article/700222159/Rookies-selling-Y-brand-just-fine.html.

9. Jeff Call, "BYU, ESPN Agree to 8-year Broadcast Partnership," *Deseret News*, September 1, 2010, http://www.deseretnews.com/article/700062009/BYU-ESPN-agree-to-8-year-broadcast-partnership.html.

10. Scott D. Pierce, "TV or not TV," *Salt Lake Tribune*, October 31, 2011, http://archive.sltrib.com/article.php?id=17759147&itype=storyID.

11. Brett Pyne (Associate Director, Athletic Communications and Football Media Relations Director, BYU), in discussion with Alyson Von Feldt, May 1, 2012.

12. As quoted in "BYU Football: Joe DuPaix Excited about First Recruiting Class," *Deseret News*, January 29, 2012, http://www.deseretnews.com/article/700220203/BYU-football-Joe-DuPaix-excited-about-first-recruiting-class.html.

13. An allusion to Joseph Smith, "I teach them correct principles, and they govern themselves," as quoted by John Taylor, "The Organization of the Church," *Millennial Star* 35 (November 15, 1851): 339. See http://josephsmith.net/josephsmith/v/index.jsp?vgnextoid=dd2f001cfb340010VgnVCM1000001f5e340aRCRD&vgnextfmt=tab2, accessed April 6, 2012.

14. As quoted in Jamshid Ghazi Askar, "Y. Coach Tells Fireside of Bigger Mission," *Deseret News*, September 16, 2011, http://www.deseretnews.com/article/700179904/Y-coach-tells-fireside-of-bigger-mission.html.

15. Ibid.

16. This quote has frequently been attributed to Muhammad Ali, http://www.goodreads.com/author/quotes/46261.Muhammad_Ali.

Chapter 12: Everyone Has a Goliath— Framing the Coaching Experience

1. Retold from 1 Samuel 17.

Chapter 13: Smooth Stone #1—Organizations Can Craft a Sustainable Competitive Advantage through Differentiation

1. Porter, "What is Strategy?" 61–78.

2. "Fact Sheet," Southwest.com, revised December 9, 2011, accessed February

15, 2012, http://www.southwest.com/html/about-southwest/history/fact-sheet
.html#stock.

3. Porter, "What Is Strategy?" 73.

4. Nick Visser, "Internet-based Used Book Seller Receives $8.5 Million
Investment," *Seattle Times*, January 17, 2011, http://seattletimes.nwsource.com/html
/businesstechnology/2013949487_trminvestment18.html.

<h3 align="center">CHAPTER 14: SMOOTH STONE #2—ORGANIZATIONS ARE PERFECTLY
DESIGNED TO GET THE RESULTS THAT THEY GET</h3>

1. See Richard E. Walton, "Work Innovation in the United States," *Harvard
Business Review* (July/August 1979): 88–98. Paul was greatly influenced early in his
career by Walton's three-level concept of work improvement, which is adapted here.
Colleague Herb Stokes brought it to his attention and showed him how Procter &
Gamble had combined it with the work of Jay Galbraith to create a General Systems
Model of organization design. Paul adapted the Procter & Gamble model to create the
OSD Model.

2. See Jay Galbraith, *Organization Design* (Reading, MA: Addison-Wesley, 1977).
Galbraith names five systems, and his model is often called the "Five Star Model."

3. Professionals at Procter & Gamble in the late 1970s combined Galbraith's five
star model with Walton's three levels and augmented the result with some concepts
from "socio-technical systems design," another discipline of work design. Paul adapted
their model, which was introduced to him by consultant Herb Stokes, and named it
the Organizational Systems Design model. See Alyson Skabelund Von Feldt, "Hill's
Richmond Start-up History: Design Document and Ethnography" (internship report,
BYU, 1992).

4. January 2008 newsletter of the BYU Management Society's Silicon Valley
chapter, available at https://marriottschool.byu.edu/mgtsoc/members/chapter_webpage
.cfm?chapter_id=9.

<h3 align="center">CHAPTER 15: SMOOTH STONE #3—ORGANIZATIONS ARE MADE UP OF BUSINESS
PROCESSES, AND ALL PROCESSES ARE NOT CREATED EQUAL</h3>

1. Lee Tom Perry, Randall G. Stott, and W. Norman Smallwood, *Real Time
Strategy: Improvising Team-Based Planning for a Fast-Changing World* (New York: John
Wiley & Sons, 1993).

2. Kathleen Slaugh Barr and Cheri A. Loveless, "Family Work," *BYU Magazine*
(Spring 2000), http://magazine.byu.edu/?act=view&a=151.

<h3 align="center">CHAPTER 16: SMOOTH STONE #4—
KNOWLEDGE IS THE PUREST FORM OF COMPETITIVE ADVANTAGE</h3>

1. William Montgomery Snyder, "Organization Learning and Performance:
An Exploration of the Linkages between Organization Learning, Knowledge, and
Performance" (dissertation, USC, 1996): 11–16.

2. Snyder, "Organization Learning," 30–34.

3. Ibid.

Notes

4. Ibid., 32.

5. Ibid., 32, 47–49

6. Ibid., 48–49.

7. Ibid., 35–43.

8. Keith Devlin, *Goodbye, Descartes: The End of Logic and the Search for a New Cosmology of the Mind* (New York: John Wiley & Sons, 1997), 177–84.

9. Carl von Clausewitz, *On War* (New York: Everyman's Library / Alfred A. Knopf, 1976), 161.

10. Keith Devlin, *The Math Gene: How Mathematical Thinking Evolved and Why Numbers are Like Gossip* (New York: Basic, 2000), 187–89.

11. Devlin, *Math Gene*, 200.

12. See Devlin, *Math Gene*, 187.

13. Lehrer, *How We Decide*, 34–42.

14. Ibid. Devlin argues that the importance of instinct acquired through experience makes the development of artificial intelligence any time soon very unlikely because tacit expertise is not reducible to rules that can be followed by a digital computer; see Devlin, *Goodbye, Descartes*, 182–83.

15. See Lehrer, *How We Decide*, xi–56. Cf. Devlin, *Goodbye, Descartes*, 180–84.

16. "Xerox: Harnessing Communal Expertise Sharing to Enhance Services: Ethnography in Action," PARC website, accessed October 1, 2011, www.parc.com /content/attachments/xerox_cs_parc.pdf.

17. Alex K.,"Google's '20 Percent Time' in Action," Google Official Blog, May 18, 2006, http://googleblog.blogspot.com/2006/05/googles-20-percent-time-in -action.html; Bharat Mediratta, "The Google Way: Give Engineers Room," *New York Times*, October 21, 2007, http://www.nytimes.com/2007/10/21/jobs/21pre.html ?_r=1; and "Engineering in Silicon Valley: How Does Google's 'Innovation Time Off' (20% time) Work, In Practice?" Quora, accessed May 3, 2012, http://www.quora .com/Engineering-in-Silicon-Valley/How-does-Googles-Innovation-Time-Off-20-time -work-in-practice.

18. Everett M. Rogers, *Diffusion of Innovations*, 5th ed. (New York: Free Press, 2003), 150–55.

19. Rogers, *Diffusion of Innovations*, 153–55.

20. Daniel Pink, foreword to *The New Social Learning: A Guide to Transforming Organizations through Social Media*, by Tony Bingham and Marcia Conner (Alexandria, Virginia: ASTD; San Francisco: Berret-Koehler, 2010), xiii–xiv.

21. Adapted from Jeanne C. Meister and Karie Willyerd, *The 2020 Workplace: How Innovative Companies Attract, Develop, and Keep Tomorrow's Employees Today* (New York: HarperCollins, 2010), 153–54.

22. Meister and Willyerd, 177–79.

23. As quoted in Meister and Willyerd, *The 2020 Workplace*, 177–79.

24. Ibid., 166–67.

25. Clayton M. Christensen and Henry J. Eyring, *The Innovative University: Changing the DNA of Higher Education from the Inside Out* (San Francisco: Wiley, 2011), 229–35.

26. Ibid., 259.

27. Clark, Hunsaker, and Schmidt, "Peer Instruction," 103.

28. Seth Godin, *Linchpin: Are You Indispensable?* (New York: Portfolio, 2010), 151.

29. Ibid., 154.

30. Ibid., 50–173.

31. Ibid., 77–79.

32. Ibid., 57.

CHAPTER 17: SMOOTH STONE #5—
EFFECTIVE LEADERS CAPTURE HEARTS AND MINDS

1. See, for example, Peter Senge, Art Kleiner, Charlotte Roberts, Richard Ross, George Roth, and Bryan Smith, *The Dance of Change: The Challenges to Sustaining Momentum in Learning Organizations* (New York: Currency/Doubleday, 1999), 5–6.

2. John P. Kotter, *Leading Change* (Boston: Harvard Business Review Press, 1996): 9.

3. Gary Hamel, "Moon Shots for Management," *Harvard Business Review* (February 2009): 93.

4. Edward L. Deci with Richard Flaste, *Why We Do What We Do: Understanding Self-Motivation,* (New York: Penguin, 1996), 126–30.

5. Jim Clifton, *The Coming Jobs War: What Every Leader Must Know about the Future of Job Creation* (New York: Gallup, 2011), 7–15.

6. Ulrich and Ulrich, *Why of Work*, 3.

7. Ibid., 6. See also Gretchen Spreitzer and Christine Porath, "Creating Sustainable Performance," *Harvard Business Review* (January–February 2012): 92–99.

8. Daniel H. Pink, *Drive: The Surprising Truth about What Motivates Us* (New York: Riverhead, 2009), 129–31.

9. Meister and Willyerd, *The 2020 Workplace*, 50. Cf. Petra Wilson, "Unlocking the Talent of Generation Y," *Engineering and Technology Magazine* 3, no. 14, http://eandt.theiet.org/magazine/2008/14/generation-y0814.cfm.

10. Justin Fox, "The Economics and Well-Being," *Harvard Business Review* (January–February 2012): 78–83.

11. Ulrich and Ulrich, *Why of Work*, 9, 25.

12. Cf. Pink, *Drive*, 137–38.

13. Meister and Willyerd, *2020 Workplace*, 35.

14. "Monthly Report in USD: 2012–13 Issue 137 USD," Data and Reports, Grameen Bank website, accessed May 9, 2012, http://www.grameen-info.org/index.php?option=com_content&task=view&id=453&Itemid=527.

15. Muhammad Yunus with Karl Weber, *Creating a World Without Poverty: Social Business and the Future of Capitalism,* (New York: Public Affairs, 2007), 43–60.

16. Antony Bugg-Levine, Bruce Kogut, and Nalin Kulatilaka, "A New Approach to Funding Social Enterprises," *Harvard Business Review* (January–February 2012): 119–20.

17. John P. Kotter and Dan S. Cohen, *Heart of Change* (Boston: Harvard Business School Press, 2002), 29–30.

18. Deci, *Why We Do*, 2–4.

19. See Deci, *Why We Do*, 10.
20. Ibid., 34.
21. Ibid., 65–73. Cf. Gilbert, "The Science behind the Smile," 87.
22. Csikszentmihalyi, *Flow*, 152.
23. Gilbert, "The Science behind the Smile," 88.
24. Pink, *Drive.*
25. Loehr and Schwartz, *Power of Full Engagement*, 32.
26. Ibid., 32–33.
27. Ibid., 166.
28. Herrmann, *Creative Brain*, 232–33.
29. Loehr and Schwartz, *Power of Full Engagement*, 5.

Index

Index

Butler, Peter, 332

BYU Broadcasting, 95

BYU Football: achievements of, under Mendenhall, 3–4, 264–68; Mendenhall named head coach of, 13–14, 15, 31–33; achievements of, under Edwards, 14–15; Mendenhall coaches for, 30–31; recruitment standards for, 59–62; future goals for, 274–78

BYU–Idaho, 333–35

BYU Management Society, 304–7

Cahoon, Ben, 180, 327

Call, Jeff, 80

Called to Serve display, 97–98

Camps, 118–19

Car, Mendenhall loses, 20

Carter, Virgil, 193–94

Cerebral cortex, 324

Challenge, as motivation, 230, 251, 346–47

Change. *See* Culture change

Choice, results and, 78–80, 286, 294–308

Church congregation, changes made by, 307–8

Church of Jesus Christ of Latter-day Saints, The: values of, 13–14, 37–38; Polynesians and, 15–16; Mendenhall's activity in, 24; Mendenhall's testimony of, 36–37; persecution of, 52–53

Church services, for potential recruits, 165

Clausewitz, Carl von, 323

Coach-to-player diffusion, 213–16

Codifiable know-how, 320, 321

Codifiable knowledge, 174, 177, 320, 321

Codifiable know-that, 320, 321

Collective Brands, 352

Collins, Jim, 57–58

Commitment, 54–55

Communication, improving, 185–86, 238

Companionships, 125–26. *See also* Band of Brothers

Competence, personal, 230

Competitive advantage: through differentiation, 44–49, 285–86, 289–93; through recruitment, 57–62, 155–66; through culture change, 62–75; knowledge as, 173–74, 287–88, 316–17, 338

Competitive enabling work, 154, 310, 311, 312, 313

Competitive work, 154, 165–69, 310, 311, 312, 313

Compliance work, 154, 167, 310, 311–12, 313

Conditioning, 100–101, 233–34, 253–57

Conditions, organization, 318, 325–29

Confidence, 178–79, 194

Copying others, 44–46

Cougars. *See* BYU Football

Countdown to Kickoff, 95

Covey, Stephen M. R., 258

Cragun, Shane, 162–63

Crime, 85

Crowton, Gary, 14, 21, 31

Csikszentmihalyi, Mihaly, 346

Culture change: effecting, 62–75, 77–80; outcomes and, 80, 295; through mission statement, 81–83; through values and guiding principles, 83–86

Dare2Share, 332

David, 40, 284–85

Deceuster, Joel, 306–7

Deci, Edward L., 340, 346

Defense, changes to, 249–59

Design choices: effecting change through, 78–79, 286, 294–308; and culture and outcomes, 80; mission statement and, 81–83; values and, 83–86; strategy as, 86–89; goals and objectives as, 89–90, 135–38;

Index

Index